MUGSY
My Story

OWEN MULLIGAN

with Orla Bannon

Published by Irish Sports Publishing (ISP)
Unit 11, Tandy's Lane
Lucan, Co Dublin
Ireland
www.irishsportspublishing.com

First published, 2013

A CIP record for this book is available from the British Library

ISBN 978-0-9573954-7-3

Printed in Ireland with Print Procedure Ltd
Cover Design and Typesetting: Anú Design www.anu-design.ie
Cover Photographs: © Inpho Sports Agency
Inside Photographs: Inpho Sports Agency and Owen Mulligan's Private Collection

For my mother, Heather, my biggest fan
and the best mother in the world.

Orla Bannon is a freelance sports journalist from Tyrone with over fifteen years' experience covering a variety of sports, including Gaelic games. She is a former staff reporter with the *Irish News* and *Daily Mirror* and now works for a wide range of national newspapers and online services throughout Ireland. This is her first book.

Contents

Acknowledgments

Throughout my life as a Gaelic footballer I have taken a lot of people for granted, and reliving past experiences through my autobiography has helped me realise that none of this would have been possible without them.

I wish to thank the club that I would die for, and the past and present players of Cookstown Father Rocks' who have become my best friends and who have always kept my feet firmly on the ground. Adrian Gilmore, the current club Chairman, and our main sponsor, Dominic Crilly of Steelweld Fabrications, have driven the success of the club over the last few years and I have no doubt they will continue to do so.

To the Tyrone teams of 1997 to 2012, it was an absolute pleasure to wear the Red Hand on my chest. It fulfilled my childhood dream; first, to play alongside Peter Canavan, the greatest player of all time, and then, after embarking on a journey which brought difficulties, triumphs and heartbreak, to achieve success beyond our wildest dreams. It was an honour and a privilege to be involved with such a fantastic bunch of fellas.

I wish to thank the people who made this book possible, including my sponsor and good friend, Maurice O'Kane of O'Kane Plumbing and Electrics Ltd.

To Liam Hayes and Kevin MacDermot of Irish Sports Publishing, for their support and for giving me an opportunity that few GAA players ever get – to tell my own story.

To Orla, it has been an honour to work alongside you throughout this process. We shared a lot of laughs and I will always appreciate your hard work, sound advice and professionalism in putting this book together.

To my family, including my late grandmother, Mary Mulligan, who have given me the drive, determination and inspiration to achieve all that I have. The loyalty they have shown me through the tough encounters is something that I will be forever grateful for.

I would like to express my deepest appreciation to my father, Eugene, who has been a role model to me from a young age. He provided me with the ambition and confidence to achieve at the highest level, both on and off the pitch.

I count myself lucky to be in the middle of two protective sisters, Michelle and Marie-Claire. They have given me their advice wherever possible and have always spoken their mind, which was often what I needed to hear. I can't thank them enough for their support and friendship down through the years.

I would like to offer my special thanks to my brother Stephen, who, not so long ago, put the value of life into perspective. He has always raised the bar to the highest possible level and never let me settle for second best. People often name their heroes as Steven Gerrard, Pelé or George Best, but mine goes by the name of Stephen 'Mugsy' Mulligan.

Last but not least, to my mother, Heather, my biggest fan but also my fiercest critic behind closed doors. The commitment and sacrifices she has had to make in her own life, just for me, show what a wonderful person she is.

Without her support the length and breadth of Ireland, shouting encouragement for me wherever I played and for whatever team I played, I doubt I would have achieved the honours that I won throughout my career. I certainly would not have become the person I am today without her love and guidance.

Foreword

A good teacher knows every rule,

A good pupil, the exceptions.

Martin H. Fischer

It was in September, 1997, that a rather plump, baby faced red-head walked tentatively into my classroom – welcome into my world, Owen Mulligan.

If only I was to know the impact he would make, not only on the corridors of Holy Trinity College but on the football pitches the length and breadth of the country. It soon became evident that Owen was no ordinary pupil and certainly no ordinary footballer.

Looking back, it seems hard to believe that this rather timid looking individual was set to become a household name throughout the country. It was Owen's brilliance that resulted in Holy Trinity winning our first ever Senior Vocational Schools title in April, 1998. Within months of that victory, he was showcasing his sublime skills to a wider audience as Tyrone captured the All-Ireland minor title in Croke Park. Two All-Ireland Under-21 titles were to follow and many were beginning to take notice of the young lad from Cookstown Fr Rocks.

As a pupil I can recall Owen's personality vividly, full of respect one minute and full of mischief the next. As a footballer he was no different. Owen played the game with a swagger and with a smile on his face.

He was very much part of the new order that transported Tyrone onto a level previously untouched. McAnallen's courage, Hub's energy, Stevie's accuracy and Mugsy's flair were all underpinned by a desire to be the best. Owen brought a charisma and a charm to our game that few could equal.

Six years on from our first introduction, I would be lining out alongside Owen in the Tyrone full-forward line on what was to prove to be Tyrone's greatest day – granted he was a little slimmer, not as pale and somewhat more blond than ginger! The memories shared that day will never fade as we became the first ever Tyrone side to collect the ultimate prize in GAA – The Sam Maguire Cup.

As someone who often stood out and at times was incorrectly labelled as an 'individual', Owen was totally unselfish and indeed was always the ultimate team player. He was never afraid to get struck hard or to do the donkey work. Indeed, a criticism I often levelled at him was that, if anything, he was too willing to pass when a shot was the better option.

While at Holy Trinity College, Owen was one of a large number of boys whom I had the pleasure of educating in my form class. Like many of them, it's fair to say that Owen's love of the National Curriculum came second only to kicking the size 5 O'Neill's.

As a pupil in my form class, Owen had many willing and able accomplices but when it came to football he was simply in a class of his own.

Having had difficulty insuring that Owen read the odd book at school, like many of his 'aul' teachers I will take great pride in the fact that he has now written his own book! I, for one, cannot wait to cast my eye over the many stories that this book will reveal and I am in no doubt that it will be a true reflection of the man himself – honest, colourful and full of the unexpected.

I conclude with one quote that encapsulates Owen and one that will forever remain with me. You won't be surprised it comes not from any literary genius but from the excellent commentary of Darragh Maloney during the epic 2005 All Ireland quarter-final against Dublin, when those fortunate enough to be there witnessed one of the finest goals ever scored in Croke Park: 'Magic-Magic Mulligan!'

Enjoy!

Peter Canavan

Prologue

I woke up with a plastic sheet around me.

The room was freezing.

Where the hell am I?

A cold, sharp, shock to the system, then a sickening feeling building in the pit of my stomach as I began to unscramble my head about what had happened the night before.

Slowly, it dawned on me. I'm banged up.

Well done, Mugsy, I thought. *You've really done it this time.*

The night had started with no big drama.

Tyrone lost an Ulster Championship quarter-final to Down after a replay and extra time on the Saturday night.

It was early summer in 2008, and even though the year would end with Tyrone winning a third All-Ireland title in the decade, I had been out of sorts for months. Out of sorts and out of my mind doing stupid things. Messing. Not thinking. I was injured, I was unfit and I was spending money I didn't have. I was doing it all with a smile on my face, but I wasn't really happy.

I wasn't involved in the Down game. There was talk I had skipped off to a beach party in Portrush, but that was just one of dozens of crazy rumours I've had to put up with over the years.

The truth was a lot more painful.

For weeks I'd had a sciatic nerve problem in my hip which meant I couldn't walk and couldn't sleep. I was driving to the hospital at three o'clock in the morning screaming in pain. Louis O'Connor, our physio, didn't know what was wrong with me. No one did.

Tyrone's defeat in Newry left me wondering if I would see any football at all that year. Maybe Tyrone's summer would be over before I could find out what was wrong with me. All sorts of doubts ran through my mind as I headed out to my local on the Sunday afternoon to watch Armagh play Cavan on television.

I was on really strong painkillers but I had about ten pints of Guinness.

I moved to another bar and met up with a few school friends I hadn't seen in ages. I started drinking brandy shots with Red Bull. Should have known that was the time to go. Brown spirits never agree with me.

Then the craic started.

We started playing this stupid game, throwing a bar stool high in the air and trying to catch it with one hand. My timing couldn't have been worse. As I threw the stool, the door of the bar opened and I split this guy on the lip as he walked in. I recognised him immediately and ran over.

'Jesus, lad … I'm wile sorry.'

He was sound about it but ten minutes later a mate of his, who was a bouncer, came over to me, sticking his chest out. It was nothing to do with him but we started a pushing and shoving match. I managed to leave quietly and moved to the Conway Inn. Who was in there but the same lad I'd had the row with.

We apologised to each other and started drinking together but, when the slagging started up about different women, the atmosphere turned sour again. Any wee thing was annoying me at that time. I was seething when the bouncers got involved but I still had enough wit to know it was time to leave.

As I walked out, I saw a boy I knew driving past and was glad when he offered me a lift. He was a tiler and had a lot of tools in the car. When he stopped at the lights, something snapped inside me. I jumped out and that's when I made one of the stupidest mistakes of my life. I grabbed the plasterer's scraper he had sticking out of his boot and ran up the street, limping and holding this long, thin scraper that had a sharp end at the top.

I wanted a row.

The bouncers saw me coming and ran inside and locked the doors. I smashed two big windows to smithereens with the scraper. I didn't try to make a run for it, I just stood there, waiting.

The bouncers came out and grabbed me. I shouted to some of the Cookstown lads to help me but nobody moved. I knew if I'd had my full strength I could have shaken these boys off but my back and hip were too sore.

The bar owner was a big, big Tyrone fan but he came out shaking his head.

'I'm sorry, Mugsy, I can't stand by you this time. You've gone too far.'

When I woke up the next morning in Cookstown police station, I knew that well enough.

I have a fair idea who contacted the papers but it was already headline news around Tyrone anyway. I was the hot topic of conversation, though most people had the wrong story. As usual.

The rumour was that boys had been slagging me off about being finished as a footballer, that Tyrone were done and I was washed up. The fact was it had nothing to do with football.

It was a relief not to be at training that Tuesday night. I couldn't make it because I was booked in to see a specialist at Chelsea about my mystery injury. But when the physio couldn't do anything for me, I came home depressed, disillusioned and fearing the worst from Mickey.

Instead he was brilliant, but he warned me I had some choices to make. 'I don't want to know the ins and outs of what happened, Mugsy, but you shouldn't be getting yourself into these situations. I've told you about this countless times. You need to get your head back into the football.' I knew it, too.

About a week later, Noel Napier in the Ulster Independent Clinic answered all my prayers.

I walked in with a limp but after getting his injection, I walked out, straight as a rush. That night I trained injury-free for the first time in months. The relief was massive. If I had been Mickey Harte dealing with me, I'd have given me the road a few times. I deserved it more than once.

The only way I could repay him was to get my head back in the game.

I was working on the roof of a house the day I heard Mickey Harte was the new Tyrone senior football manager.

I could have jumped as high as the house.

If anybody is going to manage Tyrone to a senior All-Ireland title, it's him, I reckoned. I knew Mickey was going to bring in a load of our Under-21 team straight away. A few of the older boys who had played for so long under Art McRory and Eugene McKenna were going to be disappointed.

In the end, Mickey brought nearly our whole panel in. It didn't matter who was annoyed. This was about winning a first All-Ireland for Tyrone.

One of our first team meetings was in Paudge Quinn's in Ballygawley. It was announced that Peter Canavan would be our captain. Happy days. It was the obvious choice and the right one. The man is a legend. With so many players new to senior inter-county football, we needed him and Chris

Lawn, or 'Cricko' to every young and old man on the Tyrone team, more than ever.

I felt shivers of excitement when Peter said his first words to us: 'I don't want to be a great captain. I want to be captain of a great team ... an All-Ireland winning team.'

I was delighted. This was exactly what we needed to hear.

The man was always a leader whether he was captain or not, but I had an unshakable belief that we now had the right manager and the right captain. I looked around the room at Cricko, Canavan, Hub Hughes, McGuigan, Ricey, Dooher, Gormley, Jordan. Born leaders. Exceptional talent.

If it's ever going to happen for Tyrone, it's now.

With these lads.

We're the ones to do it.

I don't think Tyrone would have made the breakthrough and won All-Ireland titles without Mickey Harte. There was a special group of players emerging who'd won all before them at Vocationals, Colleges, county minor and Under-21 level, but Mickey was the one who brought it all together and made it happen.

He took a different approach. He was light years ahead of everybody else in his thinking. I was being managed at Cookstown by people who were running us round the field. But Mickey had us doing wee drills like bouncing balls off wet surfaces just to get the feel of what it was like. He was doing those wee things way before anybody else. All the drills we did were with match situations in mind. Everything was game-related when nobody else was thinking about that.

We didn't have any challenge matches at Under-21 or senior level, when they were the norm in every other county. Mickey used to say, 'There is no better challenge than what we have here. Why play against players who are happy they've already established themselves in a county team, when we have hungry men here ... fighting tooth and nail to do the same?'

I thought it was a brilliant idea.

Our in-house matches were so heated. Blood was spilled, hair and teeth were lost, the 'verbals' were hot and heavy. We treated those matches as wars – then we'd shake hands afterwards. Our intensity in 2003 surprised everybody, and those in-house games were where it came from.

Mickey never minded us boys having our say. He'd encourage us to debate an issue – as long as the final outcome was the one he wanted.

'Should youse be able to take a drink, boys?' he'd ask.

'Aye, Mickey, we've decided we can have two pints.'

'You see those two pints, are they affecting youse do you think?'

'Ach … not really,' one of us would reply.

'Well, what's the point in having a second pint when youse are saying you don't really need it?'

Confused silence.

'And if that's the case … is there any real point in having one pint?'

Before we knew where we were, we had ended up slapping a one-month drink ban on ourselves. That was part of his genius. What a negotiator.

After that first All-Ireland winning year, it was mostly left up to the players to be responsible. There was no talk of drink bans and, by and large, everyone respected this by not going overboard, though I broke out occasionally. When drink bans were put on by players, I didn't break them.

Everyone thinks I'm a party animal but, for a party animal, I've been on some amount of winning teams and I can back it up. So, I have been disciplined. It can't be all bad, it can't all have been crazy nights out.

You can't win as much as I've won if you're out partying all the time.

The only time we had a drink ban imposed was in the build-up to the Ulster final in 2003, and I was practically a monk that whole year.

◆ ◆ ◆ ◆ ◆

I love to be the life and soul of the party, but I like my own space, too. Never more so than in the dressing room before big matches. My pre-match ritual of lying underneath the bench in the dressing rooms in Croke Park became fundamental to me.

I always sat beside the water tap, too, no matter what. For years to come, that was my spot in the dressing rooms every time we played there. All the boys knew it. Even when I played there with my club, Cookstown Father Rocks, in the 2010 and 2013 All-Ireland Intermediate finals, I did the same.

If someone was new into the squad and didn't know the craic, they were soon informed. Someone would smile over in my direction and issue a warning, 'That's Mugsy's seat there.'

On match days, the whole place is 'busy, busy, busy'. There is a lot going on in there, and I often felt I had to get away. I wanted to get into a wee place, out of the road, so that's when I started climbing underneath the bench. I lay on a towel with another towel over my head. It helped me to relax. I'd just be thinking about the game, my opponent, how I might score. Just trying to get into the zone.

Everybody had different preparations. Some boys sat reading a wee prayer before big games, even I would give that a go sometimes. Others would read a book. Some lads would kick a ball about. Davy Harte was big into that and it used to annoy me, but I never said anything. If that's what some boys wanted to do to help them get ready, that was ok. Everybody deals with it their own way.

My way was to be in my wee spot under the bench. Call it superstition if you like, but it didn't feel like that. It just helped me to focus on what I wanted to achieve in the game.

I liked the dressing room to be calm.

Even now, I'd know what kind of mood Cookstown are in – whether we have a good chance of winning a game or not – depending on how boys are in the room. I liked having my own place in the dressing rooms in Croke Park, it became so familiar to me over the years as Tyrone contested big match after big match. I always stayed in that same spot, whether I was starting games or not.

It was the same on the bus, I sat in the same seat for over fifteen years. Nobody went near my seat: back of the bus, bottom left. Hub beside me, always Hub, with McGuigan and Philly Jordan in front of us. I freaked out if anybody else tried to sit there.

When someone new joined the panel and sat there by mistake, I'd be down the bus like a shot, 'Up you get, lad … that's my seat'.

The back seat was home to the card school, too. Canavan was in the middle of it, like 'The Godfather'. He never sat down the back but he'd come down for the cards, always with a smile, ready for the action. Tommy

McGuigan, Colm 'Cobble' McCullagh, Leo and Brian Meenan, Hub, Canavan, Mickey Coleman, Ricey, Pistol Pete Loughran as well. It got hot and heavy sometimes.

Maverick became our game of choice. Big Joey McMahon was a great man for that. Everyone had to pick a card and turn it round to show the group. You'd get a second card and then you'd bet a pound, two pounds or a fiver, depending on whether you fancied your hand or not.

The aim was to pick a third card somewhere in between the first two. If you got caught out and drew the same card as before, we called that the 'double bubble', which meant you had to put the jackpot in. I was out working on building sites and hadn't that much money. Before you knew where you were, you might be down £200 and scrambling, asking for the lend of a tenner on the way home.

Mickey didn't like it. He would hear the roars when someone was caught out on the big jackpot. He would say, 'You should be concentrating on the game instead of maybe losing money'. We all knew he was right and it died out after a few years.

Mickey brought in a lot of wee things to help the younger lads gel with the older boys in the squad. Michaela Harte compiled a tape that we played on the bus going to matches, with every player's favourite song on it.

I chose 'Knocking on Heaven's Door' by Avril Lavigne, which was in the charts at the time. Given how the year turned out, it was pretty appropriate.

Some of the lads had bad ones. Everyone hated when Mickey McGee's song came on, it was just 'boom, boom, boom', a pure banging match from start to finish. Enough to give you a headache.

There were other wee touches behind the scenes which people laughed at but which were adding up to help us grow into an unstoppable force that year. One of those things was folding our jerseys before and after matches. Mickey had started that at minor level and we carried it through into the senior squad. People might have laughed but it was about showing respect for each other and the jersey, and we really bought into it.

I used to look at my jersey and think, *I wonder who all has worn this same number before me?*

In that year's Division One League final we hammered Laois. I scored three points and was named Man of the Match. Twelve months earlier, when we had won it under Art McRory and Eugene McKenna, it felt like a one-off. This time it felt like it was the start of something special.

One night sticks out in my mind as being crucial in putting us on the road to glory.

A few weeks before the Ulster final, I was renovating the house I'm living in now. I got a phone call asking me to play in the Street League, a Council-run community soccer tournament I used to play in. Initially I said no, but when I was offered £50 I soon changed my mind. Cricko always drove me to training but that night I told him to go on ahead, and to tell Mickey that I was working late.

I pitched up to the soccer game. Little did I know there was a boy from Moortown, Cricko's club, playing in the game. I didn't find that out until two nights later when Cricko picked me up for training.

We chatted over the usual banter until he steered the conversation round to my absence on Tuesday night.

'Well, did you work late the other night?'

'Aye.'

He swerved the van off the road, scaring the life out of me.

We were driving from Dungannon to Edendork at the time and I'll never forget the spot on the road where it happened.

His whole head was bright red, veins bulging out everywhere. A pure psycho face. I thought he was going to kill me.

'Don't you lie to me!'

I stuck to my guns, stupidly.

'What are you on about lad?' I said.

'Don't you fucking lie to me!' He was roaring into my face. 'You're one of our best forwards … and you're out playing soccer? You're a total disgrace. If you have any balls at all you'll tell the group at training.'

Jesus Christ.

The training that night was going shite. Mickey called the boys together.

'What's going on boys … this isn't going well. Is it these club matches at the weekends, are they making you tired?'

I looked around the circle, wondering if any of the boys felt as guilty as me. Nobody spoke. Mickey was too cute for that.

'Tell me this then. Were any of you out at the weekend?'

A few hands slowly crept up over boys' heads.

They all started coming out of the woodwork, wee shamed faces on them. 'I had a couple of pints Mickey … I had a couple of pints … me too Mickey.' It was like an AA meeting.

I could feel Cricko glaring at me. Mickey was annoyed. He was shaking his head.

'That's not good enough boys. We have an Ulster final in a few weeks. Has anybody else got anything to say?'

Cricko's eyes were burning into me.

No matter what Mickey said, I knew it wouldn't be as bad as what I'd get off Cricko on the way home. I took a deep breath. *Here we go.*

'I have something to say, Mickey,' I began. 'I wasn't working on Tuesday night … I was playing soccer … and I had a couple of pints afterwards.'

Mickey wrecked it.

'For God's sake, Mugsy, you always have to take it to the next level, don't you?' Mickey went mental. That's when Chris Lawn gave what became known among the boys as his 'Braveheart' speech.

He called the boys together, his face full of passion, still angry with me for skipping training to play soccer.

'*We don't have Celtic crosses and all those Armagh boys do and that's what eats me up. Me and Peter went on that All Star trip with them this year and we felt like second class citizens.*

'*Do youse want to go this long in your careers, like me and Pete, without an All-Ireland medal?*

'*We have to give every sacrifice for the next three months, boys. Everything. Our jobs, our families, our wives and girlfriends.*

'*Nothing is going to come before this team for the next three months.*

'*Nothing. It's only three months, boys. Three months to change our lives … forever.*'

We had that much respect for the older lads. Whether they were subs or injured or not playing, they always spoke in the dressing room. Canavan and Cricko, and Collie Holmes was another one who drew enormous respect, too.

Lawn gave it loads of passion. Everyone took a deep breath. It was a 'Holy fuck' moment. I'm a strong believer that it was a massive factor in us winning the All-Ireland in 2003. It was the sort of thing we needed to hear.

Training was unreal in the weeks that followed. It was brutal in fact, but we loved it. We were single-minded about what we were going to do for the rest of the year.

◆ ◆ ◆ ◆ ◆

As a team we were developing a bit of a reputation for giving 'verbals'.

Mickey never told us to do it or encouraged us: You can't teach a player that, it's either in you or it's not.

I had been at it long before Mickey became senior manager. In my first year in the senior squad in 2001 I got into a row with Eamon Coleman during the Ulster semi-final against Derry at Clones. Coleman ran onto the field to give out about something Pascal Canavan did and I swung him around. I didn't mean to swing him as hard as I did.

Gareth Doherty, a brother of Fergal's, was marking me. He was doing well enough to be fair, but I was acting the maggot.

'Make the switch Eamon,' I said, 'or you're going to lose this game.' Big Anthony Tohill came over and made sure that was the end of my chat.

I was at Eamon Coleman's wake years later and there on the wall was the photo of me and him 'going at it' in Clones.

Tyrone were successful at giving verbals because we could back it up. My golden rule is, if you're not playing well, keep your mouth shut. You have to be able to back it up.

A lot of us started it at minor level and we had a few boys in the team who liked to talk. I hardly ever started the verbals, but if someone said something to me I'd go at it so hard that I'd usually end up getting a box on the back of the head. No one is telling me that if a man is slagging off your ma or your girlfriend that you're not going to slag him back.

I think the best verbals are always game-related. I have never been into insults. Hub was given verbals once about his brother being killed in a car accident and he just turned around and busted the lad.

But if you can get into somebody's head and put them off their game, then I think it's valid.

When I'm going well in a match, I can get really chirpy.

'Here lads, get the ball in to me, I'm roasting this man. He'll be sleeping with no sheets on the bed tonight, he's roasting. Get the sun cream out!'

If I get a goal or a nice point I might turn around, pat my marker on the ass and say, 'Keep the head up, big man, you'll get the next one.' That drives them mental altogether.

If a defender is playing badly and trying to give me stick, I'll give him a good touch. 'You are talking rubbish there, man, you haven't touched the ball and I've scored five points, what are you mouthing for?'

If you're playing badly, keep your mouth shut.

Club is far worse than county. Sometimes I might shout over to the opposition manager.

'You can't be serious, you're not leaving this man on me. You have to make a switch here, man.' If their physio came out I'd say the same thing, and if it's a female physio I might ask for her number. It's probably the reason why some people think I'm a cocky so and so.

Ricey McMenamin is the master when it comes to giving verbals.

The great thing about Ricey is that he can always back it up. He's still at it in club games. It never bothered him that he developed a reputation or was unpopular with the media or other teams' supporters. He could back it up every day of the week. To me, he is one of the greatest players Tyrone ever had.

Still, not everybody was into it on our team. Stevie O'Neill never did it. The older boys like Canavan and Cricko didn't either. But nobody told the rest of us to stop. Why would they?

We were winning.

I first met Peter Canavan when I moved to Holy Trinity College in September, 1997.

He was my form teacher and took me for about half of the classes in the GNVQ in Leisure and Tourism I was doing. It wasn't the best course in the world, it was basically just a pass to get a few boys like me onto the football team. My Da had gone to the same school and always spoke very highly of it. I knew it was a good school but, in the back of my mind, I knew I was there for the football. Me and Canavan didn't get on too well at first — not in the classroom anyway.

Our class was full of wing nuts. There was Gavin 'Horse' Devlin, who was in my class all the way through from St Pius', Fran Loughran and Aidan Quinn, Raymie McAleer, Gavin 'Minty' Quinn — we thought we had the run of the school.

Most of the time we'd be hanging around the foyer messing about when we should have been in class. We were playing blind man's buff one day when Canavan came around the corner and one of the boys grabbed him thinking it was one of us. When the lad took the blindfold off and realised it was Canavan, he nearly died but we were relieved when Canavan started to laugh.

We did different dares on him but, at the same time, you knew not to misbehave in his class. He was strict. While other teachers let you off with things, he didn't and you had more respect for him because of it.

I would always keep the head down in his class, writing away, asking questions, trying to impress him. Then, two classes later, I'd be sent to him by another teacher because I'd played up. As my form teacher, he was the one who had to deal with it. When he'd see me coming, he'd shake his head.

'What have you done now? You don't say a word in my class.'

I was shy enough at school but, as the years went on, I started to speak my mind. I was never two-faced but I was always messing about and had to sit up the front on my own, in almost every class.

I was caught mooning at Martin McElkennon out of a classroom window and got suspended. McElkennon was training the Tyrone minors at that time and I was in the squad. He had a team from St Ciaran's in Ballygawley up at our school and when he walked past our window, I couldn't resist.

Another teacher saw me doing it and told Canavan, who brought me to the Principal and I got a two-day suspension. I knew I'd done the wrong thing.

Canavan took no shit and I'm sure he got a hard time from other teachers about us, in fact I know he did. Other teachers would say, 'Who do those boys think they are? They should be out on building sites ... they're only here for the football'. Canavan knew he had a football team on his hands. He had to defend us many a time in the staff room, even though he knew we were eejits. I didn't really want to be there, although somehow I survived all the assignments and passed with a merit. But when the bell rang and it was time to go out onto the football pitch, that is when I came into my own. That was where I felt smart.

Although Canavan and I didn't get on too well in the classroom, on the football pitch it was usually a different story. Though, even on the school field, we had the odd falling out.

We were training one day and he kept saying, 'Last score wins, last score wins,' but the game was going on and on. I was getting fed up with it. There was no end in sight for this game so I put the ball over the bar and shouted to him, 'I suppose that was fucking wide?'

He went mental. He stopped the whole thing and called me over, glaring at me.

'Who do you think you are? The cheek of you talking to me like that. I'm not having it.' The rest of the boys were staring at me, jaws on the deck. I'd just bawled out Peter Canavan.

He gave me some roasting for that and I deserved it. I went home from school that evening raging with myself. I had so much respect for him and I knew I had let myself down.

People always talk about the master and pupil relationship between us and think he must have taught me every move while I was still at school. That's not the case. I think our partnership was as good as it was because we got to know each other's games so well and were able to read each other's minds. By the time we came to play together, it just seemed like the most natural thing in the world.

I was still at school the first time I lined out alongside him.

Colm O'Rourke's Ireland squad were playing a warm-up match in Omagh before the International Rules series against Australia and the Tyrone minors were on as a curtain-raiser. We had just won the All-Ireland title and we were playing against a Rest of Ulster select in a charity game with proceeds going to the Omagh bomb fund, the tragedy having occurred two months earlier.

After we'd played our match, I showered quickly so I could go back out and watch the cream of Ireland. Then there was a knock on the dressing room door.

The Irish squad needed a few of us to help make up the numbers and they asked for Aidy Lynch and myself to play in the match.

I was stunned and said no straight away, but, despite Mickey's thoughts about International Rules, he encouraged me to play. I think he thought it would be a good experience for us to play alongside some of the best players in Ireland, so I said I'd give it a go.

There was some array of rich talent playing that day and there was us boys standing like clowns in the middle of it.

Every kind of emotion shot through me. I was seventeen years old standing on the same field as Jim McGuinness, Anthony Tohill, Jarlath Fallon, Michael Donnellan, Niall Buckley and Gary Coleman. I was excited, embarrassed, proud, awe-struck, frightened, you name it. I just wanted to get the ball and give it right away. Gary Coleman was marking me but I didn't want to get too involved in the play and mess up a move.

Canavan was Ireland's vice-captain that year and he was on the field.

I saw him running up the wing and looking up to pass the ball. I knew it should be my ball. I was free. I wanted him to pass to me but, in a way, I was hoping he wouldn't.

Please don't pass this ball to me, What if I drop it?

I put my hand up as if I was in class wanting to ask a question. Sure enough, it was coming in my direction. It was a hard enough pass but he hit it with the outside of the boot and I jumped for the ball. Gary Coleman was coming steaming in but I just closed my eyes and it landed straight into my chest. Pure relief. I took the mark and scored an 'over' which felt class.

I didn't tell anybody at school on the Monday that I had played a match with our form teacher over the weekend. I didn't feel the need to broadcast it.

Talk went around the county that some of the Tyrone minors were joining up with the Ireland squad. As if! We were only there making up the numbers but it was a special day for me because of the calibre of players I got to play with, which is why I still have the jersey.

I have kept plenty of jerseys over the years, but the only ones I've put in the safe at home are my Tyrone 2003 and 2005 All-Ireland final jerseys, and that yellow jersey from the trial match, because it was the first time that I ever played with Peter Canavan.

◆ ◆ ◆ ◆ ◆

I was born in Magherafelt in Derry.

My ma is a Maghera woman and there are sixteen in her family and thirteen in my da's. Imagine trying to get All-Ireland tickets for that lot!

My ma was in a showband, she was the lead singer of the Cotton Pickers, and she met my da going to dances. My ma is my biggest fan – and also my strongest critic. She has had to do a bit of fire-fighting for me over the years with some of the scrapes I've got myself into, but she has been to every match I've played since Under-10 and is incredibly proud of me.

My only brother, Stephen, is five years older than me and he has beautiful twins, Katie and Charlie. My two sisters are Michelle, who is a year older than me, and Marie Claire, who is five years younger than me. Michelle is married to a Derry man, Neil, and they have a wonderful boy called Jack. Michelle owns two jewellery shops in Maghera and Cookstown. Marie Claire is a teacher and she is married to Adrian, who is a Fermanagh man. They are living and working in Hong Kong. I always enjoy slagging the brothers-in-law about football. Tyrone's win over Derry with the thirteen men is thrown up at poor Neil all the time, but the whole family have always been supportive of me. We are very close and we didn't fall out much growing up, but if there's an argument and I feel I'm right, I like to put my point across.

For as long as I can remember, people have called me 'Mugsy'. Our Stephen had the nickname first, then his friends started transferring it to me when I was very young, and then my own mates and teammates did the same.

I went to a wee country school, Drummullan Primary School, because my Uncle Sean Mulligan taught there and later became the principal.

Unfortunately, he passed away in 2002 and never got to see any of Tyrone's All-Ireland success, but I have a lot of happy memories of travelling with him to matches in Clones and going to school with him every day, us all piled into the back of his car, him chain smoking and listening to BBC Radio Ulster.

All the Mulligan clan went to school there. We practically kept the school numbers up on our own.

Drummullan was where I started to learn my trade as a footballer. We won the South Derry Primary Schools' Championship in 1992 and I loved it. The class was full of Ballinderry and Ardboe lads as well as all us Mulligans. We were football mad.

When we were in Primary 7, we played against Cookstown in a community soccer tournament. They slagged us off for being a wee farmer school and laughed at our jerseys ... 'Look at the state of youse'. The 'townies', like Marty McGarrity, Peter Coyle, Stevie Hughes, Sean Bradley and I, loved it when we beat them.

I had to take the Eleven Plus test that year but, rather than preparing, I spent most of my time outside playing football.

The Mulligans never lacked for brains, and my cousin Barry 'Groovy' Mulligan sat the test in P5 and passed it, but I must have been the one who missed out.

Uncle Sean took the P7s for Eleven Plus tutoring after school and, as he was my lift home, it meant I had to wait and study too. I'd watch the P6s playing seven-a-side football outside, daydreaming, wishing I could be out there. When Uncle Sean would ask me a question I wouldn't even hear it.

Eventually, he knew he was fighting a losing battle.

'Go on ahead out there and play football, you have no interest in being in here.'

This continued for months before I sat the test. I'd go home and my ma would say, 'How did you get on?'

I would reply, 'Oh great, I had a great day today, I got a couple of good questions right.'

Every morning, I'd leave my football gear on the bed, ready for me to put on when I got home from school. Stephen, Michelle and Marie Clare would go into the house to start their homework but I'd be straight outside, mimicking Jimmy Smyth, who I loved as a TV commentator. I'd try to put on his accent and recite his commentary as I kicked ball around the house. I was happy playing by myself, hitting free kicks, going on solo runs, kicking the ball high into the air and trying to catch it. I'd dummy round trees and flowerbeds and try to hit every ball into the top corner. When I scored a goal, I'd run over and celebrate in front of the evergreens, imagining they were supporters in the crowd.

I took the ball everywhere: I took it to school in my bag, I took it to the shop, I even hid it in the hedge beside the Church when I went to Mass on Sundays and picked it up again on the way out.

We started out using two t-shirts as goal posts, then we moved on to using chalk to draw onto a wall. When we got a door on the garage it was great, it had squares on it and I would practise hitting the top corner. A couple of the panels had glass in them and I broke them every few months. My da's heart was broken too.

During the summer months all the cousins got together to play for the Mulligan Cup.

It was a five-a-side tournament we played out the back of Church Street, in the house I'm living in now. We cut the grass in straight lines so it looked like a proper pitch. My da was a site manager with McAleer and Rushe and he made us goalposts, with the green mesh used for scaffolding as our nets. He lined the pitch out with chalk and we had sideline flags. It was real professional.

We thought we were playing in Croke Park.

My da videoed it and was commentating at the same time, like he was Michael O'Hehir. He interviewed us at the start of the game, 'Who's your favourite player? Are you confident of winning today?'

We took it so seriously. We had a cup, medals, the lot.

My cousins 'Groovy', Judith Rodgers and I were on one team and we were always Tyrone. Our Michelle and Stephen were on the other team and they had to be Derry, Dublin, Kerry or whoever. The younger ones, David and Brian Mulligan, would be allowed on as subs.

We played for the Ulster Championship and then progressed to the All-Ireland series. It took about eight or ten matches to win the Mulligan Cup. It lasted the whole summer. All the aunties and uncles were the supporters. There'd be the odd row on the pitch, of course, and that usually led to a replay.

A great uncle of mine, Pat O'Neill, refereed our matches. I think I was his favourite nephew because he let me away with a lot, but we nearly had to report him to the Games Administration Committee in Croke Park one time when he counted the scores up wrong. In the end, he wasn't allowed to referee the replay so Uncle Sean took charge. My team lost!

I had the Tyrone strip on, the shirts, shorts, socks, everything. I wore No. 9 because I loved Plunkett Donaghy and I was a midfielder in those days.

Plunkett was my hero at that time along with Stephen 'Scotchy' Conway, who played for Cookstown and Tyrone.

I wore a lot of our Stephen's old football boots but I was in my element when Ma bought me my own, a pair of black and white Mitre. We lived next door to Granny and Granda Mulligan and I ran in to show them off, though Granda was shocked when he heard they cost £6.

I insisted on taking free kicks off the ground the same way Scotchy did. I used to set mine up on a wee cup to get a bit of height on the kick.

Stephen was the oldest and he used to run the field, trying to take on three of us at a time. He took it more seriously than the rest of us. One day, I was practising out the back, and he came out roaring at me to move because he was trying to grow the grass in that goalmouth. He told me to go and practise in the other goalmouth instead. He wanted the pitch to be perfect for a Mulligan Cup match taking place a few days later.

My da had always promised he'd get proper timber to build us some really big goalposts and, one day after school, I walked into the garage and saw two huge pieces of timber. *These must be the posts my da was talking about*, I thought.

I took the timber out of the garage, got the green scaffolding net and started hammering nails into the uprights, trying to make the goalposts. I wondered why it was so hard to get the nails into ordinary timber but I kept going. Finally, I dug holes in the ground and stuck the posts into them. I was delighted with myself when I finished it and shouted for Stephen to come outside to see our new posts.

It had taken me two hours to build them but, one hour later, I was grounded and had a very sore backside.

I knew by Stephen's face I'd done something wrong.

'You are dead,' he said. 'They're solid oak door frames and they're supposed to be going down to Dublin for McAleer and Rushe. They cost a fortune!'

My da went mental. When he calmed down a few days later, he got us new timber and Stephen and I made the posts ourselves.

To complete our garden pitch, Da put floodlights up around our house. In fact, they were extra security lights because we lived next door to a hotel, but I was in my element playing matches until all hours of the night.

I had my first floodlit game long before they were ever installed in Croke Park.

I went to secondary school in St Pius' in Magherafelt. All my mates were going to Holy Trinity College in Cookstown or St Patrick's Academy in Dungannon. I didn't have the brains to get into the Academy and my parents opted for St Pius' instead of Holy Trinity. I didn't care at the time which school I went to.

I found it hard at school. I found it difficult to listen and to take things in. Sometimes I wondered what it would be like to be smart. Some lads took great pleasure in answering questions and passing exams, but being out on the pitch was where I felt I could express myself.

Right, I'll show youse who's smart now.

If I'd had the same drive in the classroom as I did on the pitch, I probably would have been a barrister or a brain surgeon by now.

I half thought I would like to be a PE teacher, but I had no real desire to do any particular job and I didn't want to go to college. St Pius' was a football hotbed so that's all that mattered to me. Master McAuley hardly ever selected me for my own year's football team but I always got onto the team of the year above me.

Brendan Convery, a Lavey man, took that team and he always picked me. There were some great players on the team, like Niall McCusker and Johnny Niblock, who both went on to play for Derry. It got hot and heavy in the playground sometimes between the Tyrone and the Derry lads. Our big rivals at the time were St Pat's Maghera, who were captained by Fergal Doherty.

I hit it off straight away with Master Convery. I liked his wit and sarcasm and I was delighted when he took us on a school skiing trip to Bulgaria when I was in third year.

He had to bail me out of trouble on the second day we were there.

I got bored of the wee nursery slopes and wandered off with two mates, Raymie McAleer and Martin Harney.

I went to lift my skis off the rail and spotted a real cool, trendy pair next to mine. *Wouldn't mind having a wee go on those.* What I didn't realize wass that taking a pair of skis over there is like stealing a car.

The skis were deadly fast and I fell a few times, cutting the face off myself, but it was great craic and we lost track of time. By the time we got back to the hotel that evening, there were search parties out looking for us. The police were there too, wanting to press charges for the theft of the skis, because the owner was going mental.

Master Convery went through us, but he managed to persuade the police not to press charges. Our punishment was that we had to stay in the hotel for the rest of the trip and weren't allowed out to ski.

The rest of the class laughed and waved goodbye to us every morning as they headed out to the slopes while we stayed cooped up in the hotel.

Or so they thought.

Once they all left, Master Convery took us three lads out on our own. He was a deadly skier so it was like having our own personal tutor for the next five days. He taught us how to stop – which was a big problem for me – and how to turn. We always made sure we were back in the hotel before the rest of the class returned in the evening.

On the last day, we were allowed out to join them on the piste. The boys got some shock when they saw us gliding around like professionals while they were all slipping and sliding about the place. We had the last laugh on them, thanks to Master Convery.

◆ ◆ ◆ ◆ ◆

Going to Clones to watch Tyrone was what did it for me. I was hooked.

I suppose it's your parents who get you into it. They got the t-shirts printed up for us from local shops and bought the flags. My da had the work van and we all piled into the back of it.

Da was so superstitious, he always had to take the same route. If there were road works or we were diverted off the main road for any reason, he'd go nuts, thinking this meant Tyrone were going to get beaten. He also liked if the minors were beaten, because he was sure that meant the seniors were going to win.

Damian 'Kojak' Morgan was a local singer around Cookstown and he usually came with us. He'd bring the guitar and play all the Tyrone tunes in the back of the van, and then when we got to Clones he'd go into the bars and get the songs going again. I couldn't wait for the match to start.

I loved watching the Tyrone bus climbing the hill on its way to the ground and seeing the players get off the bus, all zoned out, totally focused on the game.

I was eight years old when Scotchy Conway hit a '45' to draw the match against Donegal, in 1989. The ball hit the post and then rolled across the crossbar to salvage a draw. I was standing behind the goals and had a great view of it. I went home and tried to practise it flat out, deliberately trying to hit the post to see could I get it to roll onto the crossbar.

Watching Tyrone win a big Ulster Championship match in Clones was the best feeling in the world. When I got home, all I wanted to do was go out into the back garden and practise what I'd seen on the pitch that day.

They were magical summers. Watching us beat Derry with only thirteen men in the Ulster semi-final in 1995 was the best game I ever watched as a supporter. I loved the way the whole team pulled together. All the talk was that Tyrone were a one-man team and too reliant on Peter Canavan, but every man stood up that day and they played like a real team.

Growing up, our big rivalry was always with Derry because of where we lived and with so many of the Mulligans having gone to school there.

Shay Forbes landed in to St Pius' the day after the match with his Tyrone jersey on and his school tie over the top of it and got suspended right away. I couldn't stop laughing the whole day.

We didn't miss one of the games in 1995.

I broke my right ankle playing football that summer but that wasn't going to keep me from going to watch the team in the All-Ireland semi-final against Galway.

Petey McAleer drove down to Dublin with his son, Ollie, in the front and his other son, Raymie, and his cousin, Lee Casewell, Barry Devine and I all piled into the back. We threw blankets and pillows down and made a big bed in the back of the van to make it easier for my plastered foot. I soon forgot about the plaster when the team won. I threw the crutches at Petey McAleer and ran down onto the pitch to celebrate with the players, not that we got near them.

I was told I'd have the plaster on for three weeks but, in the end, it was more like three months. I didn't give it a chance to heal because I kept playing football on it. The doctors couldn't understand why the bone wasn't knitting but I knew all right. I'd be out the back with one of my da's socks over the cast, playing away. In a way, it wasn't a bad thing because I started to practise kicking the ball and soloing with my left foot.

I was still on crutches going to watch the All-Ireland final but I was so excited. Those boys were heroes to me. Peter Canavan was God, and we were sure he would lead us to the promised land.

We had been watching Ulster teams win All-Irelands flat out. The year before, we watched on the big TV in the Glenavon as Down won their second All-Ireland in four years. Donegal had won in 1992. When Derry won in 1993, they got some reception driving through Cookstown. I don't think they could believe it themselves. I knew their bus driver, Benny Vincent, and he gave me a wave. All I could think was, *Imagine being on that bus.*

I thought 1995 would be like Derry's win, only better. This time it would be our boys driving through Cookstown on an open top bus with the Sam Maguire Cup.

We had tickets for the Canal End and I stared across at the Dubs on Hill 16, fascinated by the colour and the atmosphere they brought. I was lucky enough to get up close and personal with the boys on the Hill in later years and there is no greater spectacle.

We lit a red smoke bomb at the start of the match and we planned to light the second one at the end when Ciaran Corr was lifting the Cup.

Canavan was sensational, hitting eleven points, but with time almost up we were still a point behind. If we could claw our way out of this one, I was convinced we would hammer Dublin the next day.

There was time for one more attack.

I was right behind the nets when Sean McLaughlin's equalising point was disallowed. Tyrone people around me were going bananas, thinking it was a score to force a replay, but I froze to the spot. I saw right away that the referee had disallowed the point. Paddy Russell judged Canavan had fouled the ball in the build-up to the pass to McLaughlin. We were disgusted.

We never got to light the second smoke bomb.

We were as far away from an All-Ireland title as ever. I didn't know Peter Canavan or any of the players, but I was gutted for every single one of them. It wasn't fair. We were watching Ulster counties win flat out.

Why did we have to be the ones sitting with no All-Ireland title?

My life was all about football and having the craic.

Being born in June meant I was always the youngest in my class and I had just turned sixteen when I sat my GCSE's. I didn't exactly light up the sky with my results, but I was going to be moving schools to Holy Trinity in September, where I knew I'd be playing football for Peter Canavan.

After I left St Pius' I got a summer job working in Unipork. Sometimes I hid in the lockers at work, skiving. I could sleep in a locker standing up, like a horse, no bother at all.

For extra money I agreed to go into 'the kill', but I only lasted about forty minutes. There was a lot of blood and I couldn't handle it at all. I spent the rest of the summer packing sausage rolls, getting £200 a week, which was a complete fortune to me.

One day I was off work, I crashed my ma's car. My parents were away at a work dinner in Belfast and I invited a few boys round. Raymie McAleer, Barry Devine and my cousin, Deccie McGarrity, came over and when I went to get them a drink of juice out of the cupboard, I saw my ma's car keys just sitting there. *Bingo. Wouldn't mind a spin in that.* It was a white Toyota Carina and I'd fancied getting behind the wheel for some time. This was my chance.

We headed out towards Drum Manor Forest Park and, although I stalled the car a few times, I soon got the hang of it. As soon as I started to relax, we drove up behind two cars that were racing each other down the road. I panicked, swerved up to the kerb and just about missed hitting a phone box.

It scared the life out of me. I knew we'd had a narrow escape so I turned the car around and headed for home, but I could tell there was something wrong. The steering wheel was hanging to the left and I couldn't straighten it up.

I shouted at the boys at the back, 'Is there anything hanging off her?' They looked out the side and back windows and couldn't see anything.

I decided to stop.

Raymie McAleer climbed underneath the car to have a look.

'Is everything all right down there Raymie?' I said, pulling the mat back underneath my feet. I saw Raymie's face looking up at me. The two of us freaked out.

I threw the mat back down.

Despite having a two-foot gash in the floor, we somehow got the car home. I went straight into our garage and got a hammer to chip away part of the wall outside the house, thinking I could get away with some half-baked excuse.

Michelle phoned my ma and she came straight home. I explained I'd been messing about with the car outside the house and had hit the kerb and the wall. She was annoyed, saying, 'Let that be a lesson to you!'

She got the mechanic to come down to the house to take a look at the car and told him what had happened. He took one look at the damage and said, 'Where did that boy say he hit the car?' She told him again. 'No, I'm afraid not, there's not a chance he did that damage doing five miles per hour.'

She came in to the house with a face like thunder.

It was time to come clean. I had to pay £100 a week, half my week's wages, for the rest of the summer to pay for the damages. It proved to be a very expensive mistake, though, as things turned out, it wasn't to be my only mishap behind the wheel of a car.

3

A lot of people think it was success at Holy Trinity that propelled me onto the Tyrone minor squad in 1997, but my performances with the Cookstown Under-16s, minors and Under-21s also helped get me noticed. The mentality around Cookstown was always that football was a bit of craic, the players never took it seriously enough. I had watched great players from the town play, like TP Sheehy, Barry O'Hare and Benny Sheehy, who captained Tyrone minors in 1992. I saw them play for the county and always thought that if they could do it, so could I.

Our Stephen and Henry Bradley were taking our Under-16 team and they instilled great belief in us. Henry was good at psyching us up before matches. He'd say, 'We're on a train journey, and this is one station we're not stopping at'. Another classic line of his was, 'For too long we've been the bridesmaids of Tyrone football, well, today we're going to get married!'

They made us boys believe that we could win something. Lads like Sean Bradley, Ryan Collins, Kevin Kelly, Barry Devine and Marty McGarrity were there when we won the Under-16 League and Championship double, the first Grade One titles that Cookstown had won in a long time. We also won a Grade Two minor title in 1997 under Eugene McGirr, Gusty Quinn and John Foley. They dropped me for the minor final against Moy because I missed training, even though it was only because I had to go a County Board meeting about a suspension I picked up in a League match.

I was ripping to be dropped, but I came on and scored a free kick to draw the game for us and hit 1-2 in the replay.

That year I played for the club minor and Under-21 teams when I was fifteen. I came on in the Under-21 Championship against Carrickmore and scored two goals. It was brilliant playing alongside boys a few years older than me, like Paul McGurk, Jim Eastwood (of TV show 'The Apprentice' fame), Niall Quinn and Colm Devine.

Those boys were a few years older than me and were out drinking pints but my ma was strict. There was no way I was going to be allowed out at fifteen or sixteen years of age. She'd say to me, 'Sure why don't you go out the back and practise your football?'

There is just a wall between our house and The Glenavon hotel and I'd hear the disco going on next door, but I wasn't bothered. I was happier out the back practising free-kicks.

A lot of boys I played with on the Under-16 and minor teams were probably better than me at that stage. There were a lot of other boys in Cookstown who should have gone on to have success with Tyrone, but I don't think they wanted it as much as me. Cookstown was my number one priority, and I just hated getting beaten.

I was asked to play for the minors against Errigal Ciaran. I knew I was too young but my da told me to go ahead, he reckoned I wouldn't start but that it would be good experience for me. I ended up starting at full-forward and scored 2-3. Mickey Harte was there to watch some of the older Cookstown lads but I must have caught his eye.

Harte's call came soon after Paul McGirr's tragic death while playing for Tyrone minors in the Ulster Championship.

I didn't know Paul personally but I was standing on the terrace behind the goals in Healy Park when the tragedy struck. I was directly behind the nets and saw the tackle: A loopy, fisted ball came in and it looked like Paul might have been going to fist it in, but the Armagh goalkeeper came out for it at the same time. It looked like a total accident.

I knew there was something wrong when I saw some of his family coming on to the field but I had no idea how serious it was until later that night. I was sitting in my best mate Raymie McAleer's house, talking about the game when there was a newsflash on the TV, saying Paul had died. We were stunned.

I was enjoying a rare night out in the Black Horse with our minors, who were celebrating their big win, when my ma phoned the bar looking for me. 'Mickey Harte is after ringing … he wants you to ring him back,' she said.

I thought it was a wind-up but I sprinted all the way home. What did Mickey Harte want me for? I had only celebrated my sixteenth birthday a few weeks earlier, did he really want me for the minors?

I was panting and out of breath when I called him back. He wanted to invite me onto the minor panel to play in a few challenge matches. I couldn't believe it.

Without Paul McGirr, maybe they needed to bulk out the squad. I was sorry to begin my Tyrone career in such circumstances, but excited to be finally pulling on a Tyrone jersey.

I played in a challenge match against Mayo in Donegal and that's when I scored my first point for Tyrone. It was only a challenge match, but I was over the moon. I didn't really do myself justice though, certainly not enough to force my way into Mickey's plans at such a late stage in the season.

Mark Harte was the star forward on the team. He kicked the equalising point against Kerry in the All-Ireland semi-final to take the game to a replay in Parnell Park.

All the boys were making me feel welcome but I was incredibly shy. They had been together all year and I didn't really feel part of it. It was like starting a new class in the middle of the school year. I was joining a group that had already gelled and had its own wee groups.

I got friendly with boys who were in the training panel with me, like

Mickey McGee, Philly Jordan and Brendan Donnelly. We were in shirts and ties while the rest were togging out.

Six days after the drawn match with Kerry, Kevin Hughes' brother, Paul, was killed in a car accident. Everyone asked if I was going to the wake. But I didn't want to go. I didn't really know Hub at that stage. My mum said I should go but I felt I didn't know Hub well enough and I stayed away.

Paul McGirr had died only a couple of months earlier and now here was another tragedy for the group to absorb. I don't know how the boys coped as well as they did but that was when I realised there was something special about Hub Hughes. It wasn't so much what he said, but his actions spoke louder than any words.

He was offered the chance to sit out the replay in Parnell Park, and everybody would have understood if he had. Instead, not only did he play, but he produced an outstanding performance, he and Mark Harte were both brilliant.

We won the game after extra time and all the Killeeshil and Tyrone fans ran onto the pitch and lifted Hub up on their shoulders. What a performance. Everyone was crying in the dressing room and it started to dawn on us that, despite all the sadness and the tragedy, we were in an All-Ireland final.

Fr Gerard McAleer was joint-manager of the team and he helped us to deal with the tragedies, but they weren't used to psych us up for the final. We were too young to have that on our shoulders, though I wondered if we were destined to win after all that had happened.

I didn't expect to be togged out for the final against Laois, and no one was more shocked than me when I was given a place in the match day squad.

As we got off the bus at Croke Park, I saw a few Cookstown boys hanging around outside. I was busting to tell somebody and I whispered to them that I was togging out. They thought I was winding them up. Only just turned sixteen and togging out in an All-Ireland final? Unreal.

I didn't get on but I warmed up. Mickey knew I was very young but I was buzzing just to be involved.

The final proved to be a bridge too far for the boys. There were a lot of tears afterwards when Laois denied us a fairytale end to the season.

We got to watch the senior final afterwards and I saw one of my heroes, Maurice Fitzgerald, in the flesh. Along with Joe Brolly, he was the forward I most admired at the time. The next day I saw Maurice at the lunch the GAA hosted for the four minor and senior teams who'd contested the All-Ireland finals. I wanted to go over and ask him for his autograph but I thought the boys would take a hand out of me, so I left empty-handed knowing it was an opportunity missed.

It was 1998 that it really started to hit home to me that maybe I could be a serious player for Tyrone. I was flying at all levels; with Holy Trinity, Tyrone Vocationals and Tyrone minors.

I was starting to make a name for myself in midfield for Holy Trinity. The school's Under-16 team went on a good run and got to the Ulster final. They were giving us stick, chanting at us at every opportunity, 'We're in the final! We're in the final!' They won Ulster but, when they were beaten in the All-Ireland semi-final, Canavan decided to call a few of their players into our squad.

Even though Canavan was training us, it was hard to get the boys to commit one hundred per cent. We had the nucleus of a great team but we didn't realise how good we were. Canavan told us that with a sprinkling of the Under-16s to join us, we could win the All-Ireland. We didn't believe him at first.

We reached the Under-18 Vocational Schools final, called the Markey Cup, and faced Dungannon Tech in the decider at Clones. After going there for years to watch Tyrone, I couldn't wait to play there for the first time.

Myself and 'Big B', Brian O'Neill, had a great understanding in the middle of the field. Canavan pulled me over at training one day and said, 'I need you to do a job for me, I need you to mark Hub Hughes'.

Hub was already a star of the Tyrone minor team and captain of the Dungannon side. I remembered how brilliant he was against Kerry in the All-Ireland minor semi-final the year before and was nervous about marking him for the first time. In the end we both played well, we sort of cancelled each other out, with Holy Trinity winning the Ulster title.

That was when we started to believe Canavan that we could win the All-Ireland. We had some great players. We had a lad from Moortown called

Sean Teague, he was a real sticky marker and I thought he had a brilliant future ahead of him, but he died tragically a few years ago.

When we beat Kerry's Causeway Comprehensive by two points in the All-Ireland semi-final in Athlone, we were just one game away from an All-Ireland medal. We faced Davitt College from Castlebar in the final. There was a big crowd in Markievicz Park, certainly the biggest I had played in front of at that stage of my career, but it was a poor, low-scoring game.

I had scored four of our six points but we were still losing by a point and it didn't look good. The Mayo team should have had us beaten, but Ryan Quinn came on as a sub and won a free about thirty yards out.

Now it was over to me. It was the first time I felt real pressure on a football field. Up until then it had all been one fantastic rollercoaster ride, but this was serious. I felt confident stepping up to take the kick. The angle was quite difficult but I stroked it nicely between the posts. The final whistle blew, to relief all round.

The replay was in Clones and we came out onto the pitch a different animal.

Canavan was showing a real ruthless streak as manager which kept us on our toes. He dropped Stephen 'Shorty' McNally, who had been one of his best players all the way through school, and brought in Ryan 'Stringy' Collins, who hadn't been able to commit to football earlier in the year because of school work.

Shorty took it brilliantly, he was a real team player, and Stringy repaid Canavan's faith in him by scoring a goal in the replay.

We were All-Ireland champions, what a feeling! I took the Cup up to my brother, Stephen, who was sitting in the press box. It was a special moment, given everything he was going through.

Stephen was diagnosed with Hodgkin's Disease when he was seventeen, after finding lumps on his shoulder. He never let it beat him or get him down. The day he had the biopsy done, he played in a club minor Championship match against Edendork, coming on for the last ten minutes for my da, who was manager. He'd heard a few days before that a Tyrone minor selector was going to be there in Ardboe watching Stevie McGirr, Barry O'Hare, Benny Sheehy and him, so Stephen was desperate to play.

The football kept him going and when the cancer returned five years later, it helped the whole family that I was so involved with Holy Trinity, the Tyrone Vocationals and the Tyrone minors. Stephen had only got out of hospital a few days earlier when he came to Clones to watch us in the final that day. He shouldn't really have been there but that's what the football meant to us.

His illness was very serious second time around. It was a bit of a miracle, as my ma would say, that he came through it.

I had just started at Holy Trinity when I realised there was something badly wrong. My ma and da were never at home, they were up at the hospital in Dungannon the whole time with Stephen.

When Canavan called me over in school one day and asked if I was coping all right with everything at home, I was seriously worried. It seemed everyone knew more about what was going on than me, but I knew the family were trying to protect me.

Carol Doey, a good friend of our family, gave healing rubs to Stephen and she gave me rubs before games and after games. She was a great support to us at that time.

Stephen and I have always been close. I looked up to him and we had a great brotherly rivalry while we were growing up. In the early days, he lorded it over me in terms of medals. He played as a half-back with St Pat's Academy and won an All-Ireland Freshers title with Queen's. He was the only man on the Freshers team who didn't have county experience yet he more than held his own.

His bedroom was across the hall from mine and to me it seemed like it was stacked with stuff. I used to wonder would I ever win as much as him. Even my da had more medals than me. He'd captained Tyrone to the county's first All-Ireland Vocationals title in 1967 and also won an Ulster minor title the following year.

Stephen enjoyed teasing me about my lack of silverware. He used to say, 'You'll never have an Ulster medal'. He kinda stopped it in 1998 when I won three All-Ireland medals!

Winning the first one with Holy Trinity was the start of an unbelievable run. I was still only sixteen but I was enjoying the taste of winning, and had another All-Ireland final to look forward to with Tyrone Vocationals the following week.

Enda Kilpatrick and Terry McCann, who were in charge of the team, helped transform the thinking within Tyrone that All-Irelands could be won.

When word came through that our match against Offaly was going to be played in Croke Park, as a curtain-raiser to the Division One League final between Offaly and Derry, I felt a tingle of excitement.

Being togged out for the minors the previous September was one thing, but I was going to be starting this time. Starting and playing in Croke Park.

Then disaster struck.

The Monday before the final I went to minor club training. Stephen was joint-manager but, due to his illness, he wasn't really able to commit that year and I was minor captain. I really shouldn't have been training with another All-Ireland final coming up so soon but I didn't want the lads to think I had my head in the clouds and had forgotten about them.

I went up to take an Aussie Rules-style catch, climbing up on a boy's back, but I got hit from behind on the way down and lost my balance, falling and breaking the radius bone in my right arm. I was rushed to the Royal Victoria Hospital in Belfast for an emergency operation and had a plate and six screws inserted, with twenty-eight staples for good luck.

I was devastated. I had so wanted to emulate my da and win the same All-Ireland Vocational Schools title he had won 31 years earlier. I cursed my bad luck. Was I ever going to play in Croke Park?

I didn't have a realistic chance to play with the Tyrone minors in 1997 but this time the opportunity had been cruelly snatched away from me.

I was feeling sorry for myself in the hospital until a boy landed in the next bed to me, who had been kneecapped. I think he was one of the first in the north to get maggots in his knee. The doctors put them in his knee to clean the wound and then stitched him back up again. I was fascinated by the procedure but I kept to myself, I didn't know anything about him.

He had some members of the media looking for interviews with him and he was delighted with himself, nodding over to me, 'I'm famous … I'm famous'. When the TV cameras arrived the next day, though, the boy started shouting, 'I don't want any press in today'.

He needn't have worried as it turned out to be Jerome Quinn, looking to do an interview with me for BBC Northern Ireland. The boy was stunned. I was probably still doped up from the operation but I managed to enjoy my TV debut anyway. When Jerome left, the fella in the bed was staring at me, 'Who the hell are you anyway?'

I laughed. We got friendly after that and, let's just say, it was an interesting few days. He told me plenty of stories.

I attended the All-Ireland Vocational Schools final in Croke Park the next Sunday with my arm in a sling. Hub replaced me in midfield, as he had been suspended for our extra-time win over Cork in the semi-final. The boys carried me shoulder high across the pitch in Croke Park after they hammered Offaly without me. I was delighted for them but sick at the same time. I left Croke Park that afternoon wondering if I'd ever be back there.

The injury set me back big time. I was out for a few months but, worse than that, I was nervous about going up for a high ball.

It signalled the end of my midfield days. I just didn't have the confidence to go up for the big high balls any more, but it was an area of the field where Tyrone were blessed with talent. Enda McGinley was a forward in those days but he was always a great fielder, and then we had Hub and McAnallen and Ryan Mellon.

Mickey was brilliant and kept me involved with the minors even while I was injured.

My ma felt sorry for me after I broke my arm and bought me my first pair of Predator boots. Before that, I had been wearing Stephen's hand-me-downs. The new boots were the real deal and I absolutely loved them. When my da found out they cost £110 he flipped, even though I had chipped in £30 myself. He soon calmed down when, the first day I wore them, I came on as a sub against Derry in the Ulster Championship in Clones and pulled off a kick dummy before curling the ball over the bar.

Around this time some players began to stand out. We played Antrim in the Ulster minor final and boys like Brian McGuigan, McAnallen,

McGinley and Hub were looking like senior stars in waiting. Big Packie McConnell was starting to command the area, and I felt like I had a senior career ahead of me, too.

The norm was a handful of minors to make the step up to senior level, but we already knew our group was a bit special. We felt like we'd all make it.

We loved to win and some of us loved to celebrate. We had some lethal nights out after minor and Under-21 matches.

Hub was friendly with boys like Joe Campbell and Kevin 'Herby' O'Brien from Dromore who were in the squad. Those lads, and McGuigan and Horse, would throw their kit bags in our hall after matches and then we'd head straight up to the disco in The Glenavon. Ma didn't mind any of them staying over so long as they phoned home to tell their parents where they were.

Fr Gerard McAleer always tried to keep a close eye on me and make sure I wasn't drinking because he knew I was younger than most of the other boys. But, from the moment Hub bought me my first drink in a pub in Dromore, a vodka and Lucozade which didn't taste great, I've never looked back.

If anything needed to be smuggled around Ireland, that Tyrone minor team would have been the best at it. We took a lot of spirits onto the bus home, drinking out of Lucozade Sport bottles. We'd go into the toilets and tip anything half decent that we could mix with Lucozade Sport into the squeezy bottles.

One day we stopped in Cavan after a match and Hub came out of an off-license walking like a cowboy. He had stuff stashed everywhere; quarter bottles of vodka and gin in his socks and everything. He was finding it hard to get up the steps of the bus without clinking.

We collapsed into the back seat, relieved, but then we saw Fr Gerard come marching down towards us with a face like thunder. 'Kevin Hughes, Kevin Hughes, you leave that back right now.'

Oh no, I thought, *If he searches us we're dead.*

'What is it, Father?' Hub said.

'That glass you've got in your hand, it's stolen property. That's a disgrace!'

'Oh, sorry Father, would you mind leaving it back for me?'

Hub handed him the glass.

'No problem. Thank you, Kevin.'

Hub started to smile as he pulled out one bottle after another. 'Well, he didn't see this one, he didn't see that one…'

We messed about a lot, but football was still the main thing in our lives. Nothing came before that. Once we got a wee taste of success, we wanted a whole lot more.

Hub and McGuigan missed our All-Ireland semi-final against Leitrim but we were able to bring Ryan Mellon in. That's the kind of quality we had. I was buzzing about finally getting to play in Croke Park.

The excitement got the better of me, rushing a thirteen metres free into Hill 16 and kicking it wide. I was ripping with myself but finished the game with 0-3 as we made it to our second All-Ireland minor final in a row.

All I could think about was getting back to Croke Park for an All-Ireland final. After two near misses in the previous twelve months, nothing was going to stop me this time.

Things could not have gone any better. I scored 1-4 in that All-Ireland final, the kind of thing I'd dreamed about when I was kicking ball in our back garden. It was deadly. I scored the goal into the Canal End in the opening quarter, Aidy Lynch's punch pass setting me up. I saw the Laois goalkeeper, John Graham, going low, so I blasted it into the roof of the net.

For years I'd watched the All-Ireland minor final on TV, seeing Cookstown boys like Benny Sheehy and Barry O'Hare playing for Tyrone in Croke Park, and now I'd gone one better. I'd scored a goal in an All-Ireland final. Even if I never kicked a ball again, I thought, at least I've put my name down in history.

The goal set us on our way as we got revenge on Laois for defeat in the final, twelve months earlier. The only disappointment was to be taken out to midfield in the second half. I was on fire inside and felt so, so fit.

I was ripping about it, but I got over it quickly enough when I heard my name being called out as the Man of the Match. I wasn't able to speak when I collected the award at the Spa Hotel that night but I was thrilled. There had been other contenders that day but it was a great honour for me.

Hub's tradition of wearing stupid hats started that year and he had a big floppy one on at the banquet. People got to know about it and would be waiting after games to give him the most ridiculous thing they could find.

At our homecoming the next evening, I saw some of my club mates partying on the street in Aughnacloy. It was the start of many great nights there as we carried one piece of silverware after another across the border into that town.

Most of the lads moved on to Under-21s in 1999 with Mickey, but a few of us were still underage and I was appointed captain of the Tyrone minors that year by new joint-managers, Martin Coyle, who had managed me at Cookstown, and Liam Donnelly.

I had captained Cookstown minors and I enjoyed doing the same job for Tyrone, especially when we won the Ulster minor League title and I got to lift the trophy. But we weren't able to retain the Ulster minor Championship title. A Benny Coulter-inspired Down team beat us on a baking hot day in Casement Park, and went on to claim the Ulster and All-Ireland minor titles themselves.

I still won two Ulster titles that year, with Holy Trinity and Tyrone Vocationals, but my thoughts were already turning towards joining Mickey and the rest of the boys in the Tyrone Under-21s.

Time to get busy winning again.

We weren't in the least surprised to find ourselves back in the winners' enclosure when we stepped up to the Under-21s.

The team was backboned by the minors who'd lost the 1997 All-Ireland final, top players like Mark Harte, Darren O'Hanlon and Richard Thornton, and we coasted through Ulster, with me scoring 1-2 in the Ulster final against Donegal. I played what I think was one of my best ever matches for Tyrone in the All-Ireland semi-final against Galway in Carrick-on-Shannon.

Brian McGuigan had to go off and I moved out to centre half-forward. We were two points behind at half time but after Cormac gave a great speech, we came out and outscored them 1-7 to 0-1 in the second half. It was that Under-21 team's finest hour, I thought.

I was disappointed with how I played against Limerick in the final. I didn't score and could easily have been taken off but it still felt brilliant to have another All-Ireland medal. Everyone was delighted, in particular for the lads who had missed out on the 1998 minor success, and with more good players to join us for the following year I knew that we would have a great chance of putting Under-21 titles back-to-back the following year.

Once we'd won the Under-21 Championship in 2000, I had a free summer for the first time in a few seasons.

Stephen's best friend, Eamon Eastwood, went to Sydney that year and joined Penrith Gaels and later, when Cormac died, he formed the McAnallen's club, in 2005.

Stephen also went to Australia in 2000 and was playing for the Brisbane Shamrocks, who had been set up by our da's cousin, Gerry O'Neill, and Nicholas Carpenter. Both men and their wives, Ann and Sally, were very good to Stephen and me when we were there. The team was made up of former Aussie Rules players, ex-Army men and some first- and second-generation Irish.

Stephen was desperate for me to come out and join him at the Willawong, which was the Shamrocks' home pitch, and I didn't need too much persuading.

Before I arrived, Stephen made out to the boys that I was some kind of huge sports star in Ireland. *I can live with that*, I decided.

In the end, my ma, da, my girlfriend, Edele, and I all headed out. I was there for three months and absolutely loved it.

We arrived on the Friday and Stephen had me out training on the Monday, presenting me to the boys as if Pelé had just signed for the Brisbane Shamrocks. Stephen had them believing that they were going to win the Championship and that I was the missing link.

I could tell they were expecting a lot from me but it didn't take me long to get into the swing of things. They were a great bunch of lads and we were soon pulling together like a real team. We started to beat everyone in sight, and Stephen and I ran the show.

Our manager, Stevie Talbot was from Kerry. Alan Colleran, who played for Galway Minors, was full-back. Nicholas Carpenter's son, Glen, was also on the team. Adrian Darbellay, or Darbs as we called him, and Matt Ogilvie were our resident Aussies. Mattie Walsh was another Aussie but he had a

Meath accent. Sam Porter, a local politician in Brisbane, was a big part of the club, as was Scotty Ingram.

We adopted a song from an Australian rock band called Hunters and Collectors as our theme tune, 'Throw Your Arms Around Me'. Mattie O would sing it after matches and we would come in for the chorus.

We had a lot of sing-songs at the Willawong.

The lads out there were brilliant to us, they accepted us right away. They nicknamed Stephen and I 'Sinn' and 'Fein'. People in Ireland have spelt my name wrong all my life, I get Eoin all the time, but at least everyone could pronounce it. Not in Australia. The Aussies couldn't pronounce Owen at all. I was getting Oliver and all sorts until they settled on 'Fein'.

That summer in Australia was the first time I really got to play senior football with Stephen. He had battled cancer twice and was ill quite a lot when I was growing up. We were both relishing this opportunity to play together, and we took the football seriously. The standard of football was poor enough but as you got to the semi-finals and final, it quickly improved.

The games got hot and heavy sometimes. I would try to protect Stephen and he would try and watch my back, too. A team called The Souths were our main rivals. When we played them, it was a 'killing match' before the throw-in.

We had nights out, for team bonding purposes of course. I probably bonded a wee bit too much when I got a tattoo of a shamrock on my back to show my commitment to the club.

We won the Queensland Senior Football Championship, beating The South's in the final. It was great to win, but it was the camaraderie between all the boys that made those few months special.

While I was out there, I got invited to attend trials for the Brisbane Lions AFL side. I wasn't convinced I wanted a future in Aussie Rules, or that I'd be any good at it, but I was chuffed when one of their scouts came to watch me play a few games for the Shamrocks.

Stephen did all the wheeling and dealing with the club, who sent us two jerseys and two tickets to come to The Gabba to watch the Lions in an AFL game. At the ground, Brisbane Lions coach, Shane Johnston invited us to the meet the players and then took us to a warm-up room.

'Let me see the way you kick,' he said to me.

It was a big long hall that had a circular target at the end of it, which the players used for kicking practise before games. I had watched a bit of Aussie Rules on TV and noticed the way the players kicked through the bottom of the oval ball.

Here goes, I thought. I drove through the bottom of the ball, hitting it straight through the middle of the target.

Johnston spun round.

'Have you played this before, son?'

'No, I've just watched a bit of it at home.'

He must have thought it was a fluke because he asked me to kick it again. I drove straight through the target again, this time hitting the bulls-eye ring.

'Ok,' he said, 'show me how you fist the ball'.

I fisted the ball so it would spin too. I could see he was starting to get a bit excited. He arranged for Stephen and I to line out for their Junior side, the Jindalee Magpies, for a few matches alongside most of the club's rookies.

It was exciting news but I kept it quiet. I didn't want anyone at home to find out. I had a fair idea Mickey would go nuts at the thought of me staying over there. I adapted to Aussie Rules quickly enough. I thought it was just like playing full-forward in Gaelic. I could get the ball to spin back and could curl it with the outside of my boot. The coach couldn't understand it. During one of my first training sessions, he called me over.

'Are you sure you haven't played this game before?' I told him I hadn't.

I found it so easy just to catch the ball and stop. At home I was used to catching the ball and getting killed. Here, you had so much time and space on the ball. I scored one point straight from the sideline and the players all went mad. 'Aw mate, that was from the boundary … that's a peach.' The coach was standing clapping.

It didn't amount to anything in the end. The coach told me to go home and try to make Ireland's International Rules side, which I knew I'd no chance of doing at my age. He said they would keep an eye on me and possibly invite me back the next year.

Five years later, Sean Cavanagh was the one being linked with a move to Brisbane Lions. I didn't say anything to him about my connections out there, but I have no doubt Sean could have made it in the AFL. With his athleticism and physique, I think he could have been a star at Brisbane.

◆ ◆ ◆ ◆ ◆

The first time I met Ricey McMenamin he was hung over and throwing up on the pitch.

Art McRory and Eugene McKenna called me up to the Tyrone senior squad when I came home from Australia and Chris Lawn drove me to my first training session, on a freezing cold Saturday morning in Augher. It was the first of hundreds of journeys we would make together over the next five years.

I was a bundle of nerves on the way there, worrying about meeting Canavan.

After years of winding him up at school, I didn't know how he would react to me being in the squad. I thought he must have hated me.

In the end, it was Ricey who caught my attention. He looked like he was still drunk and was getting sick all over the place. I wondered who the hell this lunatic was.

Art McRory was standing over him, pushing his glasses up the bridge of his nose, giving Ricey deadly stick. I knew Ricey had marked Canavan in the club Championship and marked him really well. There were rumours that all sorts had gone on.

If he had the nerve to put it up to Canavan, he must be some boy, I thought. I was fascinated. I didn't know him to talk to, but I wandered over all the same.

'Jesus, lad, were you out last night?'

He moaned something at me. There were dribbles coming out of his mouth but he staggered on trying to do the run anyway. I couldn't stop smiling. *I'm going to enjoy this boy*, I told myself.

In those days it was daunting being in the senior squad at only 19 years old.

I didn't know anybody and felt I shouldn't be there. Ger Cavlan looked out for me, the way 'townies' do for each other. He was from Dungannon and we managed to strike up an instant friendship and sat together on the bus.

My full senior debut was a League match against Dublin in Parnell Park in October, 2000, a game I remember most for Cricko getting sent off for a straight red card.

I was still getting to know Chris Lawn and couldn't believe it when he got sent off so early. I thought the guy must be nuts. I had seen him playing in club games and watched him closely. I knew he could handle himself and made a mental note never to get into a row with him.

He was a tough man-marker during our in-house games. Sean Teague, who captained us to the Ulster title in 2001, was another one. He'd hit you a bang in the ribs and say, 'Mugsy, you'll be getting this the whole game'.

It toughened me up. I grew up fast.

That League game in Parnell Park was the start of a long love affair for me with the Dubs. Despite Cricko's early dismissal, we played the whole game with fourteen men and won by three points. I played well and scored 0-5, with four points from play. I absolutely loved it.

The game was as good as won when someone came at me from the side and left me lying stretched out. Eugene McKenna came running on.

'Are you all right, Mugsy?' he said.

I sat up, beaming.

'I'm grand. This is class.'

Eugene said, 'Welcome to senior football … you'll get a lot more of them.'

There were high expectations of players like myself, Kevin Hughes and Stevie O'Neill. People expected if you were playing for Tyrone seniors you were going to be like Maradona, up and down the pitch. One night, a girl at a birthday party said to me, 'I don't think you're Tyrone material, you'll never make it at senior level.'

Her name was Marie Ross. I still see her to this day and we have a laugh about it. I was annoyed but I didn't want to have my say until I had won something.

After we won the first All-Ireland in 2003 I saw her one day when I was going around with the Cup. I winked at her. She looked at me and smiled as if to say, *I know what that's for.*

There were a lot of people like that.

I found it easier playing with my own age group at minor and Under-21. The step up to senior was a big one. I was playing with and against men who were ten, twelve years older than me. It was physically demanding.

I was studying joinery at Dungannon Tech and didn't tell anybody I was playing for Tyrone. We played Kerry at home in the League in Dungannon that November and I scored 2-1. When I went into the Tech the next day, a few boys were straight on to me.

'You never said you played for Tyrone.'

I shrugged my shoulders. I was never into bragging about playing for Tyrone.

◆ ◆ ◆ ◆ ◆

I started to feel like I was being pulled in all directions with the Under-21s and seniors; club and county, all wanting a piece of me. Any time I had a bad game, I thought I was tired.

On the one hand, it was a carefree time, but we took the football incredibly seriously and we worked hard at our training sessions at Dungannon Academy.

We lost the Hastings Cup final to Mayo in the spring of 2001 and I had a terrible game. I was thinking of going to Mickey to tell him I needed a break. I knew I still had another year at Under-21 level left anyway, and I already had an All-Ireland Under-21 medal in the bag.

I was glad I hung in. That Under-21 team was a team that didn't know how to lose. We beat Monaghan in the Ulster Under-21 semi-final, with me scoring four points, and despite Ciaran Meenagh being sent off after only sixteen minutes. Any other underage team would have folded that day but, for young lads, we were already very experienced.

If the other team scored a goal, nobody panicked. We knew we'd peg it back no bother. Mickey instilled that belief in us. He made sure we kept going to the end. I think that's why so many of us were called in to the seniors. We had a steel about us from early on. When you looked around and saw all the players we had on the bench, you knew you had to perform.

Mickey is not the sort of manager who will take you off straight away, he sticks with you. There were a few times, in later years, that I felt hard done by when I was taken off, but it wouldn't have happened in the early years. Then, even if I'd had two bad games in a row, I wasn't taken off and I imagine the other boys were saying, 'What does that man have to do to be dropped?' But I wasn't a pet, definitely not.

Mickey was already starting to hear stories. Cookstown boys get a raw deal, like most 'townies' do, because they have more craic. The Errigal and Carrickmore boys had nothing else to do but play football and they tended to go with women from their own area, which I would always have given them stick about. In towns like Cookstown, there were plenty of distractions.

I was immature at times, throwing clothes in the dressing room and messing about, but Mickey never gave out to me. He treated everyone the same and he had a lot of faith in me. If you were putting it in at training, he would have seen that and stuck by you. If I had a bad game or two, I would try my hardest to pay him back in the next game by scoring 1-3 or 1-4.

The outbreak of Foot and Mouth disease meant our Ulster Under-21 final was put on hold. Fermanagh, as our opponents in the final, were going to be nominated to represent Ulster in the All-Ireland series, even though we were reigning All-Ireland champions. We were only reinstated after Mickey fought to get us back in, but the delay meant I had to focus on the Tyrone senior team.

The older players had big faith in Art and Eugene. Some of them were still there from 1995 when we lost the All-Ireland final to Dublin and they had been through a lot with them. I took Eoin Gormley's place, and he was some player. I felt awkward about going over to talk to him. He was probably thinking, *Who does this boy think he is?*

It was weird playing with men that I'd watched and supported for years. They made the younger lads feel welcome but I was shy and full of self-doubt. Did they think I was some cocky lad, full of himself?

A week or two before we played Armagh in the Ulster championship, Art and Eugene took us away for a training weekend to Bundoran.

We were staying in the Great Northern Hotel and had a real good training session followed by an in-house game. There was no talk of drink bans and Michael Owen had scored two late goals to win the FA Cup for Liverpool the same day, and I reckoned that deserved a little celebrating.

So, Calvo, Hub, Gary Fitzpatrick – another Cookstown man – and I snuck out and went into the town looking for a quiet pub. A few hours later we were strutting our stuff in the disco in the Holyrood Hotel. I looked around and it looked like everyone in the squad must have had the same idea! There was Pascal Canavan and Peter, too. The senior players and the younger lads had sneaked out in their wee groups, and all ended up in the disco.

The shy young boys and the legends were suddenly mixing and having a laugh. It definitely helped us gel. The following Sunday I scored my first senior Championship goal on my debut. It was a really hot day and I had the ginger skinhead on me. I was up for it. Armagh were a big team at the time.

I remembered Mickey's advice to me about stepping up to senior. 'You have to be really alert, you have to be on your toes all the time.'

His words were in my head as I slid in to score a goal after just twelve seconds. The ball was going out wide over the end-line when I reacted by sliding in for a soccer-style finish.

I didn't get on the ball as much as I'd have liked in the match and was taken off at half time. But, as the bus pulled out of the ground, I wondered if I had just experienced the highlight of my senior career, scoring a goal in Clones against Armagh.

It turned out to be a good day for the Mulligan family. My uncle, Sean had backed me to score the first goal for the seniors and backed my cousin, Barry Mulligan, to score a goal at any time in the minor match, which he did. He cleaned up.

The following weekend I was back in Clones, this time with the Under-21s for the delayed Ulster final with Fermanagh. When Tyrone were banned from competing due to the Foot and Mouth outbreak, we were annoyed that Fermanagh had seemed all too keen to be nominated as Ulster champions and progress to the All-Ireland semi-final.

By the time the game finally came around, we couldn't wait to play them. Ryan McCluskey is a great defender but I did well on him that day, scoring

1-7 and was named Man of the Match.

I was on top form against Cork in the All-Ireland semi-final in Parnell Park and scored eight points as we won 0-14 to 1-2. We beat Mayo in the final to win back-to-back All-Ireland Under-21 titles.

Life was going well for me.

I'd already won six All-Ireland medals at the age of 20, I was going steady with Edele and I was enjoying the joinery course. Marty Fox from Clonoe taught me and for the first time in my life, I took the assignments seriously.

I was working for Gerry Mallon from Kildress and served my time under Dermot McGurk, one of the best joiners I have ever seen in my life. They were big Tyrone fans and it was a boom time in the building trade; we worked flat out. Marty Fox wanted me to go on and teach joinery but I couldn't see myself doing that. I didn't think I would have the temperament or be smart enough for it, although I hear my assignments are still being used as examples in the joinery course.

My ma wanted me to go on to college like my sisters and Stephen. But she always said that, though they got their degrees, I was the happiest of the lot of us, because I was doing what I wanted to do.

When my cousin, Barry Mulligan didn't get the exam results he wanted and was sitting in our kitchen, upset, wondering what to do, I came in from the building site and handed him my lunch box and said, 'There's nothing like the Rover lunchbox.' Barry wasn't going to go down that road, but it worked for me. My life pretty much revolved around joinery and football.

In 2002, I was still playing for the Under-21s and giving them total commitment ahead of the seniors. I still didn't feel totally comfortable in the senior environment.

In the spring I used the Under-21s as an excuse when I didn't want to go away with the seniors for a League match against Cork in Pairc Ui Chaiomh. I told Mickey I felt tired.

'You shouldn't be doing that,' he told me, 'The Under-21s come first.' I could have hugged him. I didn't even ring Art to say I wasn't going.

Enda McGinley was captain of the Under-21s, with Cormac and most of the boys who had won back-to-back All-Ireland titles being over-age that year. We weren't expected to win anything because the Down players who'd won the All-Ireland minor title in 1999 were in their last year at Under-21 level and expected to make a big push.

They had hammered us in the Ulster minor semi-final three years earlier, but Mickey told us this Ulster title was ours for the taking. We believed everything he told us and I scored eight points as we beat Down in the first round in Newry.

Enda sustained knee ligament damage in the game and missed the next game against Monaghan so I stood in as captain. Enda was back for the final against Cavan and when we won it, he said he wouldn't go up to collect the Cup without me because I'd been captain in one of the games. I thought that was a real classy touch by Enda. In the end, we lifted it together. All-Ireland ambitions were a step beyond us, though, and Dublin beat us by four points in the semi-final in Cavan. With my underage career now behind me, I was a fully-fledged senior footballer, or at least I should have been. Art and Eugene had given me a chance the year before but, in 2002, I was on the fringes and felt out of my depth, like I wasn't good enough for it.

If Art and Eugene had stayed in charge beyond that year, I don't think I would have made it as a top county footballer because I don't think I was their cup of tea as a player. But they did give me my debut and I'd won an Ulster championship and a Division One League title under them before I was 21.

Winning the League title that spring was quickly forgotten about when we lost to Armagh in the first round of the Ulster championship a few weeks later.

We progressed through the back door and were red-hot favourites to beat Sligo in the fourth round qualifier. I was told during the week I would be starting at centre half-forward because there was a doubt over Pascal Canavan.

Our Stephen was getting married the day before the game and I was best man. I was told not to drink.

When we arrived in Croke Park the next day I was told I wasn't starting. I was fuming until I heard it was Pascal who was in. His injury had cleared up. He was a legend in my eyes, so I was fine with that.

It turned out to be Pascal's last game in a Tyrone jersey and I was always sorry he didn't stay on and get the All-Ireland medal he deserved in 2003. Seamus McCallan was another one who maybe went a bit too early.

Pascal gave some performance that day in Croke Park, scoring the first two points as we opened up a 0-9 to 0-3 lead, and Peter scored six points. We were coasting, but the game turned into a pure disaster.

We collapsed.

Eamonn O'Hara was inspirational for Sligo and he turned the tide. I was brought on after sixty-four minutes for Declan McCrossan. Here I was, at 21 years of age, trying to make an impact in difficult circumstances. I showed for the ball but misjudged it, and it bounced over my head. I felt stupid, but not as bad as I felt a few minutes later when I was taken off again – the biggest humiliation of my career.

That was the most embarrassed, the most insulted, I have ever felt on a football pitch.

What a joke. It was the ultimate insult.

Ciaran 'Dinky' McBride came on instead of me.

Afterwards I wanted to know why I'd been taken off. Eugene McKenna told me, 'Ah … it's Dinky's last year … I had to give him a run-out in Croke Park'.

What? I was disgusted. What a pathetic reason for bringing anybody on.

So what if it was Dinky's last year? I didn't care. The game was probably already gone but we should have been trying to make something happen. We were well on top and let it slip.

It felt shit to be taken off like that. I was very young but I don't think it should happen to any player unless you're injured. I still get stick over it from boys around Cookstown.

I won two big titles under Art and Eugene in successive seasons but I don't think I would have become the player I did if they had stayed in charge. For one thing I wouldn't have played under them if they were still there in 2003.

I was too sore about the Sligo match. Art is a pure gentleman and I had good craic with him. I'm not saying they were bad managers, far from it. I just was ripping at the Sligo experience.

That September, I sat in the Conway Inn in Cookstown watching as

Armagh won their first All-Ireland title.

I wasn't thinking that it should have been us, because I don't think we had the players to go all the way that year, but Armagh's success was definitely the spark that ignited us.

If they can do it, so can we, I thought.

People might not believe this, but off the pitch I am incredibly shy.

If I was walking around Belfast, say, I'd always wear a baseball cap in case anybody spotted me. People have this impression I love getting attention but, most of the time, I just want to blend in with the crowd.

On the pitch, it's a different story.

I want to be noticed.

Always.

I've never minded too much having ginger hair. It's not really bad ginger – it's not Neil Lennon hair! I didn't start dying my hair bleached blond because I didn't like being ginger. I did it because it got me noticed on the pitch.

The very first time I did it was for a bet.

I'm a big Liverpool fan and the Spice Boys were all dying their hair around 1996, guys like Robbie Fowler and Stan Collymore. Paul Gascoigne did it during the Euro '96 soccer Tournament and I thought it looked class. It was around that time I decided to give it a go.

I played a lot of soccer back then, travelling to Toronto with the Cookstown United Under-14s to play in the Niagara Pioneer Tournament, and playing in the Milk Cup for Craigavon Youth and Tyrone. One of the lads dared me to go for the full white head, so, Terry McCabe, a son of Kevin McCabe who played for Tyrone in the 1980s, shaved my ginger locks off with a disposable razor and did the bleaching job for me.

The peroxide used to sting the life out of my scalp.

I wanted to stand out and, in the early years, I thought it would also help me to get Mickey Harte's attention. It didn't do me any harm. I stopped it for a while but by 2003 I was flat out bleaching it. I got slagged of course.

Boys would trot over to me on the field.

'Look at the cut of you, are you a spice boy, or what?'

I was called a 'queer' and a 'faggot'.

My standard response to that was, 'Ask your ma if I'm a poof'.

In later years, I started wearing a hairband because my hair was getting long and it was falling into my eyes. I got a lot of verbals about that. I could even hear it in the crowd, supporters laughing about it, but I was well used to getting slagged at that stage. It was nothing new.

I introduced waxing and a bit of male grooming to the Tyrone dressing room, too. I got a fair amount of slagging about that at first.

The farmers wouldn't dabble at all, and the Errigal boys were too civil to do it, but gradually, bit by bit, the rest of them followed.

The younger lads are at it all the time now.

I shaved lines through my eyebrows and was one of the first to wear 'skins' under training gear on cold winter nights. Conor Gormley used to shake his head and say, 'Look at the cut of you, you're some eejit wearing them.'

Then, who runs out with them on one night, only Carrickmore's finest! We had a good laugh about that.

We weren't a team of clones. We were individuals, we had characters and Mickey didn't mind us expressing ourselves. He respected that we were all different.

We looked at the Armagh team and thought they were a team of robots. We had personalities and we weren't afraid to show them. We'd do dozens of media interviews before and after games when other counties were running scared in case they'd say the wrong thing.

I was beginning to get a lot of criticism for diving. The media were picking up on it, saying I was holding men by the arm and pulling them down on top of me. I'm sorry, but if you're stupid enough to put your arm in, I'm going to go down.

A lot of them were fouls, but I made the most of it.

The Armagh fans gave me a lot of stick for throwing myself about but it's not like I was diving into a swimming pool. If a man is willing to commit, I'm going to grab his arm and go down. It's the defender's fault. If he is up my ass, of course I'm going to go down and win my team a free. I wanted to show him that if he stayed too close to me, I was going down – which meant he was going to fall down too.

I didn't care about getting a reputation for that – we were winning games.

I wasn't told to do it, or coached how to do it. Mickey taught us to tackle properly so if our opponents couldn't do the same, I made them pay for that by winning my team a free. Mickey used to teach us that if you were running alongside someone, to always put in your hand that was next to the man. You never put an arm across your body, it should always be the arm next to the man.

If you can take a man's ground, he is automatically going to put the wrong hand in. If an arm comes across like that, you take the man down with you. It looks like a foul all day long. A good defender won't do that. They will be quick with the hands, in and out, with wee sharp jabs. Others aren't so clever. You'll see the big dopey arms coming in across your body.

If my man was on a tick or a yellow card, I'd remind him about it and worry him all day long.

Maybe I was going down easier than others, but I didn't mind the flak at all. I just felt that if you take a man's ground, you have a good chance of winning a free.

After a while referees caught on to it and would say, 'Christ, Owen, you went down too easy there'.

The best referees are the ones that interact with you. I always liked Pat McEnaney for that. He was a good referee and he is good craic. At least he treats players with respect and like we're human beings, unlike some of them.

'Nice legs, Pat, did you get them shaved for the day?'

He never fell for that.

'I'm taking none of your shite today, Mugsy.'

I'd run away laughing.

I liked Gerry Kinneavy too.

I'd shout over, smiling, 'Hey, ref, this man is hitting me hard, I'm fearing for my safety here.'

He'd smile back at me. 'You're ok, you're big enough to take care of yourself.'

I never waved the imaginary yellow or red card at a referee, trying to get an opponent sent off. I never bounced the ball after winning a free either, though I know one or two of my teammates did.

But I'd chat away to referees, at club and county level, trying to get them on side. I got to know which ones I could play.

For instance, if the other team got a score I might say, 'That was some score there, ref.' If he talked back to me, and said, 'Yeah, some score all right,' I knew I had him. I'd probably get the next two frees off him. Call it being cute, street-wise, call it whatever you want, it worked.

If I lost a game under a referee, then the next time he was refereeing us or was even a sideline official, I'd remind him about it.

'Now, you know you tried your best to get us beaten the last day,' I would say.

Or I might trot past the ref and say, 'That's his fourth foul on me, I'm keeping count of these, are you?'

Some referees would tell me to shut up, that I was annoying them all day. McEnaney or Kinneavy would just laugh and say, 'Stay on your feet, Mugsy.'

Sometimes it backfired. Then I might try and offer him a drink of water to try and get him back onside.

Football has become so serious and intense in the modern game, but there should still be room for a bit of banter. I once said to a Dublin referee in a club match, 'By the way, you have to be the best looking referee I have ever seen.' He just stared at me, shaking his head. 'I've had a lot of things said to me,' he said, 'but you are some wind-up merchant.'

I would far rather have a referee having the craic with me or even telling me to shut up than one not talking to me at all.

John Bannon couldn't wait to get the yellow card out for verbals. Far more sensible refereeing in my view is someone who says, 'You're talking shite all day, I'm taking none of your crap, Mugsy, that was a foul.'

Then I'd accept it and keep quiet.

I wasn't that smart at school but on a football pitch I always used to think, 'If I was a back, what would I hate?'

Whatever I thought a defender wouldn't like, I would try and do it.

Canavan, Joe Brolly and James McCartan, they were the men I watched. They were class at winning frees like that. Paul McGurk, who played for Cookstown and Tyrone, had told me about his experience marking McCartan and Mickey Linden in the Ulster championship. I absorbed every piece of information I could.

I watched a lot of players but I always had a soft spot for Brolly, the way he played. I loved that he was a showman. When he blew kisses to the crowd after scoring the goal in the 1998 Ulster final a lot of people, my da included, thought he was a clown, but to me it was pure class. He was the first one I saw laughing at his opponent and it got me thinking, 'He is really getting into their heads.'

The kick dummy became my signature tune on the field.

Stephen 'Scotchy' Conway, who played with Cookstown and Tyrone, was the man I modelled it on. I played with him for the club in the latter stages of his career and he would have me in stitches. Men would be lying flat out on the ground all over the place as he dummied past them with the right foot, then the left.

There is nothing as good as getting somebody with a really good kick dummy. You can see them out of the corner of your eye going in for the block. Sometimes you can just bounce it past them, but that doesn't look as good. If you want to really annoy them, the kick dummy works every time.

I love it when a defender lets a big, 'Fuck!' out of him in mid-air after he realises he's bought the dummy. He'll be giving out to himself while you're putting it over the bar with the outside of your boot.

Magic.

I loved getting Hub or Ricey or Cricko with the kick dummy in training because they were hard men to get … they were my prizes. Hub was that committed he would buy it sometimes, and then he'd be raging with himself.

I would just look back at him and say, 'How much did you buy that one for, did you go to Costcutter for that?'

Scotchy was also the first one I saw showing the fist dummy and the wee feint, which I also pulled off to good effect once or even twice! He was brilliant at them.

In the 2003 Ulster championship we played Derry in the first round. Paddy Bradley caused us serious bother scoring 1-6 and it finished in a draw. Niall McCusker, my former teammate from St Pius', held me scoreless. It was a wrestling match from start to finish. I was going down the tunnel in Clones at the end of the game and some Derry fan shouted, 'Where's the blond bombshell now?'

You cheeky bastard, I thought.

I knew I hadn't played well. Mickey played me a bit further out the field in the replay in Casement Park so I wouldn't get the same attention and we beat them easily enough.

In the Ulster semi-final against Antrim, Calvo was brilliant and Peter and I scored 1-10 between us. We were starting to develop a really good understanding.

During that Ulster campaign, the whole master-pupil thing about Canavan and myself was kicking into overdrive in the media. We were instinctively on the same wavelength, no doubt about it, and I had studied his game meticulously for years.

I used to get off the school bus from St Pius' watching him driving around Cookstown in his sponsored car thinking he was a genius.

By the time he taught me in Holy Trinity, I was in total awe. How could you not want to learn from the best? I spent years watching him in club games and for Tyrone, long before I ever played with him, learning how to read him.

I got to read him so well that I nearly knew what he was going to do before he knew himself. I'd watch him and think, *How did he get free there?* I started to copy how he turned and moved, trying to practise it when I got home.

When I started training with him I learned a lot more. Any time I had a knock and was sitting out a session, I'd just watch him, trying to pick up on wee things. I'd wonder, *How the hell is he getting that free?* He'd spin and get out sharp, far better than anybody else.

I was soon able to read his spins and turns.

Every time I looked up, the wee man was free.

You'd look up, left and right, and the wee man had spun clear and wanted the ball. Whatever way he moved, he'd get free. I always thought that if you were a back and your man just stood still waiting on the ball to come to him, it was happy days for you. A back is going to like that. I reckoned a forward should always be running and moving.

Canavan was like that. A wee run here and a dart there. He tormented his man.

People always throw it up to me that I was never the same player after Canavan retired. Maybe that is partly true.

It used to give me a lift seeing him come on because I knew he was going to create space. I'd think, *This man is going to get the ball ... and all hell's going to break loose. I'm going to get all the space.*

That's usually what happened.

I loved playing with him. If he saw the whites of your eyes, he'd give you the ball. The same with McGuigan. Just the whites of your eyes. Those boys didn't care if they were on the scoresheet or not.

That hasn't always been the case in recent years. I think there are players in the Tyrone squad now who are happy if they lift the paper the next day and see 0-2 after their name, regardless of whether the team has won or lost. Or if they get a decent player rating they're happy enough. I mean, who gives a damn about a rating? Complete bullshit. It should be about Tyrone winning.

Some of the younger lads need to learn to be more ruthless. They're taking the easy option too many times, fisting the ball over the bar when they're clean through on goal.

If a player was through on goal and fisted the ball over the bar like that, Canavan used to go mad.

Go for the far corner, man. Who's going to say you did the wrong thing? Take your goal chance, make the 'keeper work. Players are holding on to the ball too long. They're taking too much out of it and running down blind alleys and getting turned over.

Canavan would have given out to me or anybody else in the dressing room if we did that. At half time in the 2003 All-Ireland quarter-final against Fermanagh, he was raging that I didn't pass to him.

I wasn't going to make the same mistake again. In the second half, I had a good chance to put the ball over the bar. I could have done it myself but he was in a better position so I passed it to him to put over.

I hated making mistakes in front of him. I wanted to impress him every single time we played together.

It was the same with Stephen Conway when we played for the club. I hated giving him a shit ball. Scotchy wouldn't have said anything, but he'd just give you a look that said, 'Fuck me, give me that into my chest.'

He always told me if anybody blocks you, take that as an insult. You should never get blocked on a football pitch.

I was learning from the best.

◆ ◆ ◆ ◆ ◆

To win an All-Ireland, there is always one game in which you will need a bit of luck, and for us that year it definitely came in the Ulster final against Down.

Coming from nine points down to draw the game set us on the way to the All-Ireland. It was an epic comeback but, for me, it was tainted a wee bit by what happened to Chris Lawn. He was totally hung out to dry for the four goals we conceded in Clones.

There had been talk we were suspect under the high ball and Down pumped it in flat out. Dan Gordon fisted two balls to the net and there was total chaos in our defence. As full-back, Cricko had to take his share of the blame but others could have done better too.

Ten minutes into the second half, we were nine points behind and it looked all over. Canavan turned in some performance to save us.

His father, Sean, had died the week before. I don't think Peter had had a lot of sleep and he was asked whether or not he wanted to play, but it was never in doubt. When we were rocking and doubting ourselves, he spun on a sixpence and won us a penalty out of nothing.

Only he was ever going to take that penalty.

I thought, *I'll not begrudge this man if he misses this one, after all that's happened. He's only after burying his da … he can't be totally tuned in.*

I then watched in awe as he stuck it in the top corner. I turned and skipped back into position. *You wee legend. Is there nothing this man can't do?* I thought.

That was what kick-started the whole fight-back.

It was some comeback to get a draw, but everyone knew there would be changes for the replay. The papers went to town on Cricko. Everybody said he was finished. He was ripping.

He was quiet that week going to training. He knew what was coming and sure enough himself, Declan McCrossan and John Devine were dropped for the replay. Pascal McConnell came in, and Cormac was moved to full back. Fair play to Cormac, he wasn't nervous at all about the switch from midfield. It was just another day at the office for him. If Mickey wanted him to go and mind the house, he was up for it. It was a move which definitely helped us win the All-Ireland that year.

But it pisses me off when I hear people say Cormac was Tyrone's best ever full-back. How could he have been? That's total nonsense, Cormac only played a few games for Tyrone in that position.

If Cormac had gone on to enjoy a long career, then maybe you could argue the point. But, sadly, the way things worked out, there can be no argument. I've had this debate in bars many times with people and Chris Lawn is the best full-back Tyrone ever had. End of.

He marked me loads of times in in-house games and he always stood me up. He never put his wrong arm in to tackle me and he never fell for my dummies. Other players were diving around and lying on the ground looking stupid, but Cricko never fell for them. And despite what happened against Down that day, he was also brilliant in the air, which he got a chance to show in the All-Ireland final two years later.

Mickey told us in the build-up to the replay that we were going to blow these Down boys away and we did. We totally annihilated them. Ciaran Gourley came in to the defence and was superb, while Canavan and I did the business up front, hitting 0-15 between us – Canavan getting eleven points. I thought it was one of my best ever performances for Tyrone.

After that game I really thought that we could win the All-Ireland. We celebrated that Ulster title, but what happened to Cricko took the edge off it a little for me.

◆ ◆ ◆ ◆ ◆

I did my driving test four times in a week before the drawn match with Down.

Sean Kelly, a Cookstown man, used to drive us younger boys to county training at minor and Under-21 level but I knew it was time to get my test.

Pat Canavan from Ardboe, a Tyrone fanatic, was my driving instructor.

I didn't want anyone seeing me driving around town with the 'L' plates up so he agreed to take me for lessons at half seven in the morning.

I thought that was sound of him so after a couple of lessons I gave him a Tyrone jersey. Next time he arrived wearing it and sticks the chest out, 'Here, sign that.' And me trying to keep a low profile!

My driving test was scheduled for the Monday before the Ulster final. I failed, for going around a roundabout in third gear. Pat was disappointed.

'Lad, I want you to go into this match stress-free. I don't want this test hanging over you. We'll leave it until after the final, ok?'

I agreed.

He phoned me a few hours later.

'Lad, I've pulled a few strings here. You're doing it again on Wednesday.'

'I thought it took weeks to get a retest, Pat.'

'Don't you worry about that. I need you going into this match with a clear head. It's sorted.'

I got a different examiner this time.

I thought it was ok to do a three-point turn in as many turns you like, so long as you do it correctly, but obviously not.

The examiner shook his head at the end. 'Everything was perfect there, but you did that three-point turn in about eleven manoeuvres. You can't do that.'

Pat came running out when we pulled up at the test centre, his eyes wide open. 'Well, everything all right?'

'Sorry, Pat, failed again.'

He phoned me early the next morning.

'Right, Musgy, third-time lucky. I've got you in again this afternoon. Unless … am I putting you under too much pressure here?'

I was happy enough. I hadn't told anybody I was doing my test, not even my ma. *Today is bound to be the day*, I thought.

This time the gods really conspired against me. We were turning into the bus station when this elderly woman steps out in front of me. I calmly put my foot on the brakes and waved her on, like a good boy. The examiner waved her out too. She takes a step out on the road and then stops. She waves me on.

I go to drive on and the woman takes another step.

The examiner slams on the brakes.

I looked at him. 'Aw, now that wasn't my fault… You saw what happened there. You can't fail me for that'.

It was at the very start of the test. We went through the rest of it and everything was one hundred per cent. As we pulled back into the test centre, I was happy.

'Owen, I can't pass you. You're not allowed to wave anybody on like that. You can't give hand signals.'

I was gutted – but I was more worried about meeting Pat.

He came running out again, unzipped his jacket and started pointing at the Tyrone shirt. 'Well, well? Are we set for Clones?'

I shook my head.

'You are joking me. What the hell went wrong this time?'

He went mental, but an air of resignation quickly settled in.

'Right,' he said. 'We'll definitely leave it until after Sunday then.'

I said ok.

On Friday morning, my phone rang.

'Don't tell me, Pat. There's a cancellation?'

'Aye, you're in.'

I arrived at the centre for my fourth test of the week.

This time it was a female examiner wearing a nice wee skirt.

'Are you the footballer? You're playing this weekend in the Ulster final aren't you?'

'Aye, that's right.'

Oh lethal, I thought. *I'm in here.*

I started chatting the hind leg off her.

'Have you done the test before, Owen?'

I smiled. 'Well if you really want to know, this is my fourth test in the one week'.

She laughed at that.

'Ok, you're going well. Just keep it calm.'

Afterwards she said the words I'd been waiting to hear all week.

'Owen, you'll be glad to know you've just passed your driving test.'

'You don't know what this means to me,' I said and gave her a big hug.

Pat was happier than I was. He danced around the place.

I just felt relief. Relief and delight that no one had seen me spend an entire week driving around Cookstown in a driving instructor's car with the 'L' plates up.

On the way to training the next week, Cricko picked me up as usual.

'Well, any craic Mugsy?'

'I got my driving test last week.'

'Och, you should have said, that's great lad. First attempt?'

'Aye.'

That night at training Cricko got the dreaded news. Down's four goals had cost him his place. He was dropped for the replay.

He was quiet on the way home, really down in the dumps. He wondered if that was the end of his Tyrone career.

I wanted to cheer him up and I knew exactly how, so I told him the real story about my driving tests. He laughed the rest of the way home.

◆ ◆ ◆ ◆ ◆

I have a very low attention threshold. I always have to be at something.

At school, some of the teachers used to let me leave the classroom and go outside and kick the ball about rather than distract the whole class.

So, when Mickey decided we should learn 'Amhrán na bhFiann' before the All-Ireland semi-final against Kerry, I didn't exactly take to it like a duck to water.

Michaela Harte was brilliant at Irish and she was our teacher.

She took it line by line, helping us with the pronunciation and the meaning behind every word.

I thought it looked well, all of us standing in a circle singing it together. It was another thing that brought us even closer as a squad, another good idea of Mickey's. Of course, the smarter boys picked it up right away. Only problem was, I hadn't a clue. Right up to the week before the Kerry game I still hadn't learned it.

Desperate, I turned to Mickey Coleman for extra tutoring. Mickey loves the rebel songs and a bit of singing, I knew he'd be the man.

'I can't get on to this at all Mickey, I never did Irish in school.'

Coleman brought his guitar everywhere. He was humming the tune and strumming the guitar. Still I wasn't picking it up.

'You're one thick eejit, Mugsy. It'd be easier to get a mouse to play this guitar than teach you this.'

Eventually, I got there.

We practised it all week. We gave it a rattle most nights at training. No one thought it was stupid. Mickey was the Messiah. He told us to do it and we did it. I thought it made us look like brothers in arms, real passionate.

The best way to learn was by singing it all together. Once I was confident enough I knew the words I looked around at the rest of the boys' faces, everyone singing away. We'd go into a huddle before or after training. Someone would just start it up and we'd give it a wee blast.

We were facing into the biggest match of our lives and we were more united than ever.

Fourteen minutes into the game, Canavan damaged ankle ligaments in a tussle with Seamus Moynihan and had to go off.

We went into the game pumped up and ready to show Kerry that Tyrone were now a match for them and we weren't going to roll over.

Our All-Ireland minor semi-final replay win over them in 1997 was when we started to believe we could match Kerry, and this was the day we let them know it was going to happen at senior level too.

They were taken aback by our physicality and intensity from the start. We chased in packs after the man in possession, making sure not to foul him, but with so much aggression that Kerry were rocking.

There was so much adrenalin pumping through my veins that I even put Darragh Ó Sé on the floor … me that didn't even do weights. There were about nine of us around this Kerry legend and I was the one who put him down. I gave Enda, and the other boys who were into their weights, a good bit of stick about that when the game was over.

Our work-rate that year was surprising everybody. We were like men possessed. Nothing was going to stop us.

We had Horse back after a three-month suspension and he was such a great organiser on the field and had such a great understanding with McGuigan, that I knew this would help us. At times it seemed like the ball was on a piece of string between the two of them and with Horse there to keep giving him the ball, I knew McGuigan would look up and give Peter and me the ideal pass inside.

Mickey kept drilling into us that defence started with the No.15 and that was me. The forwards swarmed and tackled and when we got the ball back, we punished Kerry, scoring the first six points of the game.

They had shipped four goals against Roscommon in the All-Ireland quarter-final and we could see in the Kerry boys' faces we had them rattled.

Canavan was in brilliant form that summer and if he hadn't gone off early, I have no doubt he would have roasted Seamus Moynihan. But even the loss of our talisman didn't faze us.

The intensity was unrelenting with the numbers of frees conceded spiralling to over one a minute. There were so many stoppages in the game that eight minutes of injury-time had to be played at the end of the first half.

We were well on top at half time leading by 0-9 to 0-2 but when I went back into the dressing room I could see by Peter's face that he was gutted at being able to play no further part. He stood up to speak.

I always hung on his every word when he spoke, but this was special. There was so much passion and emotion in his voice, the atmosphere in the room was electric.

'Boys, look at the journey we've come on this year and we are so close. I have never asked anybody to do anything for me in my life that I couldn't do myself, but I'm asking you boys to do one thing for me now. Get me to another All-Ireland final.'

There was nearly a stampede for the door to get back out and finish Kerry off. We'd have done anything that man asked of us. I couldn't wait to get back out there.

Kerry were slow coming out and we were full of nervous energy. We got into a huddle and Horse started singing the anthem. We all burst out singing it and then we split, ready to finish what we started. And we did.

We won by seven points, pulling up.

We were taken aback by the level of criticism we got in the days and weeks after the game.

Pat Spillane called it 'puke football', which annoyed some of the lads, but it didn't annoy me. I couldn't have cared less. We were heading for our first All-Ireland final.

We got more stick about verbals and diving about the place and we did not get much credit for the way we were playing. But we knew what was happening. We were winning because we had better players than everybody else. We went on to win All-Irelands because we had the best group of footballers in the country.

Someone in the media described us as a pack of ravenous dogs. Mickey absolutely loved that. It was team, team, team with him, all the way.

Canavan was the same. He went mad if there was any selfish play. He had the stature and the respect to be able to turn around and say, 'What the hell are you doing? Pass the ball'. After he retired, I don't think anyone else had the stature to say that.

McGuigan was top-class, the ultimate playmaker. He could look up and put the ball straight into your chest. Ger Cavlan was another one with that ability.

Hub knew his own strengths, too. Tyrone fans always used to shout, 'Don't shoot … don't shoot!' when he was on the ball, but I grew up with the man and I know what an important player he was to us. For years he put his body on the line for Tyrone and he would go through you at training. A real warrior. He knew his shooting wasn't the best and he got the biggest cheer from the fans when he'd stick one over the bar. He always enjoyed that.

Philip Jordan was unreal, he had some engine. Ricey had his enemies but he is one of the best players Tyrone ever had. What a leader. The opposition hated him but every team would love to have a Ricey on their side.

The Errigal boys were the total opposite to me but I had good craic with those boys. Mark Harte was a very clever footballer who didn't get the respect he deserved. Enda McGinley and I played against each other all the way up from Under-14 at club level and for the Vocationals, he was in the forwards and I was in midfield in those days. He was always a class player.

It was always team, team, team with Enda. He'd be thinking, 'What can I do for this team?' He was under-rated and maybe not trusted as much as he should have been. I know he'd have been first on my team sheet every day.

With all this talent around, I was sure we could do it. Canavan told us how important it would be, 'Boys, if we win this All-Ireland, it's going to change our lives forever and it's all going to be for the better.'

The most pressure I have ever felt in my life was in the build-up to that first All-Ireland final.

It was like having a weight pressing down on your chest, making me breathe hard every time I thought about it. The county was crying out for an All-Ireland. Armagh's win the year before had upped the ante and the place was frantic in the days and weeks leading up to the game.

If we were ever going to get this monkey off our backs, now was the time. I knew we had the players to do it but we would still have to go out and play the match of our lives.

It was a lot to handle at twenty-two years of age.

I was laying slabs at a friend's house until the Thursday before the final. We needed to get the job finished on time, which was good because it kept me away from a lot of the hype.

My ma took care of my All-Ireland final ticket allocation for me. I had enough on my plate without worrying about who should get what. The weight of expectation from the fans was brutal. I felt under wild pressure.

I absolutely hated the open night in Carrickmore.

Thousands of fans screaming and wanting a piece of you, dozens of media people probing, asking questions I didn't want to answer. Mickey, as usual, had all the bases covered. He got us coached on how to talk to the press but I very nearly didn't go.

The whole thing was completely mad that night, thousands and thousands of supporters going completely mental. While signing a few jerseys on the field, I wondered to myself, *How mad would it not be if we won this thing?*

Cookstown was awash with Tyrone bunting, far more than I remembered in 1995, which made me proud. Scotchy Conway had been part of the 1995 team who narrowly missed out. The thought of becoming the first Cookstown man to bring the Sam Maguire back to the town was just too good to even dream about.

Holy relics were being sent flat out to Mickey before the final. Nothing was forced on us, he gave us the option whether we wanted to take them or not, but I always did. Everybody did.

My ma was big into that as well. She gave me a miraculous medal at an early age that I still have tucked inside the sole of my right boot, to this day.

For a while I was running around with that much stuff in my kit bag I could have opened my own stall at Knock. Holy water, prayers, wee crosses, miraculous medals, Padre Pio relic, you name it, I had it. There was hardly enough room to get my gear in but it was all helping to keep me relaxed.

Cricko was the man who kept me sane during those few weeks.

Canavan is the best player I have ever seen and the best player I have ever played with, but I don't think I would have been the footballer I became only for Cricko. I always found it a real good release talking to him. He kept me calm, kept me focused. He'd give out to me about drinking or playing soccer and going with women.

'Bloody hell, lad, how do you find time to fit it in! That's your lot now, you need to pull the horns in.

Our belief in ourselves grew as the year wore on.

The game has moved on now but our tactics that year were so spot on.

Everyone knew to move the ball on quickly. Give the ball, and you knew if you made a run you were going to get the ball, because everyone was working so hard to shut down the opposition and make space.

It was always all about the team with Mickey, he never took any of the credit. He'd say, 'These boys are working hard, these boys want to win'.

He would build things up when he spoke to us, telling us, 'Youse are still getting no credit for this, everyone is against us'.

When I left home on the Saturday morning before my first All-Ireland senior final, I stuck to the same tried and trusted routine.

My ma got my boots ready. I wore the same navy pants throughout the whole 2003 season and I wore the same socks.

I hated the big thick socks we were supposed to wear and I always wore a thin pair, like a child's socks, so that I had a better feeling in my feet. They only came half-way up my calf, but they gave me deadly grip.

Before matches, I always went in to my Granny's house. I'd done it for years when we lived next door to her and Granda and, even after we moved house, I still did the same. I gave her a big hug, trying not to let her see how nervous I was.

My ma blessed me with holy water as I was heading out of our house and Granny stayed at home, praying flat out. I looked back at the front door, wondering when I came back through it on Monday night would I be an All-Ireland champion or not.

Once we got together as a squad, we were in our own wee world, away from all the outside pressures.

Cricko's and Canavan's experience was invaluable. At the team hotel they spoke to us about the devastation in the Tyrone dressing room after the 1995 All-Ireland final defeat.

Going back in there after the game it had been so, so cold, they said. They kept talking about the cold, that this time they wanted to experience the light and the joy. They didn't want to feel that coldness again.

I thought it was deadly. It fired me up. When those two boys spoke, everybody listened. All year we had been building up to this moment.

Mickey told us we would win and we believed him.

I got my usual good luck texts from the family.

My auntie Una is the seventh child in my da's family and always considered herself lucky number seven, and she always texted me before big games to wish me luck. Then one from my da, 'No-one remembers who sets the scores up, it's who scores them'. It was always left to my ma to send the loving ones. 'We're so proud of you, of what you've done for this family and the club. We're so proud of you no matter what the result is. Good luck – and say your prayers!'

We were focused.

Canavan and Mickey protected us from the whole furore surrounding his ankle injury. I knew something was up with Peter's ankle but I didn't ask him about it. It was all the supporters and the media wanted to talk about, but I ignored it. We had hammered Kerry in the All-Ireland semi-final without him for most of the game so I knew we could do it again if we had to, but it never crossed my mind that he wouldn't start. *That wee man's leg would need to be hanging off before he misses this game*, I thought.

◆ ◆ ◆ ◆ ◆

I was pacing the corridors, unable to sleep. The four walls of my bedroom were closing in on me and I'd had to get out.

At one o'clock in the morning I should have been tucked up in bed, resting before the biggest match of my life. Instead, I was walking around the hotel trying to get rid of some nervous energy. I was never a great sleeper before big games but this was as big as it got and I was a bundle of nerves.

After all we'd come through, it would come down to this seventy minutes against Armagh. So be it. We had prepared as thoroughly as we could, nothing had been left to chance, yet, here I was, climbing the walls. Maybe I was missing my room mate, Chris Lawn? I usually shared with Cricko but that night we were all given a room to ourselves.

When we'd gone back to our rooms after the team meeting we each found an envelope beside our bed. Someone had come in and left one in each player's room, with comments from Mickey and all the players describing your qualities and talents. It gave me a real confidence boost to read all the nice things the lads said about me, a brilliant idea by Mickey.

They were supposed to be football-related comments but I noticed that Mickey Coleman had written on mine 'good craic'. That made me laugh.

We were told to switch our phones off but there was trouble at home and I wanted to know what was going on. A mate back in Cookstown had got into a scuffle and I wanted to make sure everything was okay.

The later it got, the more guilty I felt. I should have been asleep like the rest of the boys. I wondered if they were all sparked out or if some of them were tossing and turning in their beds.

On my third walk around the lobby, I saw Cormac coming round the corner.

'Well... Are you nervous Mugsy?'

'Aye, I haven't turned an eye.'

Cormac was in the same boat.

'It's probably the first time I've ever been nervous before a match,' he said.

'Is it the McDonnell thing?' I asked.

'Yeah, sort of, but it's a good kind of scared. What about you, are you nervous about Bellew?'

'Yeah, but it's the same as you. It's a good kind of scared.'

We looked at each other.

I thought back to Cormac's speech at our homecoming in Aughnacloy when we won the All-Ireland minors in 1998. He got up on stage that night and said a great line out of a Queen song, 'It's been no bed of roses, no pleasure cruise'.

There had been plenty of highs since then but I wondered would we be singing that song 'We Are the Champions' in a few hours' time.

'All you can do is your best, Mugsy,' he told me.

'It's going to be tight but I think we're going to do it. I just know it.'

We shook hands and went our separate ways.

Five minutes into the All-Ireland final and I am having the most physical confrontation of my life.

Francie Bellew is trying to intimidate me but I'm up for the fight.

Joe Kernan and the Armagh supporters have been hyping him up as this scary brute who is going to crush me into the dirt. I can hear the Armagh fans singing 'Francie's gonna get you... Francie's gonna get you,' but it's just making me more determined to have my say.

I've always given as good as I've got when it came to the verbals, but this battle was about raw strength and sheer guts.

Not a word was spoken. Actions were going to speak louder than words. I knew he wanted to scare me.

I had the bleached blond hair and was the young pup coming up. He was dying to teach me a lesson. I didn't give a damn. I knew he wasn't the fastest. I knew I could get out in front of him.

The first time I had marked him was in the League earlier that year, when we had to clap Armagh onto the field as All-Ireland champions in Omagh.

Bellew was pulling my jersey that day, nothing serious, but I'd never let anybody off with that. He told me, 'Watch your elbow'. I did well on him, but I got booked and was then taken off. He was a tight marker but he wasn't the paciest defender. I'm not saying I was the fastest, I have never relied on pace, but I knew how to get out in front and I was sharp.

Now here we were again, on the biggest stage of all. It was a complete pulling and hauling show between us from start to finish, a man on man wrestling match. Nipping, and wrestling.

Armagh set the tone for the day when they ran out into our warm-up area in front of the Hill. Tyrone had done something similar to Dublin in the 1995 All-Ireland final but there was already a huge rivalry building between us and Armagh, and it got hot and heavy in there.

I was focused on taking a few shots at the posts and I didn't see them coming until the orange jerseys were in amongst us. It was a shouldering match to start with, but there were fists and punches thrown. It was as if they were trying to send out a message, 'We're the All-Ireland champions, this is our territory.'

I thought it was disrespectful. We might have had a lot of young players, but it's not like we were naïve or inexperienced.

We took that kind of crap in our stride.

I trusted the men I was going into battle with. We had been backing each other up all year. Still, this was on a bigger scale to anything we'd been used to. Those few moments before the throw-in I struggled to keep the nerves at bay. I knew deep down Canavan wasn't right and I felt the scoring burden was on me because I'd made a name for myself in the earlier rounds.

I tried to block out the wall of noise and tried not to look at the orange, white and red splashes of colour everywhere. I didn't think President Mary McAleese would be the first to make me crack a smile, but it seemed she was a fan of my blond hair.

After a lot of handshakes she got to me at the end of the line and started laughing, 'Well now, you will be easily spotted today, that's for sure.'

Francie was on top of me from the word go. My legs were heavy and I couldn't breathe. It took me six minutes to get a touch. I came deep looking for the ball and laid it off to Horse.

Relief.

A couple of minutes later I gave John McEntee a wee kick, pure petulance because I wasn't having things my own way. On another day I'd have been booked. Already the frustration was building. I just could not shake this man off.

Everywhere I turned, he was stuck to me. I was starting to believe the pre-match hype, that this man was stronger than me, that he would take no prisoners, like everybody said.

Then, a lucky break.

McGuigan, as only McGuigan could do, fizzed in a lovely low ball. I am out in front and Francie was right behind me. I gathered the ball but let him go first, so he came into the back of me. I wrapped my leg around him and went down.

I bounced straight up with my arms stretched out.

'Ref! What are you going to do about this?'

Brian White brought out the yellow card.

I smiled to myself.

Right, I'm on the pig's back here. Let's go.

The Armagh fans gave me a lot of stick for diving. Maybe the hair made people think I was copying soccer players, but it's not like I did an Italian dive or a Spanish roll. It wasn't that dramatic. But I did go down easily and got Francie Bellew booked.

I used the booking to my advantage; I knew, and he knew, he wouldn't be able to go after me after that. I knew if I could get into his head, I might get some peace to play my own game.

'You may go easy on me here, lad,' I told him. 'Come on, you're getting too close,' I went on.

Those were probably the only words I said to him all day. He never spoke. He just hit me harder than ever.

In my head, I was thinking, *Next ball, I'm going to go straight for him.* I had visions of going straight for the jugular. It's all I was thinking about. *If I can get out in space, I can get past him, no problem.* But the Armagh blanket was everywhere and I wasn't getting the ball the way I wanted it.

I made a grab for his balls.

I'd be big into that on the pitch. It really, really hurts. If someone starts nipping me, I'd pull them out. I only did it the once on Francie. He hit me so hard in the back I knew to leave well alone.

Calvo scored one of his usual wonder points and out the field it was getting hot and heavy. The ground shook when McGinley and Tony McEntee collided but McGinley got up and played on. When we found out later that he had broken a bone in his neck during the incident, no one could believe he had played on, but that was typical McGinley.

McGuigan was taking no crap from Kieran McGeeney. The All-Ireland winning captain was standing there with this cheeky cub from Ardboe in his face, wagging a finger at him. I watched him leave McGeeney on the ground and skip past him to score a great point to put us 0-5 to 0-1 up.

I felt a surge of confidence. This was going to be our day. But I still felt pure frustration personally. I wasn't playing well. I wasn't making an impact.

Canavan tried to get me into the game, hitting a free short to me. I got it away to McGuigan and he was hauled to the floor.

Penalty! But the play went on and big Sean Cavanagh missed a good goal chance. Still, we were well on top. The first-half was played at a furious tempo and I hadn't even noticed that Peter was struggling with his ankle. I was stuck in Bellew mode.

Frustration got the better of me eventually and I started acting the 'Big I am'. Peter was getting ready to convert his fifth free and I was close in to goal, getting mixed up with Bellew and Paul Hearty.

I took a drink out of a water bottle and then shoved it into Hearty's face. I left him raging. I was lucky. Not even a booking.

I badly needed a score to settle me down.

Our lead was 0-8 to 0-4 at half time but I was pissed off heading back to the dressing room. This was not how I had imagined the first All-Ireland final, this was not how I imagined *myself* in an All-Ireland final.

I knew I wasn't having a good game but just in case I didn't, Canavan came over to remind me.

I always admired the way the wee man could handle himself when backs would be trying to take lumps out of him. He was no size but by God he was strong. I realised it when he grabbed me by the two shoulders.

'What the fuck are you at?'

He was shaking me hard. He'd just had an injection on his ankle but rather than get himself right he was trying to shake some sense into me.

'You're getting too involved with him, Mugsy, play your own game. You're going back to your old ways getting too involved with players. You were warned about this. Just relax… don't worry about him. Get on the ball and do your own thing.'

He gave me some telling off, just like the old days.

Why are you always messing about in other teachers' classes? You don't mess about in mine. You can't keep going on like this. You need to grow up.

That was Mr Canavan's voice!

I never felt that smart at school but we weren't in school now. On the football pitch was where I felt smart … that was where I was top of the class. I went out determined he would be giving me top marks for how I played in the second half.

We ran back out for the start of the second half and Canavan led us down the tunnel with Ricey behind him, and me next.

Canavan's words were ringing in my ears. I knew he was right. Enough of worrying about Bellew. I needed to do my own thing.

The ball was thrown in before I even noticed that he was not on the field.

Then I spotted McGuigan back on. He'd been struggling with 'flu all week and was replaced by Stevie O'Neill near the end of the first half, but when I saw him on again, it dawned on me that Canavan must be off.

I thought to myself, *Time for me to raise my game.*

Five minutes in, I fed Stevie with a nice ball and he put a goal on a plate for Calvo, who dragged his shot wide.

With Canavan off, I was on free-kick duty all of a sudden and was feeling totally confident. *I'm not leaving this All-Ireland final without scoring, I don't care whether it's from play or not*, I promised myself.

We were awarded a free and Bellew made the kick a bit easier for me when he refused to budge and the referee, Brian White, moved it forward. I had honed my free-kick routine for years, always putting my left thumb over the 'O' and my right thumb over the 'S' on the O'Neill's size 5 when I had the ball in my hands, which I grew to believe stood for 'Owen Scores'.

I had practised it thousands and thousands of times, all for this moment. I felt a huge weight lifting off me as it curled in beyond the far post in front of the Hill.

We then got a free over on the right-hand side, ideal for a left-footed kicker. Realistically it was Stevie's shout but I jogged over to the ball.

'Just set that down, Stevie,' I told him. 'I'll hit that.' He looked at me and threw the ball over. I stuck it over and we were 0-10 to 0-7 ahead, inching ever closer.

Straight away Armagh were down to fourteen men. A red card was flashed at Diarmuid Marsden and he was off while Philly was lying on the ground.

I didn't see what happened but nobody seemed to be complaining. Philly got a lot of stick over that incident but he had every right to go down. Any man who says he wouldn't have done the same thing with an All-Ireland on the line is a bull-shitter.

Minutes later Dooher got told off for diving. What a joke, Dooher is no diver. But that was the reputation we were getting.

For all our dominance, we still hadn't put Armagh away. I blew a great chance to slay the dragon with about six minutes to go. Calvo pounced on a loose ball and put it on a plate for me. Hearty was that far off his line I was thinking of the spectacular. *You're going to get chipped here*, I thought.

I got caught in two minds. I worried that if I chipped him, a defender might come sprinting out of nowhere and clear it off the line making me look stupid. All this flashed through my head in a split second.

I resisted the temptation to go for the chip and noticed there was massive space in the top corner. I tried to curl it in.

Wide.

I collapsed to the ground, cramping up. I was accused of faking it, people thought I went down because I was annoyed at missing the goal. It was a bit of both. I cramped up straight after I'd hit the ball but as I lay stretched out on the turf, I was wishing I could turn back the clock and go for the chip.

We should have been out of sight but, somehow, Armagh were still in the game. Then I heard the roar.

I hadn't noticed Canavan warming up but the cheers made me look around and that's when I saw the wee bald head of him standing there, itching to get back on. I couldn't believe it. We weren't told about the plan to take him off and bring him back on again, we were as surprised as the supporters.

Another masterstroke by Harte.

I was pumped up. *Oh happy days! This is deadly. We're going to do this. Let's go.* I knew the wee man was there to bring us home, to get us over the line. It was meant to be. But we weren't home yet.

Stevie McDonnell had been hot all year and was in serious form. With three minutes to go, Tony McEntee hand-passed to him and he drew back his foot to pull the trigger at the Canal End.

I was far away from it but I just froze to the spot. I couldn't move my legs. I was just waiting, waiting for the net to ripple. *Disaster*, I thought. *The ball is going to hit the net any second.*

Then Conor Gormley came out of nowhere, and I mean nowhere, and blocked the ball away. It was no easy block, it was a full stretch block. Block of the century! The form McDonnell was in, that shot was going in the top corner, nowhere else.

I started roaring at the top of my voice, 'Gormley you LEGEND! YOU FUCKING LEGEND!' No one could hear me over the noise in the ground but I just kept saying it, over and over again. Gormley saved us, no doubt about it. That block won us the All-Ireland. There should be a statue up in Carrickmore to that man.

All we had to do was see out the last couple of minutes. Eventually, I got booked for hauling Bellew down. Canavan also got booked. People called them cynical fouls, but you do what you have to do. The prize was massive. We'd talked about knocking down Heaven's door and here we were, kicking it down to bring Sam Maguire to Tyrone.

The whistle went and my legs left me.

I dropped to my knees, unable to breathe. All the hard work, all the sacrifices, all for this moment. History for Tyrone. As players, we had reached the pinnacle of our sport. I felt a feeling of huge satisfaction and contentment wash over me.

The supporters were on the pitch before I had time to catch my breath. I tried to make my way over to the Hogan Stand but they were pulling me in every direction. They all had tears in their eyes. Immediately, I saw some familiar faces from home … Chubby McCrystal, Aodh Scullion and Niall Glackin hugged me tight.

Next thing I knew I was being carried shoulder high like a rock star, slowly moving over towards the Hogan. All around me was a sea of white and red but, as the stands emptied, I could see Tyrone and Armagh fans, shaking hands. After the near hatred in the build-up, that was nice to see.

The first player I met at the bottom of the steps was Cricko. He was going completely crazy. I was delighted he was the first person I saw. Not only were we great friends, but I felt a great sense of satisfaction that I'd helped him achieve his dream – him and every other Tyrone person who ever dreamt of that moment.

I didn't enjoy the final and I didn't play well, but at that moment I felt a kind of euphoria no drug could ever give you. You can only do something the first time once, and being part of the team that brought the first All-Ireland to Tyrone was something that can never be taken away from any of us. Being the first is so, so special. The county needed it badly and we had delivered.

The view from the top of the steps was breathtaking. I couldn't see any piece of green. The pitch had been swallowed up by Tyrone people hugging and crying.

I looked at Canavan's face as he lifted the Sam Maguire Cup, his face full of every emotion you could think of. It meant so much to him. The 'best player never to win an All-Ireland' tag had just been lifted off his shoulders. In his speech, he spoke of all the players who had gone before us and that he was lifting it on behalf of every one of them. *You legend*, I reflected.

Lifting the Sam Maguire on the steps of the Hogan, holding it over my head for the first time, was an incredible feeling. I had touched it a few times in 1993 when Derry won it and used to think how amazing it would be to lift it as a champion, in front of your own supporters. Now I was doing just that. I would get used to the feeling of that big Cup in my arms, but the first time I held it was amazing.

I felt so proud to be the first Cookstown man to lift it in the air.

I couldn't wait to take it up to our own pitch at home, but that moment on the pitch in Croke Park was one to remember. I felt sorry for the likes of the Dublin and Donegal lads that they didn't get to experience that feeling in the years after us. Not allowing supporters onto the pitch after an All-Ireland final is a disgrace in my view. That's what memories are made of. That's what makes the occasion; supporters saluting their heroes and the players soaking it all up. I have that picture from 2003 up on the wall in my bar and at home, and every time I walk past it, I get a shiver up my spine.

When we got Sam into the dressing room, we danced and sang and got photo after photo taken. Joe Kernan came in and told us to enjoy it, that Armagh had had a brilliant year and that we would too. Top man.

Mickey brought us into the warm-up area beside our dressing room and we went into a huddle, with the Cup in the middle of the floor. I couldn't stop looking at it. I'd seen pictures of it hundreds of times and now it was ours.

'You have done yourselves proud boys, look at what you have achieved,' he told us. 'This is only the start of it.'

I thought my first All-Ireland final day couldn't get any better, until Hub was announced as the Man of the Match at the banquet that night. I went straight over to him to shake his hand. I was over the moon for him. After all he had been through, it was a brilliant achievement.

Some of the boys' women tackled Cricko about his 'Braveheart' speech. He wasn't happy. He wasn't happy the boys had told their women and I suppose he didn't want his own wife to hear it either.

But it didn't matter. We had made sacrifices along the way, but we had done what we set out to do.

The journey home the next day was class but the celebrations didn't really start until we got to Aughnacloy. I remembered how brilliant it was when we brought the Tom Markham Cup there five years earlier and knew it would be even better this time.

We got onto an open-top bus and I saw the twin Glackins from Cookstown, Mick and Paddy, on their knees beside the memorial to Aiden McAnespie on the side of the road beside where he had been killed.

'Thanks young Mulligan,' one of them shouted. 'You don't know what you've done for Cookstown and Tyrone.' I was starting to get a sense of what we had achieved and what it meant to people.

The scale of it really hit me when we got to Omagh and saw the thousands and thousands of people packed in, the whole way down the street. I came out onto the stage and there were people not just halfway down, but the whole way down, as far as the eye could see. Lads were climbing up on lamp posts, and onto the roofs of shops and houses just to get a glimpse of us and of the Cup. It was one of the best nights of my life.

◆ ◆ ◆ ◆ ◆

Amidst the celebrations, though, my whole afternoon fighting with Francie Bellew the day before left me with a nagging feeling. I was disappointed that I hadn't produced my best on the biggest day. I was annoyed I had taken the bait in an All-Ireland final, when I should have played my own game. He was good and he was brave, he'd take your life, but I knew I'd marked better.

A few days after the final I got a phone call from a journalist in Dublin saying Gay Byrne had called me, 'a troublesome scamp' and did I want to respond? I didn't bother saying anything, but my ma was ripping.

I didn't know Gay Byrne was such an expert on GAA. Maybe it was the whole blond hair thing he didn't like. Me and Bellew had gone at it from the first whistle to the last. Maybe he didn't realise I was getting as good as I was giving. If a man is hitting you, you're going to hit him back. I was only twenty-two. Bellew was a grown man.

But that was his job and fair play to him, he did a job on me that day, no doubt about it. No-one knew it more than me. I just hoped that some day I might have a chance to get my revenge.

There was an All-Ireland title won in 2003 but there were also a whole lot of other things going on that year. Mickey had brought so many of our Under-21 team straight into the seniors that the age profile of the squad was very young.

Were we childish? Yes.

Were we immature? Yes.

Did we have a laugh? We never stopped.

When the fun started, our back-room team officials, Frank Campbell and Jim Curran, got it in the neck a few times from us young boys. Our kit man, Mickey Moynagh, did a lot of hard work for us behind the scenes and he was another one who we played a few pranks on.

On away trips we'd cut a piece of clothing starting with something small – maybe just ripping a sleeve or a collar. I was the one who started the craze off, but it wasn't long before Horse came to me begging to be let in on the craic. Gradually, we let a few boys in on it.

The standard plan was to go up to the reception desk in whatever hotel we might be staying in and say: 'Sorry, but I've left my key in the room.'

'No problem, sir. What's the name?'

'Frank Campbell'.

We cut the straps on Frank's kit bag once so he had to scoop it up in his arms.

We warned all the boys to be ready for it when he came into breakfast the next morning carrying it.

Mickey saw the funny side of it. We never touched his stuff. We talked about it, mind, but we knew that was a step too far.

The first few times Frank took it well but when we started to get in to the heavy stuff, cutting trousers and blazers, he got thick.

All the County Board boys would be there in their suits and poor Frank would be sitting with his Tyrone tracksuit on.

The day we cut Frank's blazer was the day that Mickey stepped in.

'That's Tyrone property, boys. It was a joke at the start but you're disrespecting Tyrone property,' he came on strong. 'It's not on.'

The blazer cost £70 to get fixed and we were made to pay for it.

Horse piped up. 'Boys, this is ridiculous. It was a joke at the start but come on, youse need to catch yourselves on.'

He threw £30 down on the table and looked around the room at us. 'The rest of you may do the same.'

Pure class. Him pretending to have nothing to do with it and him one of the main culprits.

The craic was good. What better way for the younger boys to gel with the guys who had been there for years, like Canavan, Cricko, Dooher and Calvo, than to have a good laugh with them. We got up to all sorts.

On a bonding weekend before we played Fermanagh in the All-Ireland quarter final, we swiped Canavan's phone. He left it down for two minutes. Big mistake, in a flash it was gone. He spotted me laughing and was raging.

'Give me the phone back, Mugsy, stop the messin',' he ordered.

'I don't have it, lad.'

A few of us went up to one of the rooms – Hub, Horse, McGuigan and I. We took pictures on Canavan's phone of us posing, from the shoulders down, starkers,

We went back downstairs again and waited to see who would be sitting opposite Canavan at the dinner table. It was Philly. A few touches of the button and, bang, the pictures were sent from Canavan's phone to Philly's.

His phone bleeped and he picked it up.

'Oh, holy shit!' Philly was in stitches.

Canavan knew right away. 'Is that from my phone, Philly? Let me see it.' Philly showed him the pictures but he didn't flinch, he just sat there, fuming. Then, I took a picture of the back of his wee bald head and sent that to Philly.

Philly bursts out laughing again.

Canavan swung round. 'Right, Mugsy, give me the phone.'

But we were having way too much fun to stop now. A few hours later we were at it again. We texted Finola, Canavan's wife, 'I really miss you pet.'

She texted back, 'I miss you, too.' Class.

We spied Frank Campbell sitting in the lobby. Text time. 'Frank, Peter here, there is an emergency meeting up in room 456.' Frank jumped out of his seat and marched across the lobby towards the lift. Hysterics again. It was comedy gold.

Reluctantly, we eventually gave the phone back. Canavan wagged the phone at us.

'I'm telling you now, boys. Before the year is out, you'll all be got back. You have my word.'

He wasn't too long in getting his revenge.

Coming home on the bus the next day, Canavan said he wanted a word.

'Listen Mugsy, I've been approached by Adidas,' he explained. 'They want to meet me in Cookstown on Tuesday. I'll put in a word for you… There might be a few pound in it for you. You can talk to them and you might be able to thrash out a deal.'

Canavan was planting the seed.

Welcome to Mulligans ... our family (Stephen, my ma, myself, Marie Claire, Michelle and my da) on opening night of my bar 'Mulligans', in 2010.

Come on Tyrone ... that's me on the left with Stephen and Michelle before a road trip to Clones.

Sweet Tooth ...
I'm ready to get
down to the serious
business on the
occasion of my
first birthday,
with Stephen
and Michelle.

Boy in Blue ...
I was in the
Cookstown Fr Rocks'
colours as soon as
I could walk. I'm
pictured here with
my older sister,
Michelle.

On holidays in
Portugal with
Marie Claire and
Michelle.

Two Gems ... me with the Tyrone Under-16 Grade One championship trophy and the club's Youth Player of the Year trophy with my ma and da when I was 15 years old.

First Taste of Success ... our Cookstown Fr Rocks' Under-16 Grade One champions, that's me in the middle of the back row.

School's Out ... our Holy Trinity team which lined out in the All-Ireland Vocational Schools final in 1998. I'm in the back row standing beside Gavin 'Horse' Devlin.

Carried Aloft ... my Tyrone teammates carry me across the pitch in Croke Park after we beat Offaly to win the All-Ireland Vocationals title, a game I missed after breaking my arm a few days earlier.

Cormac McAnallen and I lock arms as he speaks to the crowd in Aughnacloy after our 1998 All-Ireland minor win.

'My granny, Mary Mulligan, blessed me before every game. After our first All-Ireland win in 2003, I brought the Sam Maguire to her house along with our captain, Peter Canavan, whom she asked: 'Who are you?'

'Reach out your hands, sweet Jesus ... and guide me on my way.' My blessing from Granny Mary helped me more than anyone knows.

Meeting Sam For the First Time... Da and Ma, Marie Claire, Stephen, Michelle and I get to know Sam Maguire after our 2003 victory over Armagh.

Me, Bob and Sam in 2003.

Clockwise from top left: At last ... the minutes count down before the 2003 final; Peter the Great ... my favourite teacher, on and off the field, becomes the first Tyrone man to lift the Sam Maguire Cup; Cormac (centre) leads the celebrations in our dressing room in 2003; getting the better of Francie Bellew, for once, in the 2003 final.

The Goal ...
the moment in the
2005 All-Ireland
quarter-final against
Dublin when I
scored the goal
I'm best known for.

Nearly there...

Goal!

Time to celebrate my most famous moment in Croke Park.

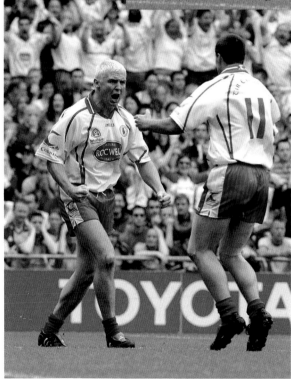

Brian McGuigan comes screaming in my direction.

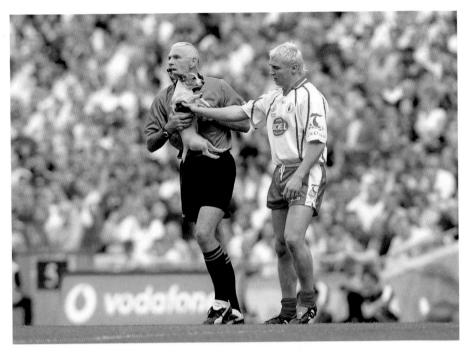

Every dog has its day! I hand over a stray to referee, Gearoid Ó Conamha, during the replay against Dublin.

Above, never in doubt ... Peter Canavan scores the winning point against Armagh in the semi-final in 2005.

Champions Again ... I celebrate the final whistle after the 2005 All-Ireland final next to a dejected Aidan O'Mahony.

Lifting Sam in '05.

Top, with Ma and Da, and my Man of the Match trophy at the victory banquet for the 2005 All-Ireland final. Middle, receiving my All Star award from Sean Kelly in 2005 and, bottom, proudly lining up to make it eight Tyrone All Stars (with Brian Dooher, Peter Canavan, Stephen O'Neill, Conor Gormley, Sean Cavanagh, Philip Jordan and Ryan McMenamin).

Mickey Harte surprises us all a second time by bringing Stephen O'Neill in so early in the 2008 final.

Tommy McGuigan scores the decisive goal against Kerry.

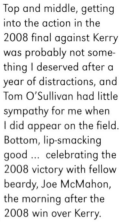

Top and middle, getting into the action in the 2008 final against Kerry was probably not something I deserved after a year of distractions, and Tom O'Sullivan had little sympathy for me when I did appear on the field. Bottom, lip-smacking good ... celebrating the 2008 victory with fellow beardy, Joe McMahon, the morning after the 2008 win over Kerry.

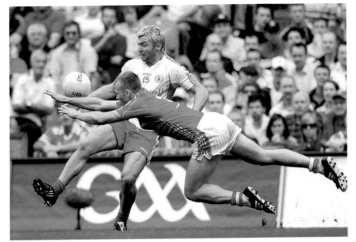

'You go that way ...'
In my whole career,
there was nothing
I enjoyed more than
perfecting a perfect
dummy solo, as
shown here against
poor Michael Shields
of Cork.

Standing proud with some of my Fr Rocks' teammates as the National Anthem is played before the 2013 All-Ireland intermediate club final victory over Finuge.

Left, celebrating scoring a point in the game. Right, there is nothing better than getting to play in Croke Park with my lifelong clubmates … and winning on the double!

Stupidly, I was sucked in straight away, dollar signs flashing in my head. 'Aye, great, no bother.'

The next week the whole team put in a good performance as we blitzed Fermanagh by 1-21 to 0-5 in Croke Park. Canavan and I both scored 0-4 and everyone was in good form on the bus home. We had an All-Ireland semi-final with Kerry to look forward to.

A few weeks passed and I forgot all about Adidas, until one day the phone rang in the week leading up to the Kerry game.

'Hi, Owen,' this guy introduced himself as so and so from Adidas.

'I've been talking to Peter Canavan about you and we'd like to thrash out a deal with you. I'm in McConnell's sports shop in Cookstown right now, but I'll be down in the White Horse shortly.'

I butted in, all excited.

'You mean the Black Horse? It must be the Black Horse you mean.'

Fine work by Canavan. Real professional, down to the last mistaken detail.

'Oh yeah, whatever it's called ... yeah ... the Black Horse. I could meet you for lunch and maybe get a couple of snaps of you, does that sound ok?'

I'm already turning the car in the middle of the road, heading back to Cookstown.

'Oh, and I don't know if you're at home at the minute, but I need you to wear a suit.'

'Aye, no problem, I can do that no problem.'

I hung up and phoned my ma straight away.

'Ma, get my suit sorted out quick. And shine my shoes. I'm meeting a boy from Adidas.'

I rushed home and jumped into the shower, my mind a whir of excitement.

Adidas, imagine. It's Adidas! I love Adidas.

I headed into the Black Horse and saw a barman I knew well. 'Well, Owen, do you want a feed?'

I shook my head. I told him I was waiting for someone.

A maths teacher I knew from Holy Trinity, Miss Gribben, walked in.

'Hello, Owen, how are you?'

'How's it going Miss, you keeping well?'

'And what are you doing in here today?'

'Oh, I'm just taking care of a bit of business, Miss.'

'Actually Owen, now that I see you, there're a few girls on the camogie team were asking me if I could get a picture of you on your own.'

'No problem, Miss.'

She took out the phone. 'Just sit where you are, Owen.' I sat, smiling up at her with a big stupid smile on my stupid face.

I looked at the phone. *That's funny*, I noted, *she has the same phone as Canavan, one of those flip-top jobs.*

It still didn't click.

A few minutes after she left, who came round the corner only Canavan, clutching the phone.

He waved it into my face, so I could see the picture of myself in the suit. He was beaming.

'What's this here Mugsy ... what's this here?'

He was delighted with himself.

'Ah lad, no.' I put my head in my hands. *How the hell did I fall for that?*

He pointed at the phone. 'That's for taking this. Never you play a prank on me again.'

All the bar staff started to clap and roar. He had tipped them all off.

He sent it to everybody in the squad that day. The picture of me in the suit and the caption, 'Caught Mugsy with the old Adidas trick'.

I got some slagging at training that night. I made a promise never to play a trick on him again.

Just another lesson I learned from the master.

Winning that first All-Ireland changed our lives. Everywhere I went, people were stuffing envelopes full of money into my pocket, women were slipping me their phone numbers, there was fan mail, endorsement deals, sponsored cars.

The first few months were manic.

I never had much trouble pulling women, but I went out with some gorgeous girls that I wouldn't have stood a chance with if we hadn't just won the All-Ireland.

C'mon Tyrone!

It was one long party.

The morning I left a nightclub in San Francisco with feathers coming out of my Tyrone suit was typical of the madness at the time.

Tyrone people out there had organised a dinner dance and some of us had been invited to travel to the States with the Sam Maguire. I fell in love with the city immediately. The place is so chilled out, it's a lot like Australia.

After the dinner dance, the sensible ones like Stevie and Cricko went back to the hotel. I'd heard about a sex club called the Power Exchange and persuaded Hub and Calvo to come with me to check it out.

The boys were up for it until they saw the entrance fee at the door. Hub's eyes nearly popped out. 'A hundred dollars, Mugsy? No bloody way.'

Calvo started to laugh, pointing at another sign.

'Well, it's actually only $20 in if you take your clothes off.' We looked at each other.

I wasn't taking no for an answer.

'Come on lads, we're only here the once. Sure we'll not know anybody anyway.'

We took the plunge and each paid $20.

We weren't expecting to see the inside of any changing rooms on that trip, yet here we were, taking off our suits and putting a cloth like a wee tea towel around us. It just about covered what it needed to cover.

We ventured out into the club with just the tea towels and our shoes on.

Upstairs there were play areas, jails, dungeons and fantasy rooms with consenting adults of all sexual persuasions getting up to all sorts. There was wild stuff going on.

Anything goes in San Francisco and it was all happening in there. I thought I was a 'man about town' but I was a long way from Cookstown.

We headed straight for the bar and tried to relax into the whole scene. A few transvestites chatted us up and we were having the craic until Hub spotted three boys he knew. We hadn't been in the place five minutes.

'For God's sake … you can go nowhere.' Hub was raging.

The boys had their clothes on. There was no place to hide and it was only a matter of time before they saw us. I decided the best thing to do was go on the attack. I walked over, clapping my hands. 'Ah lads … youse didn't pay a hundred dollars in here, did youse?'

Their jaws hit the floor. 'Oh, holy fuck … is that you, Mugsy? What are youse boys doing here?'

We chatted to them for a few minutes and headed off to see the sights.

The more drink we got, the more cocky we got, singing and cheering – but we didn't get involved in anything else that was going on.

After a few hours, we nearly got into a scuffle with a few boys wearing mini skirts and stilettos. They realised we were taking the piss out of them and they weren't long flexing their muscles. The bouncers stepped in and it all calmed down fairly quickly.

At about six in the morning we headed back to the changing room. There was total carnage in there. Wands, whips, feathers, high heels, make-up, hairspray, sequined underwear, stuff lying everywhere. And in the middle of it all, our Tyrone suits, still hanging neatly on three hangers where we'd left them, with shirts and ties all to match.

I couldn't stop smiling. Not quite like our dressing room at home. It would have made some picture.

◆ ◆ ◆ ◆ ◆

I didn't expect to get an All Star after the way I'd played in the All-Ireland final. I thought I played well throughout the League and Ulster Championship, but I hadn't exactly lit up Croke Park and that is the place where All Stars are won and lost. I was happy enough with the nomination and looking forward to a good night out. I brought my da with me and he was delighted.

Tyrone was awarded seven All Stars. The awards were announced live on the night and I wasn't in the least disappointed I didn't win one. I still felt out of my depth even though we were All-Ireland champions. *What am I doing here?* I thought. *Look at all these good players.* I couldn't be bothered with the hype and was shy about mixing with players from other counties.

I wondered, if I ever won an All Star in the future, would I even come and collect it? It wasn't my scene. A few players probably thought I was stuck up for not talking, but I'm not the kind of lad who'll walk over and start chatting to some boy I've never met before like he's my best mate.

I made an exception with Francie.

We had gone at it from the first whistle to the last in the All-Ireland final and he had won the fight, no doubt about it. He was named right corner-back on the All Star team. I went over to congratulate him and to shake hands, because I hadn't seen him after the match.

He, my Da and I had some craic, we had a right few drinks together that night. My da gave him some stick about all the nipping and tugging we'd been at during the match but he took it well, he was laughing away. That is the way it should be. Go hell for leather on the pitch surely but, once it's over, it's over. I have never held a grudge against anybody once a match is over.

We didn't drink for months before the All-Ireland but we certainly made up for it afterwards. The All Stars was just one of many nights out we had. Mickey tried his best to keep our feet on the ground. 'Boys, it's not always going to be like this. Enjoy this … soak it up, because it won't always be like this.'

What's he talking about? Of course it's always going to be like this. He knows we have a great team, a young team. We're going to dominate. We're going to rule football for the next ten years.

◆ ◆ ◆ ◆ ◆

I thought this was a natural progression in our careers, from our minor and Under-21 successes. A senior All-Ireland was the way it was supposed to be. But I never imagined all the spin-offs that came with it. Winning an All-Ireland senior title was off the scale, a whole new ball game.

We didn't give everything we had trying to win the All-Ireland for money or the holidays, or for cars or women. But, once we had done it, it definitely had its perks. Canavan had told us it would be a life changer, that people would get opportunities, and my phone didn't stop ringing for months.

My ma was like my full-time secretary, pencilling in engagements for me here, there and everywhere. It was Tyrone's first All-Ireland and people were just firing money at us.

We had heard of a few counties where there had been a fallout because it was felt that some players were getting all the money and all the appearances, and a bit of jealousy had set in. We were determined not to let that happen to us.

Canavan thought the fairest thing was that if a player was asked to go somewhere, half of the money should go into the players' fund. I always gave half, I thought it was fair enough, but I know there were players who didn't hand money over. They know who they are, too. Philly Jordan is an accountant so he was put in charge of the players' fund. When it was all divided up at the end, every single player in the squad got something like £1,500 each.

Women wanted to be *seen* with us as much as they wanted to *be* with us. It was pure attention-seeking but, I'm a man, and I took full advantage. If some gorgeous girl came over and said, 'Are you going to take me home tonight, Owen?' then, of course, I did.

There were silly ones pouring themselves all over us, but I always liked the quieter ones who were a bit more subtle about it. 'Well, where are you going tonight, Owen? We're heading to such and such … are you heading down?'

'Aye, I have a few lads here with me, we might go down for a while.'

You'd get to the next bar and chat to her for a while and she'd tell you there was a party in her house after. Then you'd land round and there'd be nobody there but her.

Yes!

My phone was melting. The boys started calling it the bat phone. 'Where's the bat signal shining tonight, Mugsy … is it in Coalisland or Brockagh … or where?' I had to get another phone about three months after the All-Ireland final and change my number.

The fan mail was pouring in. Some of it would come to the house and some to the County Board office. Dominic McCaughey, the Tyrone secretary, would walk over to me sometimes, smiling, carrying a few envelopes and faxes. It just took off, the whole Tyrone craziness.

The women weren't just throwing themselves at me, other players had fun, too. I started getting a bit of a reputation, unfairly I thought. Girls need to realise it works both ways. They start saying, 'Oh, he's a dirty so and so … he only used me for one thing.' But if they hadn't come near me, then it wouldn't have happened.

I knew I wasn't like that. Nobody said, 'Actually, Owen Mulligan went steady with a girl there for about six or seven years.'

It was so funny in Cookstown. Women would come to your house for about three weeks and then one of them would say, 'My mate says I've been seen coming out of your house. I can't do this any more'.

I have had girlfriends and I've heard them slag off good, decent lads calling them all sorts after they've been spotted out with other girls. It's hilarious. They seem to think they're the innocent ones all the time and it's the men who are always the ones to blame.

The rumours going around about me were unreal. I'm still hearing stories of things I'm supposed to have done ten years ago. It got out of hand when the reality TV star, Jordan, came to town. She came to attend some event in Clubland and the chat was that I went out with her that night. To this day, there are boys around Cookstown who don't believe me when I tell them that it never happened. I wish.

I did meet her all right and I just told her she needn't think she was the most famous blond in the place that night – that I was. She just looked at me like I wasn't half wise. She hadn't a clue who I was.

Her minders weren't long pushing me to one side.

Thankfully, some people were more generous. The first car I ever owned was the sponsored car I got from Mid Ulster Cars after the final. I'd only passed my test a few months earlier and here I was, sitting in a brand new Toyota. I used it for work and everything but I paid to get it cleaned before I left it back. I even paid £450 to get a scratch taken out of it when I returned it in the hope they might give it to me for another year if it was in mint condition. It didn't happen!

My rock 'n' roll lifestyle continued when I was asked by the GPA to take part in the Club Energise advertisement being shot in the Wicklow mountains.

I had started seeing a new girlfriend, Tina, and we drove down to Dublin in my sponsored car and were put up, all expenses paid, in The Berkeley Court Hotel for three days. Stevie McDonnell, the hurler Eugene Cloonan from Galway, and Diarmuid O'Sullivan from Cork, were also there.

We had to run and kick footballs down the mountain. One of the days we got soaked and it was freezing. Somebody joked, 'Hey, this wasn't in the contract'.

'Don't worry lads, there's an extra thousand for this.'

No way!

There was one scene where you had to do a block. On the second day of the shoot I felt like I knew McDonnell well enough to start slagging him. Someone was filming him having a shot blocked down. 'Ah, you're not used to having that done on you, sure you're not, Stevie?'

He wasn't happy.

I thought, *Uh oh, maybe I shouldn't have said that, this is still a bit raw.* I got real friendly with McDonnell after that and we went out for a few pints that night with Diarmuid O'Sullivan.

A lot of doors open after you win an All-Ireland. The Irish League soccer team, Dungannon Swifts, approached me about playing for them over the winter months. Joe McAree was the manager, a really nice man, and his son Rodney was the boy who pulled the strings for them in midfield. They seemed keen for me to give it a go, as was big Gary Fitzpatrick, who played with me at Cookstown, who also played for the Swifts.

I was flattered to be asked. I always loved playing soccer, usually as a centre-back or in midfield, but it's a skillful game and I thought that after a few years of playing mostly Gaelic I'd have lost my touch. I think it's a game you need to be playing regularly to be any good at it. I was worried boys would be looking at me and saying, 'That man can't trap a bag of cement'.

UTV sports broadcaster, Adrian Logan, told me he was taking the cameras down to shoot me playing in my first game. The pressure was on and I was starting to get cold feet. I made up a story that I needed to get an MRI scan on a hip and back injury I'd picked up in the All-Ireland final. It was complete bullshit. I just wanted an excuse to back out because I knew I wasn't good enough.

The good times kept on coming though.

Barney Eastwood is a big Tyrone fan and he organised a party in his house to celebrate the All-Ireland win. He's a Cookstown man like me and played on the Tyrone team that won the All-Ireland minor football title in 1948. He used to play soccer with my granda in the old street leagues around the town. That was all long before he became a successful businessman and boxing promoter.

A mini-bus took the east Tyrone boys up to his house in Cultra, outside Belfast; the whole McGuigan clan, including Frank senior, and myself, Jim

Curran, Mickey Coleman, Horse, Ciaran Gourley and Peter Donnelly. Patsy Forbes from Ardboe was also with us, he's great friends with Barney and had organised the whole thing.

We drank champagne flat out. It was an expensive taste we were beginning to get used to during those few months. Barney brought us into his games room. There was a snooker table in the middle of it but the room was full of gloves, replicas of World title belts, Northern Ireland jerseys and boxing bibs. Barney started pointing at all the gloves. He knew the history of each piece.

His minders were ex-boxers. He'd say, 'This man was a great boxer but sometimes you'd a bad chin, hadn't you?'

Then he'd show us a picture of a boxer and then point to one of the lads, 'This is him here. Look, he hasn't changed a bit.' I thought that was class. Fair play, I thought, he has employed all of these boys. He had a great word on all of them.

He took us across the road to The Culloden Hotel for dinner, which he didn't have to do. We were just delighted he had invited us to his house, but dinner in a place like that was the icing on the cake.

Most of us got full but it was a brilliant night. When we were leaving Barney gave us all an Eastwoods Bookmakers mug and a card. He shook hands and had a word with all of us as we got back on the minibus.

'Frank, you're still the King, the best player I have ever seen in my life,' he said, as we said our goodbyes. 'Brian, you're emulating your old boy very nicely.'

I think Barney has a bit of a soft spot for me because I'm a Cookstown boy. He put his hand on my shoulder. 'Son, it's a pity you weren't a boxer. I'd have made some job of you. You're brave and you're strong and you're committed. I'd have made you famous.'

I swallowed hard. Some words from a man like that.

'Thanks Barney, I appreciate it,' I replied.

There was still time for one more laugh. Mickey Coleman had been on the Blind Date TV programme and fancied himself as a bit of an entertainer playing gigs in local bars. 'Mickey, you're a great singer,' said Barney, 'You might make it in showbiz but I don't think you'll make it on the football pitch.' We exploded.

When we got on the bus we opened the envelopes. Each one contained a congratulations card with £250 inside. Five crisp £50 notes with not a crease in them.

Frank senior couldn't believe it. He waved the notes in the air like it was a winning bookies' docket. 'What a man! Never in my life have I got this here, boys, never!'

We were stunned.

No one could believe his generosity. He had no need to do that because it was sound of him to invite us up to his house in the first place, but that's a measure of the man. A pure gentleman.

◆ ◆ ◆ ◆ ◆

A GAA club in Chicago asked Cricko if he would take the Sam over there to a dinner dance. He had connections from playing football over there one summer and he asked me if I wanted to go with him. I jumped at it. The break-up with my girlfriend had been difficult for me and I was happy to be away from women completely.

There was no big drinking done, just a nice quiet time with good people. Cricko made a speech the night before we left and thanked everybody. That was the only night we went on a bit of a bender. We met a few Carrickmore men and then starting chatting to an Aer Lingus air stewardess who was going out with one of the Carrickmore men. We told her we were flying home the next day.

We pitched up to the airport the next morning, totally hungover and in need of sleep. She met us at the gate. 'You're going home first class, boys.' Lethal.

Cricko and I lay back on two big recliners eating steak dinners and drinking beer, smiling at each other all the way home.

I thought about Canavan.

Boys, if we win this All-Ireland it's going to change our lives forever, and it's all going to be for the better.

He wasn't wrong.

The partying stopped when Cormac died.

The last time I saw him was at training on a Tuesday night and everything seemed grand. I was up early the next morning getting ready to go to work in Belfast when I got a text from Calvo. It was about a quarter to six. I smiled. *This boy must have been out partying last night and needs a lift home.*

I read the text.

'Did you hear about McAnallen?' it read.

I texted back.

'No, what about him?'

He texted back, 'McAnallen died early this morning.'

I read it, then read it again. I read it a third time and then phoned him.

'What the fuck are you on about, Calvo?'

'I swear, Mugsy, I swear to God.'

I phoned Canavan, praying Calvo had got it wrong, but he confirmed it. I turned on the TV and there was already news on Teletext that there were complications at the McAnallen house, that something had happened at the Tyrone captain's house.

Nobody knew what had happened. There was talk of a break in, or a murder. Everyone was ringing everybody else trying to figure it out.

It was the same confusion and disbelief when Michaela Harte died some years later, the total shock, and not a single person on the team really knowing what had happened.

I slumped into a chair for the day and never moved, glued to every news bulletin I could find. I chatted to some of the Moy boys, like Philly Jordan and Collie Holmes, the boys who travelled to training with Cormac every week and knew him best.

It seemed like a long wait before word eventually filtered through that Cormac had died of an undetected heart condition. I was sceptical. It was the last thing anyone would have thought.

I still thought there must have been some kind of accident, no way could McAnallen have had some kind of heart attack. It seemed like complete bullshit.

Heart attacks are for smokers and big drinkers, I reasoned, *not boys like Cormac*. He was flying fit, there wasn't a pick of fat on him. Everyone was in right good shape but he was a top class athlete. He won every bleep test and fitness test going.

We travelled up to Cormac's home in Brantry on the buses that had been laid on for the thousands of mourners who attended the wake. I had played with this man since I was fifteen years old and I couldn't get my head around it. *Is this a bad dream, or what the hell is going on here?*

It didn't hit me that Cormac was dead until I saw him in the coffin. This wasn't the Cormac I knew, the Cormac who had his whole life ahead of him. It was upsetting but I didn't cry.

I never know what to say at wakes and funerals, I hate going to them in case I come out with something stupid. I saw Cormac's mother, Bridget. I felt awkward, unable to find the right words.

People started shaking our hands.

I remember seeing Mattie McGleenan, and then Anthony Tohill came over and shook my hand. The Ó Sé's came all the way from Kerry, which was sound of them. It hit everybody hard.

We had a team meeting in Paudge Quinn's the night before the funeral and our doctor, Seamus Cassidy, explained to us that Cormac had died in random circumstances, of a condition called Sudden Adult Death Syndrome which can happen to anybody, even very fit and healthy young men like Cormac.

We were put into groups to try to come to terms with it. I was dumb with shock. I had abused my body far more than Cormac. *Why has this happened to him and not me?*

Mickey asked Hub to speak. I'll never forget it.

Here was a lad who had lost not one, but two, of his immediate family in car accidents on almost the same stretch of road and he has to drive past those spots every day. I always expected Hub to be captain at some point. After all he had been through, I thought he would have been the right person for the job, and he spoke like a captain that night.

'Boys, I've been through this before and you just have to rise above it. You're probably not going to like what I'm going to say here, because you're upset about Cormac. But you have just got to get on with your lives. That is what Cormac would want us to do.'

There were no tears in the room. Just amazement and admiration at what he had just said. There was silence from the boys when anybody spoke. I looked around and you could see boys were just staking it in.

I only saw Cormac at the collective training sessions twice a week but other boys, like Philly, Collie Holmes, Ryan Mellon and big Sean, they saw him at the weights sessions and did all the workouts with him. You could see they were hurting.

Mickey looked pale and tired. I could see it was taking a lot out of him. Not only had he lost his captain but he had lost a real friend, someone he trusted. I shook his hand, not knowing what to say. It was tough on Fr Gerard, too. He had taught Cormac and had big respect for him as a star student and as a person. They were very close.

We wore our suits from the All-Ireland final to the funeral and I walked stone-faced, head up. No tears.

There was eerie silence, with walls of people everywhere you looked. Crowds and crowds of people lined the streets, some in club jerseys, some in Tyrone jerseys.

The Armagh team joined us in a guard of honour either side of Cormac's hearse. As we walked slowly from the chapel to the graveyard, I glanced over at the men who six months earlier had been our enemy. In order to take their All-Ireland crown away from them, we'd had to build up a hatred of them.

At that time, the rivalry was at its height but it was more among the supporters than the players. Those boys are the same as us. They would have known what we were going through and they walked shoulder to shoulder with us.

I spotted Bellew, my old sparring partner. We shook hands. All the Armagh boys said the same thing to us. 'Sorry about your teammate, sorry about Cormac.'

I thought it was brilliant the Armagh boys were there. They put themselves in our shoes and probably thought if it had been one of their young players, they would have wanted a show of support from us, too.

The worst part for me at every funeral is lowering the coffin into the ground. That is the lump in the throat moment for me every time. As Mícheál Ó Muircheartaigh gave a graveside oration, I looked around at our team and most of the boys were crying. But not me. I never cry at funerals. I just go away off on my own and do my own thing.

The next night a few of us went to McAleer's bar in Dungannon, but my evening came to a premature end.

I wasn't in the mood. Men in the bar were talking about Cormac, people who didn't know him. They wanted to know too much stuff, what was he like, did he ever do this, did he ever do that? There was a curiosity about him I found hard to handle. It was private stuff. Team stuff.

I don't need this, I thought. I ordered a taxi and went straight home.

Over the next few weeks it was thrown up to me a few times – three to be exact – why had I not cried at Cormac's funeral? A boy came up to me one night in Cookstown. 'You didn't cry at the funeral, I was watching on TV, you weren't even crying for that man. You're a disgrace, you're some mate.'

Bang. I knocked him clean out.

I got the same thing twice in Dungannon. When they started, I didn't even take time to get into a conversation or ask them what they were talking about, I just smacked them. People probably rolled their eyes, there he goes again, getting into another scrap. But I only react like that when something bad is said to me.

People mourn in different ways.

A few days after the funeral I walked the few short steps from our house to the Glenavon Hotel and ended up getting sideroads drunk. I went back to the house, poured another drink and lay down on the sofa. I lifted my dog, Bob, up in my arms and the tears started to come.

That's when I did my crying for Cormac.

◆ ◆ ◆ ◆ ◆

A Tyrone minor trial match in Newtownstewart was my first time meeting Cormac McAnallen.

Cookstown put me forward for a trial but I was wary of going because I was only fifteen. I didn't want people saying, 'Who does this boy think he is?' I already knew Brian McGuigan and had played soccer with Stevie O'Neill but it was the first time I saw Hub and McAnallen.

Cormac was centre half-back and I was right half-back. I knew nothing about being a back but he kept me right. He was captain material even then, chatting away. Always talking and pointing.

We all moved up through the ranks together. Himself and Hub were on the seniors first, followed by me and Stevie, all under Art and Eugene.

Cormac was a born leader.

He got the captaincy of the minors in 1998 when McGuigan broke his collarbone, a decision that initially didn't go down well in Ardboe.

Their club was where we went drinking on a Monday. People were always coming up to Brian saying, 'Why are you not captain?' I kind of disagreed with the decision to replace McGuigan with Cormac. Once you're captain for the year, you should stay as captain.

But once Cormac got the job, he grew into it. He was big for a minor, imposing looking. Harte confided in him and they got really close. It wasn't that he was a 'mini-me' version of Mickey, but you just didn't want to be messing about in front of him. He was so well respected.

You could always see him trying to better himself at training, using his bad hand or his weaker foot. Sometimes I'd see him running awkwardly or doing a clumsy solo and wonder what the hell he was at, then I'd realise he was soloing with his left foot. He was always striving to be better. It was pure focus with him.

When it came out after he died that he had kept jotters rating all his own performances at training and matches, I wasn't one bit surprised. That was Cormac all over.

He would always have said he wasn't the most talented player in the squad, that he just worked harder at his game than everybody else, although the Eglish boys, like Brendan Donnelly who won an Ulster minor League with him, disagreed with that. They said he was unreal.

At minor level, Dungannon Academy and St Pat's Armagh were big rivals in the MacRory Cup. Cormac, Ryan Mellon and Philly were all on the Armagh team. With the two MacRory teams, the Errigal boys and the Vocationals, we knew we had the makings of some team. It all came together.

Once Cormac got the captaincy he never looked back.

He spoke a lot of sense and he never changed when he became captain. He was the same McAnallen. He was sensible and always did things the proper way. Even though some of us didn't match his high standards, we had massive respect for him. He sat up near the front of the bus, whereas we were down the back and messing about. But he was still one of the boys.

When we'd win important matches, even at minor level, he'd come down the back and have a few drinks. We'd sing a few songs. Cormac loved singing 'The Music Man'. That was his party piece. He was always there on the nights out and when he went on the drink with the boys, he was on it. There was no such thing as, 'That's enough now, boys'. He enjoyed the slagging and the craic.

He also had brains to burn.

After we beat Cork in an All-Ireland Under-21 semi-final in Parnell Park, he waved goodbye to us as we got on the bus and he headed back to UCD. He studied at Queen's and then UCD while some of us were out on building sites. He only missed the very odd training session all the time he was in Dublin. He was that committed to the cause.

He was a very intelligent fella and he came across well in media interviews while other boys would be stuttering and stammering. At minor and Under-21 level especially, we would be shy and awkward not knowing what to say. But Cormac's interviews were brilliant. We'd be standing and staring at him as he chatted away, no bother. He talked like a senior footballer. The words came flowing out of him.

With Canavan looking like he might be out for most of the year after having surgery on his injured ankle, we were in need of a new captain. I was sad that he wasn't going to be leading us out any more but, if a change had to be made, I wasn't surprised when it was Cormac who was appointed.

Harte had huge belief in our minor and Under-21 All-Ireland winning teams, and Cormac had led us for so long. Harte always had faith in us. He knew we were winners and would fight for him.

I congratulated Cormac on getting the captaincy but he just shrugged it off, he took it all in his stride. The night he was appointed, he stood up and said one All-Ireland wasn't enough, that he was going to captain us to another All-Ireland that year and bring back-to-back titles to Tyrone. If he hadn't died, Cormac would still be captain now.

All we thought about was how it would be if we won it, how unreal it would be if we won it for that man.

I also thought about something else. I thought that if all us Tyrone boys were lined up and God said, 'Right, boys, youse are never going to win another All-Ireland unless I take one of youse,' McAnallen would have been the one to put his hand up.

I often wonder, would I have put my hand up? Probably not. I was enjoying the craic too much. But Cormac was that much of a leader, he'd have said 'Right, boys'. That's what he was like. He was all for the cause.

◆ ◆ ◆ ◆ ◆

We had a lot to get our heads around when we lost Cormac. It was hard to move on and start playing football again as if nothing had happened.

Brian Dooher was announced as our new captain.

I would have loved to have seen Hub lead us out because he had such a presence about him. If anything happened on the pitch, he was always straight in, the first man to push and shove men out of the road. He always had your back and you need men like that. People had a wee bit of fear of Hub because he was in your face.

But, as it turned out, Dooher proved to be an excellent captain. You just know leaders and he is the perfect example of someone who gives everything. He gave everything to the cause every day he went out, every last drop he had. He was the right man at the right time.

Mickey brought in a sports psychologist to help us that year. We had one-to-one meetings with him and I hated it. He told me I needed to change my game, that my dummy wasn't working any more. People were going to read me better that year, so I was going to have to reinvent myself.

I wasn't impressed.

'Well … the dummy is still going okay at club level. Boys are still falling for it that have seen me doing it for years.'

It wouldn't work any more at county level, he said. I'd have to go onto my left foot more.

I accepted that point from him but from the very start I thought he was wrong about me. There was talk he was in the background helping Mickey in 2003, and I'd have preferred things to stay that way.

In 2003 we covered everything. We used to break up into separate groups and make contingency plans for absolutely everything that might happen on the pitch.

But for me, now there was too much talk about motivation and psyching-up tools at the expense of discussing tactics and our opponents. The psychology stuff was getting in the way of the work that some players like myself thought was more important.

I missed the bonding weekend away before our first Ulster Championship match against Derry after being involved in a minor accident when a car crashed into the back of me. When the boys got back they filled me in.

The psychologist was no longer working with us. Some of the established players had made it clear to Mickey that they wanted a change in team preparations and wanted more work on the field.

We went into a huddle in our first training session after Cormac died. I looked at every face in the circle. No McAnallen. I wondered how we would ever get used to that. Mickey spoke, as always, but he never mentioned Cormac's name.

He didn't have to.

Our No.3 jersey was retired for the year and we tried to get down to the business of returning to some kind of normality. We trained, but it felt strange. Going on the bus to Castlebar for our first National League game after Cormac died was weird, too.

It was a windy day. I wasn't able to play because I'd had an injection for a hip injury picked up in the All-Ireland final the year before, but we had a good League campaign and faced Galway at home in the League semi-final, with us going for a three-in-a-row of League titles.

We never wanted any sympathy after losing Cormac and we found out that day that teams weren't going to roll over and feel sorry for us.

It got heated on the sideline between Mickey and John O'Mahony and we ended up drawing the game. The replay in Salthill was an absolute classic. We lost it 2-18 to 1-19 after extra time, but we mounted some comeback after being eight points down at half time.

My tackling had improved a lot and Mickey wanted me to play wing-forward to do a man-marking job on Declan Meehan. I was pretty ineffective but it was one of the most exciting League games I've ever played in.

We lost our League crown and then, very quickly after it, we lost our Ulster title too.

Donegal beat us in the Ulster semi-final in Clones and I was booed off by the Donegal supporters for getting Niall McCready sent off.

I could see their point. He was a very good marker, very sticky, and I wanted to see the back of him. I knew what I was at. He was digging his elbows in to me and he was on a booking. I hit him an elbow which nobody saw and he got frustrated. Soon after, I saw him coming for me out of the corner of my eye so I rode the tackle and got him sent off. It gave a bit more ammunition to those who thought I was a diver.

We got our revenge on Galway in a qualifier in Croke Park, needing some magic from Canavan off the bench to rescue us. We were limping along. Then we hammered Laois, I got a goal after four minutes, and Mark 'Sparky' Harte scored 2-3 to put us into the All-Ireland quarter finals.

There were no big 'Let's do it for Cormac' speeches before we played Mayo. That would have put too much pressure on us. Mickey never used Cormac as a psyching up tool that year and he was right. We were struggling to handle it as it was, but I was quietly hoping for a fairytale ending to the year.

I really believed it would happen when Jim Curran came into the dressing room before the match and shouted that Fermanagh had just beaten Armagh. Our match was the second part of a double-header and we had been watching some of the first game on the TV, before it was switched off to allow us to focus on our own game.

Great, with Armagh out of the picture, we can win this All-Ireland, I figured.

In hindsight, it was the worst thing we could have been told. Maybe it got into men's heads but, from the start, it seemed nothing went right. Canavan wasn't fit to start, having missed the Laois game completely the week before. McGuigan couldn't start because of a knee injury and we lost Conor Gormley in the first half. I missed a free that I fancied taking when we were level after forty-five minutes. It was a crucial miss and Alan Dillon destroyed us on his own, hitting six points.

We were devastated. We had lost our All-Ireland title. Cormac's wish had been trampled into the dirt in Croke Park.

I think we used his death as a bit of a crutch without even knowing it. After we were beaten, boys started saying, 'Sure McAnallen died, McAnallen died,' as if that was some sort of excuse. That shouldn't have been the case.

Cormac's parents came into the dressing room after we lost. I couldn't look at them. I felt guilty, I felt we had let Cormac down.

Mickey told us it just wasn't meant to be. 'There is more to life than football,' he said. We just accepted it. There were a few heads in hands and a few tears. It was a bad place to be.

But, going home on the bus, I kept thinking that we shouldn't have been beaten. We had surrendered the All-Ireland but worse, far worse, we had let Cormac down.

If he had been there, we would have won the All-Ireland title again in 2004. No one will ever tell me any different. Kerry won a very soft All-Ireland that year.

Cormac should have been leading us into 2005 going for a three-in-a-row.

10

It was tough to have to move on and start into a new season without Cormac but, in a way, it was a relief to leave a sad year behind.

Mickey didn't mention Cormac's name very often at team meetings, but he would say things like, 'You know what other men would do, you know what other men did for this cause, you know what other men would sacrifice.'

There were other changes we had to get used to. I missed Kevin Hughes, who had opted out and gone to Australia for the year, with Brian McGuigan also going away for a few months. We had big changes in the back-room team to get used to as well. Tony Donnelly came in as Mickey's assistant, and Fergal McCann as trainer, after Mickey had parted company with Paddy Tally at the end of the previous season.

Mickey also had the difficult situation of his son, Mark, to deal with. By the time Mark's career with Tyrone was over, I thought that he had got a raw deal from the Tyrone supporters.

Sparky is a really good lad, a gentleman, but he was also very under-rated as a footballer. Yes, he was small, but he had a serious football brain and he was very, very accurate. I rated him highly as a footballer.

He excelled as a minor and he was probably our best player in 2004. We were playing Mayo in a League match at home in March of the following year when so-called 'supporters' booed him. I was sitting in the stand because I was injured and I heard the whole thing.

Ok, Sparky maybe dropped a couple of balls and got beated to a few that he should have got, but nothing that many a player, including myself, hasn't done before. I think he was only coming back from an injury and may not have been fully fit.

People were shouting, 'You need to get that man off, Mickey'. To be booed by your own supporters? It was the ultimate insult. Those Tyrone supporters were totally out of order that day.

With a new back-room team in place, we had to get used to a new training regime and I found it difficult.

To me, Paddy Tally was outstanding. He'd studied sports science and had us doing resistance training with straps and tackle bags and gave us diet sheets. It was a really professional set-up.

He'd tell you the truth.

'What's wrong with you? You didn't play on Sunday, you look tired.' Tally is his own man. He didn't sit and agree with all of Mickey's decisions just for the sake of it. What's the point in having a back-room team if you don't have people who will challenge you, who will tell you the truth, who you might have the odd row with?

I always believed that if you're training a county team, you need to be able to do the training with the players. I've more admiration for a man who's doing a training session with me, running alongside me, practising what he preaches, rather than someone standing there barking orders.

When Cricko took charge of Cookstown, in 2009, he would tog out some nights and he'd ram it into our faces. Tally was the same. He wasn't too long out of football himself, he was still playing a bit for the reserves, and he'd run alongside us, roaring in our faces. Those boys didn't put any man through training sessions they hadn't already done themselves.

Even when I take our club youth teams I always run the hard yards with the boys. You get more respect that way.

I was sad to see Tally go and I missed him those first few weeks. I was having doubts: We'd gone from a man who was super fit and could run the hard yards with us, to Fergal, pleasantly plump and roaring from the sidelines.

Once I got past my own biased perceptions, it didn't take me long to realise that Fergal was the real deal. It was just that, after Tally, he was very static but that was his method and I got used to it.

Fergal soon gained respect because the training was class. All the drills he did were related to the games and no two training sessions were the same. I enjoyed going to training every single night.

If we played a match on a Sunday, he would have a drill set up the following Tuesday night specifically to work on our mistakes. 'This is where youse went wrong the other day, boys.'

I try to do that now with our youth teams in Cookstown. Whatever I see happening on the pitch, I tailor our next training session to suit. If boys are not riding the tackle well enough, I'll have the tackle bags out. That was Fergal's mission all the time and I learned a lot from him.

Tony was always in the background as a trusted ally of Mickey's, but I didn't know him until 2005. I know he freshened things up.

I like people who make me laugh and I hit it off with Tony straight away. But when it comes to the serious side, he talks an awful lot of sense about football, too. He gives stick, talks sense and has a deadly football brain. What more could you want? We felt like we were building momentum again.

◆ ◆ ◆ ◆ ◆

We had another feisty League encounter with the Dubs that spring.

The year before, Dublin had given us a guard of honour in Parnell Park in our first League match as All-Ireland champions, and then got stuck into us. Dooher was used as a punch bag and Paddy Russell flashed ten yellow cards as Dublin won by a point.

This time we were determined to put down a marker – but it turned nasty again with one of the Healy Park stewards being struck and the Dublin subs having to be moved out of their seats.

Despite all that, we managed to get some football played. I was in top form and I hit a few free-kicks into the wind with the outside of the boot and they sailed over. When the Dubs come to town, of course you're going to raise your game. I scored a goal after twenty-six minutes which was a sign of what was to come.

Mickey Coleman did great work out on the wing and gave me the ball. I burst forward and was going to pass inside to Sean Cavanagh but I threw a fist dummy. Paddy Christie fell for it, and I put the ball low in the bottom corner.

Coleman was brilliant that day and was playing very well all spring. He was getting excited at the prospect of being on the starting team in the Championship. 'Any deals going lad? I'm on top of my game,' he said to me.

I had met with an Umbro rep and it just clicked with me that now might be a good time to have a wee bit of fun with Coleman. He is the easiest man to wind up.

'Funny you say that, Mickey, a boy from Umbro came looking for me to wear boots and gloves for them this year but I'm an Adidas man.'

'Jesus, put a good word in for me, lad,' he said. 'I'm playing well.'

Canavan sat out the entire League campaign, feeling he needed to play more club games to get back up to the pace of things after missing nearly the whole of 2004 through injury. He hadn't been around much but I phoned him looking for a number for Buzzer, the lad from Eglish who he'd got to set me up with the Adidas prank two years earlier.

Canavan was curious. 'What do you want his number for? What are you up to?'

'I'm gonna get Coleman with the old Adidas trick, except it'll be Umbro this time.'

He laughed. 'Well, make sure you do it right.'

I sat in the back seat of the car with Brendy Donnelly, a mate of Buzzer's who was in the Tyrone squad at that time, waiting for the show to start. We held our phones out to try and catch the conversation on tape, because this was going to be good.

Buzzer, sitting in the driver's seat, got to work.

'How are you, Michael? It's Tom from Umbro here. I was talking to Owen Mulligan about possibly getting you a boot deal.'

Coleman was delighted and off he went.

'Well, that's great,' he said. 'It's great timing actually because I think I'm on the top of my game.'

'Yes, yes, I've been to a couple of Tyrone games this year and you do seem to be one of the main players.'

'Ah here, look, you know I don't want to be blowing my own trumpet but I'll probably be starting midfield this year.' Brendy and I managed to keep the sniggering under control.

'We're going to give you a range of boots to try. Would you be interested in white boots?'

I could nearly hear Coleman gulping.

'Ah, well, I dunno about white boots now. It would depend what the money's like.'

We were laughing so much we had to get out of the car, this was too good for us to ruin it now.

'We're going to give you a seven grand signing on fee.'

'Sorry, say that again?'

'Seven grand.'

'Well, to be honest with you, if I was getting twenty grand and the boots weren't right, I wouldn't be wearing them. It's just whatever suits my foot.'

'Would you be interested in wearing the big Umbro gloves that the goalkeepers wear, to help you catch a ball in midfield?'

'Aye, aye, no problem.'

It was too good for words. We sent the voice recording around the lads. Even Mickey Harte got wind of it and wanted to hear it. He thought it was hilarious.

At training one night shortly afterwards, he got in on the act. 'Ok, lads, get those training bibs on but, Mickey, I have to warn you, they're not Umbro.'

Coleman came over to me. 'Did you hear Mickey being smart with me there? Did he hear I'm getting that Umbro deal, or what?' I smiled. 'I wouldn't like to think you are pranking me lad,' he added, clearly becoming suspicious. When he heard nothing back from Umbro after a few weeks, he realised the whole thing was a wind-up and wanted to know who had set him up.

I denied it flat out. He'd have taken it thick if he ever found out it was me. I guess he just has!

◆ ◆ ◆ ◆ ◆

I pulled a hamstring in a League match against Offaly and missed most of the campaign. When you hurt the hammer, you're always watching it. I'm the type of player who needs to do a lot of speed work and needs to be training flat out to get sharp. The injury meant I couldn't do that.

I was a bit sluggish and heavy, and I was working on a site in Dublin which meant I was skipping training sometimes. At the start, Mickey was ok about it when I phoned to say I wouldn't be there.

'That's ok, sure you never miss.'

Then it progressed to the stage where I wasn't ringing, I was just a no-show. Then I'd turn up the next night and say nothing. A couple of other boys did it occasionally, but I was the main culprit.

Cricko and Canavan were on my case. They gave out to me about skipping training, more so as the year went on, but Mickey kept faith with me.

We opened the Ulster Championship campaign at home against Down. I hit 0-3, all from frees, and had a goal disallowed for a square ball that definitely wasn't a square ball. We struggled, and needed Canavan to come off the bench in his first game of the year to win the game for us.

I played poorly against Cavan in the semi-final. McGuigan was just home from Australia and he came on for me as we drew the match. I was dropped for the replay – the first time I'd been dropped by Mickey for a big game.

Canavan was the man starting in my place, so there was no way I was complaining about that. But I knew I was in trouble. I knew rightly the replay was going to be a stuffing match and I was out of the team. *The whole thing is gonna click here, and I'm not going to get my place back,* I thought.

Sure enough, we annihilated them. Canavan scored 1-7 and McGuigan also started as we hammered Cavan in the replay. It was frustrating that Canavan and McGuigan were back just as I was losing my place. We were like ships passing in the night. They were the men I wanted to be playing with.

The Tyrone-Armagh rivalry was at its height and when both teams reached the Ulster final the Ulster Council fixed the game for Croke Park, a decision that was justified when over 60,000 people turned up.

On three occasions we led Armagh by four points, but we couldn't put them away. Stevie was superb and roasted Francie Bellew, scoring ten points. Canavan had to go off at half time with a rib injury and I came on for Penrose, but I was off the pace. Kieran McGeeney and Paul McGrane combined for an equalizer in injury-time and it was a draw, which felt like a defeat for us.

There was a really poor crowd at the replay, only 30,000, which made for a weird atmosphere in Croke Park. There was a huge cheer from the Tyrone supporters though, when Peter and I got ready to come on together after fifty-four minutes. I turned around and smiled at him and said, 'Is that for me or for you?'

I thought, *Right, let's light this place up, we're gonna destroy these men.*

As soon as Peter went in, all the Armagh boys seemed to go for him.

He got dragged along the ground by Ciaran McKeever and I was amazed when the referee sent them both off.

It was a disgrace Canavan got sent off. Michael Collins had a poor game and it got worse when he sent Stevie off for what was supposed to be a second yellow card, even though he hadn't been booked before.

Later in the year, when we went to trials for the International Rules squad, Michael Collins apologised to Stevie for sending him off that day. Fair play to him for holding his hands up, but those decisions had cost us an Ulster title.

After lifting the Anglo Celt Cup, Geezer said in his acceptance speech that he was sure Tyrone weren't finished in the Championship yet.

I knew it. Despite such a sickening defeat, we felt pretty much invincible.

We were champions in waiting as far as I was concerned.

This team is unbelievable, I thought. *How the hell am I going to get back on this team, because we're going to win the All-Ireland.*

We were allowed to chill in Dublin that night to get over the disappointment of an Ulster medal slipping through our fingers.

The Meenan brothers, Leo and Brian, and I stayed on in Dublin and went for a quiet drink after the match to the Sunnybank Hotel. It was full of guards who had come off their shift.

I saw a fella making his way over to me, which was the last thing I wanted. All I wanted was some peace, and a quiet pint. 'You're not going to know me but I'm John McCarthy. I played on the Dublin team in the 1970s.'

He'd won three All-Irelands in Heffo's Army and he had some great stories to tell. I took to him straight away. He was interesting and seemed to know everyone in the place. He seemed a good character.

'Why are you not on that team?' he wanted to know.

He counselled me and spoke about times he was dropped by Heffernan. 'You just have to keep going, Owen, and fight your way back in. I can see you have a lot of ability.'

He told me a funny story about one time he marked Mickey John Forbes from Ardboe. The two boys were having a digging match and McCarthy fell over. Forbes said to him: 'You've just run into the hardest man in Ulster.'

McCarthy was only a cub and, at half time, he called for back up. 'This Ardboe man is giving me a hard time, can youse sort him out, boys?'

Ten minutes into the second half, Brian Mullins ran into Mickey John, who had to be stretchered off. McCarthy jogged alongside the stretcher and shouted, 'Well, Mickey John, you've just met the hardest man in Leinster.'

We enjoyed the banter that night and swapped numbers. It was just the sort of blowout I needed. Now it was time to try and force my way back into the team. We should never have lost the Ulster final but we didn't sit around feeling sorry for ourselves. All we wanted was to get back to the All-Ireland quarter finals.

What happened against Armagh was just typical of my whole year. I was struggling. My da was giving me grief that I wasn't being selfish enough.

Canavan went mad if players didn't play for the team but maybe there was a fine line between being selfish and being ruthless. I needed to go for the jugular more.

Maybe I can strike the right balance if Mickey gives me another chance, I reasoned.

I was shocked when Mickey gave me the start against Monaghan in the qualifier because I'd done nothing against Armagh. Stevie's red card was rescinded, but Ricey was banned retrospectively by the Central Disciplinary Committee for dropping his knees into John McEntee. It felt like everyone was against us, but we used it to psych ourselves up even more.

I was desperate to play well but I was terrible again. Stevie was outstanding again, and I was taken off with fifteen minutes to go. I was sick. *That's my chance gone now,* I reckoned.

I geared myself up for the axe but Mickey surprised me at training. 'You did well against Monaghan, believe it or not. I know I took you off but you were out in front, you were showing well. You're starting against Dublin.'

I was in total shock. Are that man's eyes painted on? I was brutal out there. Once I got over the shock I started to get excited. The only thing we hadn't done in 2003 was beat the Dubs en route to the All-Ireland title. There is no better fixture in Gaelic football than playing Dublin, and I was pumped up to be playing them in an All-Ireland quarter final.

We had Ricey back, after the Disputes Resolution Authority ruled that as he had picked up a yellow card during the Armagh game, the incident had already been dealt with. It was a great boost to have him back for the game, but it all went wrong in the first half. Mossy Quinn's goal in first half injury time put the Dubs 1-10 to 0-8 ahead at half time. Mickey told us to go out and win the second half, and that the result would look after itself.

I was gutted to be having such a bad game. I was absolutely rotten, nothing was going right. I got plenty of ball but I wasn't scoring.

The team made a great start to the second half and narrowed the deficit to 1-11 to 0-11 with almost forty-nine minutes gone. But I was still floundering. I spotted Canavan and Penrose warming up out of the corner of my eye. I was coming off for sure. *I'm for the road here if I don't do something.*

I think I have Canavan to thank for the fact I stayed on the pitch. He had a word with Mickey before he came on and said that, although I wasn't playing well, the two of us always played well together.

Poor Ryan Mellon got taken off instead. I doubt he was playing any worse than me. I was relieved to still be on the field when Canavan came trotting on. I always played better when the wee man was around. I hoped we could get a spark going and if anyone was going to get the best out of me, it was him. One way or the other, I needed to do something special or I'd definitely be the next man taken off.

Little did I know I was about to do something that would become the defining moment of my career.

It's the thing I'm most remembered for, but what happened in Croke Park that afternoon is a bit of a blur to me. Nothing was going right for me inside, so I came out the field a bit, hunting for the ball.

We broke down a Dublin attack in front of the Hill and Ricey mopped up, lobbing a loopy fist pass to McGuigan. He kicked it long to Stevie, who couldn't pick it up at the first attempt. Paul Griffin kicked the ball along the ground and looked to have cleared the danger, but Stevie was really persistent and won it back.

He kicked it in and I ran on to the ball, my back to goal, and let it bounce once straight into my chest. I was almost out as far as the forty-five metre line by the time I'd stopped running.

I turned sharply, leaving Paddy Christie on the ground and out of the game.

I looked up and there was loads of space in front of me.

I soloed the ball and threw the first fist dummy on Stephen O'Shaughnessy. I felt I got past him and no more.

Still loads of space.

I bounced the ball and took another solo, spying Paul Casey coming towards me.

This man is not gonna be expecting this dummy again.

I threw it again.

And, by God, did he not fall for it.

Suddenly, the goal opened up wide.

I could hear the crowd … 'GOOOOO … OOONNN … GOOOOO … OOONNN.'

The noise was like waves spilling down from the stands. Growing louder and louder, and louder.

Canavan and McGinley were steaming in and I was going to square it.

I thought of my da's words to me: 'You're passing the buck, why are you passing the ball so much when you're in a good position? Why don't you go on yourself? You can finish, for God's sake, you're one of the best finishers on the team.'

I put my laces through the ball.

The ball flew into the roof of the net.

If Cluxton had stayed where he was, he might have got to it but I think he saw the two boys coming in and had moved slightly to his right.

I might have side-footed it, but because the ball hit the roof of the net it made the goal look so spectacular.

It felt so good I didn't know how to celebrate. McGuigan then McGinley and Canavan came over to me, all smiling and laughing.

It was similar to the goal I'd scored against Dublin in Omagh in the League six months earlier, only better.

Two dummies, instead of one. And this time it was in front of over 78,000 people.

When you're in a situation like that, instinct takes over. People said I must have known after throwing the first dummy what I was going to do, because of the goal in Omagh, but it doesn't work like that. I wasn't thinking about anything.

It was as big a surprise to me as everyone else.

Like Canavan, McGinley was always good at sorting my head out during matches. If I scored an early free or a point or made a good block or a tackle, he'd always build me up and get my confidence going.

He had a quiet word in my ear after the goal.

'Right that's you sorted now, Mugsy, away you go'.

I felt the confidence surging through me. It was like somebody had injected me with something.

You know what? I told myself, *Let's do this, let's hit the dance floor.*

I had felt under so much pressure because I was playing shit, and I was having a shit season. Now I felt so light on my feet. It was like someone had lifted a big weight off my back. Balls started sticking to me, whereas a couple of minutes before they were bouncing off me.

The goal only brought us level, but it changed things. Dublin's big lead was gone and you could see their players were deflated. If either team was going to win it now, it was us.

We should have won it, too.

We had the momentum but only led by a point as the game slipped into stoppage time. Dublin were awarded a soft free and Mossy Quinn converted. We were going to have to do it all over again.

I couldn't wait to get out of the dressing room. I had felt like a spare wheel for weeks when I couldn't get on the team and I certainly didn't want to be the centre of attention now.

I got showered quickly and organised a lift home and was well up the road before the team bus was even pulling out of Croke Park. Mickey tried to ring me, over and over again, as I was on my way home, he was melting my phone but I wouldn't answer.

You have hardly spoken to me in three months, I thought to myself. *Why are you ringing me now?*

I switched the phone off when I got home and went to a quiet bar across the road from my house to have a few beers.

All the wee old men in the bar were coming over and shaking my hand, which surprised me. These men saw me all the time and they'd never reacted like this before. I didn't think the goal was that big a deal. It felt really, really good at the time because I was having such a shit game, but I'd scored goals like that before for the club and at underage level. I thought maybe it was because it was against Dublin that it was turning into a bit of a circus.

I watched The Sunday Game in the bar and saw the goal for the first time. *Was that me?* I couldn't remember half of what happened. I knew it was pretty special when they showed the goal over and over again.

I couldn't hear a lot of what was being said by the RTÉ pundits but there was a debate about whether I had fouled the ball. That pissed me off, no way had I fouled the ball, and I was happy to see Anthony Tohill stick up for me on the panel.

Mickey came straight over to me at training the next Tuesday night in Omagh.

'You didn't answer your phone to me … I was ringing you the whole night. There were journalists there waiting to talk to you after the match.'

'They'll be all right, Mickey,' I said. 'They didn't want to talk to me three months ago or last week for that matter.'

I could have been saying it about him, never mind the media.

'I don't think you realise what you've done here,' he said. 'You've scored the best goal ever seen in Croke Park. If that doesn't catapult your season, I don't know what will.'

'Yeah, well, I'm feeling good. Hopefully I'll get the start the next day.' He smiled at that.

Mickey showed a lot of faith in me to start me against Monaghan and Dublin when I wasn't playing well, but I was still upset he hadn't being showing me much attention. I always wanted to impress him at training, that was my number one goal at every training session in the fifteen years I played for him.

I was out of form and wasn't enjoying my football. I was missing sessions and it was nobody's fault but my own. But I needed an arm around the shoulder rather than the cold shoulder. I needed to know I was still wanted, that I was in his plans. I hated missing club games and I went to Mickey a few weeks before the Dublin game because I wanted to know whether I would be better off going back to the club than sitting on the bench.

He told me to hang in, that I would get my chance. He gave me that chance.

Even though I was annoyed with him, I knew I still owed him, big time.

Most managers would have taken me off against Dublin, the way I was playing. Only for the fact he still had faith in me, I wouldn't have even been on the pitch to score that goal. I was determined to repay him by helping us beat Dublin the next day.

Mickey's superb record in replays is no coincidence. His attention to detail used to blow me away. He goes through absolutely everything.

We prepared for the replay against Dublin totally convinced we were going to win the game. We watched the highlights of the drawn match, starting as usual with the things we did wrong. I was starring in the 'video nasty'.

Clip after clip I was losing the ball, I wasn't tracking back, I was a shambles.

Then we moved on to the good bits. Mickey praised us for the way we came back at Dublin in the second half, we were a different side after half time.

My goal was the last thing shown. All the boys started clapping and laughing. Mark Harte was jumping about the place. 'That is unreal, Mugsy, just unreal!' he said.

I was starting to hear stories back from family and friends about where they were or what they were doing as the goal went in. It was nearly becoming a 'JFK moment'.

My ma would never have said to people sitting next to her at matches that I was her son, even if they slagging me or any of the other boys off – but she made an exception that day.

She and my da were sitting in the Premium Level of the Upper Cusack with friends of theirs, Seamus McAleer and Kate Lennon.

When the goal went in, she jumped up and started shouting at the top of her voice, 'Oh my God! That's my son! THAT'S MY SON!'

Years ago, a fortune teller in Portrush told her that one of her children was going to be famous and would be surrounded by thousands of people standing and clapping. She wondered would it be Michelle, because she was good at piano, but thought it was probably just a load of nonsense. When I scored the goal, she thought maybe the fortune-teller had been right after all.

My best mate, Barry Devine, phoned me from Australia. 'Lad, you don't know how good that was sitting in that bar. You were getting slated so much. There was a pile of Dubs in the bar slagging you off, and you just did that. I was in tears.'

It wasn't just the Dubs who had been slating me, apparently. Our club chairman, Adrian Gilmore, who has always stood up for me through thick and thin, was sitting with a pile of Ardboe men around him. They were shaking their heads and shouting, 'Get that Mulligan man off to hell, Mickey.'

When the goal went in, he went mental. He started roaring, 'Get who off did you say? Who do you want off now?'

I couldn't walk up the town but people were stopping me. Journalists were ringing all the time, leaving messages and texts wanting to speak to me. At club training it was all anybody wanted to talk about.

One of the few calls I took that week was from my old pal in Dublin, John McCarthy. He was delighted for me. 'You absolute bastard, what did I give you that talk for? That was amazing, absolutely amazing what you just did. Youse will win it now, youse are flying.'

It was dawning on me this had been no ordinary goal.

My brother Stephen and I were chatting about it in the house a few days later. As usual, he was challenging me. 'Maybe you can do it again in the replay,' he said.

'Not a chance, Stevie,' I replied. 'That was a one-off, a pure freak. I don't know what happened out there. I wasn't thinking. It just happened.'

'You were playing shite, too. Don't mess it up the next day.'

We were both agreed there was only one thing wrong with the goal – it hadn't been in front of the Hill.

'Can you imagine scoring a goal in front of that Hill, Mugsy? That'd be the best yet,' he said. 'You have to do something special again'.

I couldn't wait for the replay.

The Dublin supporters are lethal and I couldn't wait to soak up that buzz again. When I was growing up I always loved the Dubs.

We lived in Castleknock on the west side of the city when I was two or three years of age, though I don't remember it. Stephen went to school in Blanchardstown and we stayed there for about eight months because my da was working in Dublin. We moved back to Cookstown after that.

If we had stayed there, who knows what might have happened? Maybe I would have played for the Dubs. I wouldn't have minded that one bit. I love the whole professionalism, the soccer-type chanting.

The Hill reminds me of the Kop, another place I love. The Dublin colours are the same as my own club, Cookstown Fr Rocks'. There is just so much I can relate to when it comes to Dublin.

A few days before the replay I was watching Sky Sports News and they were showing an old clip of Eric Cantona scoring the famous chip against Sunderland, where he just turns around with his collar up and arms outstretched as if to say, 'How good was that folks?' I'm no Man United fan but I thought it was a class celebration. I made my mind up that, if I scored again, I was going to do that.

Our training was brilliant now.

All the game-related stuff that Fergal was so good at was paying off. We were naturally comfortable on the ball and the wee drills we were doing made us even better. We'd practise having three men around the man with the ball, and he would have to try to get the ball out quickly, doing it with his weak hand. We rolled the tackle bags, coming out of the tackle and laying off the ball with our weak side or weak foot.

It all came together for my goal against Dublin in the replay.

Sean Cavanagh caught a Dublin kickout and surged forward. It looked like he was going to fall but, just as he stumbled and the defender came in for the kill, he managed to get the ball away to me, just like we'd practised so many times.

I rolled the defender like a tackle bag and stuck it away with my left foot under Cluxton in front of the Hill, just like I'd been dreaming about all week.

I didn't put my arms out but I stood still, like Cantona. No way was I going to disrespect the Hill, the way I'd seen other players do.

I looked into the crowd, straight into the eyes on the Hill. Brilliant.

Thousands of pairs of eyes stared back at me, thousands of Dubs just standing there with their arms folded. I could hear the Tyrone fans cheering in the stands behind me but there was total silence where I was. Just me and a packed blue Hill sharing a moment. Them hating me, me loving them.

Maybe in another life, I'd have been a hero to them but I'm in a Tyrone jersey and this was all-out war.

I enjoyed that goal far more than the one everyone remembers me for. Maybe that's because I had half-planned it. The week before, I never thought about scoring a goal, let alone a wonder-goal. Before the replay, I kept thinking about scoring a goal into the Hill. I was determined to do it.

The sense of satisfaction was huge. I loved being in the thick of the action and I was buzzing now. When a Jack Russell dog ran onto the pitch, I clicked my fingers and whistled to it. I couldn't believe it when it trotted straight over to me, wagging its wee tail.

Almost 82,000 people started laughing. Maybe the wee dog smelt my own dog off me but he was delighted with me altogether. I lifted him up and gave him to the referee, Gerry Kinneavy, who was smiling and nodding, 'Thank you, thank you very much.'

I finished the game with 1-7, with 1-5 from play, as we hammered Dublin by seven points. People are always dying to slag the Dubs off but I clapped them after every match, including that one.

My da got a bit carried away. Michelle told me he started a soccer chant as he walked out of the ground and down Clonliffe Road, 'He scored one-o-seven ... he scored one-o-seven, one-o-seven, he scored one-o-seven.'

The Dubs must have thought he was mad.

We were through to take on our deadliest rivals, Armagh. The game was only eight days after the replay with Dublin, but you don't feel tired when you have an All-Ireland semi-final coming up.

I had waited almost two years for revenge on Francie and this was going to be my day. I'd only been on the fringes of the team when we'd played them in the two Ulster final matches a month earlier but now, with the Dublin goals behind me, I was back where I wanted to be in the heart of the action.

Stevie had roasted Francie in the drawn Ulster final. I'd got so much stick about Bellew after the 2003 final that I fancied a piece of the action. *No one will remember that game if I make an impact here*, I told myself.

A lot of people have said it was the match that showed the Tyrone v Armagh rivalry at its best, but it was suffocating to play in.

They owed us one from the 2003 All-Ireland final, but those Ulster final matches were fresh in our heads. No way should we have lost that Ulster final. Now it was our turn. The stakes could not have been higher for both teams.

From early on I knew I had Bellew's number. I was able to play the way I should have played in the All-Ireland final two years earlier. I was able to turn and get away from him.

I hit a point that went over the bar with the outside of my boot and it set me on my way. I had a good goal chance, too, but I couldn't get the power behind the punch and Paul Hearty was able to save it.

Canavan came on at half time and had a hand in everything, but it was a surprise to us to see Kieran McGeeney substituted with ten minutes to go. We had talked about him being their leader and tried to target him. We tried not to give him time on the ball, because he had great vision and was a good kick passer and could set up attacks. If we could keep him quiet, it would send out a powerful message to the rest of the Armagh players. To see him taken off like that, gave us such a lift.

Armagh still led by two points with six minutes to go but we levelled it up and it looked like we were heading for our fourth replay of the summer.

Then Stevie got fouled about twenty-five metres out from the Hill over on the Hogan Stand side of the pitch.

There wasn't a doubt in my mind that I'd hit the free and send her over. I was taking the free kicks that day and was on form, hitting three points. I'd scored high pressure free kicks before, including two in the 2003 All-Ireland final, so I was relaxed about it. I went over to take the free and lifted the ball.

Canavan walked towards me but, before I had a chance to say anything, McGuigan comes haring down the pitch roaring his head off.

'Set that down, Mugsy, Canavan is hitting that, he's hitting that.'

I dropped the ball.

The cameras picked up on me shaking my head saying, 'I don't mind, I don't mind.' Canavan, the leader that he was, never broke his stride as he lifted the ball and walked past me.

He was smiling, and said, 'I'll take this, no bother.'

I trotted over to be close to the posts in the unlikely event that he missed or the ball came off the post, but I had no doubt where it was going. When I looked back at him he was chatting to Paddy Russell, the referee who'd said he'd fouled the ball at the end of the 1995 All-Ireland final. The seconds ticked away into the second and last minute of injury time. This was going to be the last kick of the game.

This man could put that over with his heel, I reckoned, *he doesn't miss these.* I'd only ever seen him miss one free like that before, against Derry in Clones in 2001, and he was suffering from blurred vision that day.

Sure enough, the ball sailed between the posts.

I think I would have converted it, but the right man took it. If Peter had missed, he wouldn't have been remembered for it. I would have.

The final whistle blew almost immediately.

The scenes were unbelievable. Canavan was carried, shoulder high, off the pitch and it was like we had won the All-Ireland again. The Tyrone supporters were going mental, running onto the pitch. We made it back into the dressing room and I don't think there was a buzz like it after any of our All-Ireland final wins.

There had been a lot of talk about Kerry but we knew it was Armagh we'd have to get past if we wanted to get the Sam back. We were on our way. Philly Jordan was going berserk, fist pumping and shouting 'Yes!' over and over again. He was always the man to celebrate the most after Armagh games. I don't think he will mind me saying he doesn't like Armagh much. I have a neighbourly rivalry with Derry because of living close to them, but the Moy is so close to Armagh that beating them used to make Philly go nuts.

The Armagh fans were brilliant to us and clapped our bus out of Croke Park. They could easily have beaten us, but everyone recognised that both sides had been involved in three special games.

Having failed to put Armagh away in both the Ulster finals, and then blowing a lead against Dublin in the drawn All-Ireland quarter final, people had started questioning whether we could close out tight games. That All-Ireland semi-final changed all that. It was just the kind of game we needed to come out the right side of.

◆ ◆ ◆ ◆

I loved the whole build-up to the All-Ireland final against Kerry.

Two years earlier the expectation and the pressure ruined what should have been the most exciting time of my life. This time, I was determined to soak it up.

I felt totally relaxed because everything was going right. The Dublin goals had changed everything for me. All of a sudden I was tuned in, I couldn't wait to go to training, I was on top of my game. I'd got my own back on Francie in the semi-final, which had given me a huge lift. We were in demand again. Nike wanted to sponsor five of us to wear their boots in the final. I said I wasn't interested, that I always wore the Adidas Predator. They were offering good money but I wasn't sure if I wanted to change for a final. This was no time to be experimenting with new footwear.

I thought I'd try them out in an in-house game and I liked them straight away. There was good grip in them. I turned sharp a few times to see how they handled, no problems. They had more studs and they were really tight around my foot. The money was appealing, too, so I decided to wear them on the big day.

I don't know what it is about me and Croke Park but it always brought out the best in me. You'd see the nerves in a couple of boys but, the bigger the game, the more excited I got.

Bring it on, I just loved it.

I've had a few bad games there but not too many. I came alive there. Clones is my second favourite ground but Croke Park is the only place to be.

I soaked up the atmosphere in the weeks leading up to the game and savoured every moment.

There was a sea of white and red following our bus on our way into the ground. As soon as I saw Croke Park in the distance, I started to get the tingles. The more supporters gathered and the more they banged on the bus, the better I liked it.

I couldn't see how we would be beaten. We had outstanding players and we were in our prime.

It was the closest team I have ever been involved in. We stood up for each other any time a scuffle broke out: it was like a family member being hit, you took it that personally. Other teams would fall out if someone gave a teammate a bollocking on the pitch. Not us, we accepted it. We knew it was for the benefit of the team.

That team was as close to perfection as you get. I loved the togetherness of it all. For me, there was only one thing, or one person, missing. Hub. He definitely would have started had he been there.

We were at our peak as a team, and McGuigan coming back was key. He made a difference right away. He could give the killer pass that no one else would even see, let alone try.

He would get mad if it didn't come off. At his fittest, he'd track back until he won the ball back again and then, instead of giving a wee simple ball the next time, he'd try something even more risky, and it would come off.

That's the sort of player he was.

Walking around the pitch behind the Artane Boys' Band, I was able to embrace the occasion this time. In 2003, I was so nervous I didn't look around me and blocked everything out. This time I looked at the stands, listened to the noise. I was relaxed and ready for battle.

I looked over at the Kerry players walking alongside us. They were some team. I respected them, but I wasn't nervous or afraid.

There was a lot of talk about Kerry getting revenge on us for the 2003 All-Ireland semi-final when we had ambushed them. They were still hurting and had said they were going to be ready for us this time.

Mike McCarthy picked me up, but I didn't care who was marking me. I was on my game and totally confident. Dara Ó Cinnéide got a goal for Kerry after just seven minutes but I got on the scoreboard straight after.

Peter hit a free straight to me. I turned sharply, one bounce and it sailed between the posts in front of the Hill. It wasn't an easy chance but it was my first point from play in an All-Ireland final, and it felt great.

McGuigan could have teed me up for an easy goal but, for once, he didn't pass to a man in a better position, he tried to shoot himself from a narrow angle.

Still, we were level at 0-6 to 1-3 after 28 minutes thanks to a wonder-point from Dooher when Davy Harte won a free in. William Kirby went in heavy on McGuigan and Canavan and a scuffle broke out. Tom O'Sullivan wouldn't let go of Canavan and ripped his jersey. I was straight over. *There is no way he is getting away with that,* I thought, grabbing him by the throat.

Kerry threw everything at us in that first half. I think they wanted to be out of sight by half time. We had come through nine tough Championship games. It was obvious they wanted to put us away early, to make us feel tired and plant a few doubts in our heads that maybe this was one game too many.

That's why our goal just before half time was such a massive score.

I was hanging around the edge of the square with my back to goal when Philly came running down the touchline, looking up to see who was free. I was pointing for him to hit it out to the wing but he drove it straight into the square, high and long. For a split second I was annoyed.

Then I thought, *Hang on a minute, that's not a bad ball.*

I thought the goalkeeper was going to come out but I felt sure I'd get there before him. I could get up well and I knew I was going to catch it.

Paul Galvin was behind me.

We had stretched Kerry so much all over the field that he ended up being left stranded as an emergency full-back.

In my head, I was already spinning for a goal when I landed. Then I saw Canavan, flying in. I saw the whites of his eyes and knew immediately he wanted it. He was the only man in the world I'd have passed to. In a situation like that, I would normally have turned and shot myself.

I feigned to turn left but stood my ground, shielding the ball from the men running in so the wee man would have a clear shot at it.

Canavan's face was a picture of pure concentration. I delayed the pass until just the right second and once he got the ball in his hands, his face totally relaxed. The assassin took over.

Galvin went for the full-length block but hit nothing but thin air. I looked over my shoulder to watch the master at work.

I thought he was going for the far corner but he went low with his supposedly weaker left foot, threading the ball just inside the near post. He had very little room to work with but he hit it precisely. Diarmuid Murphy hadn't conceded a goal all year and it was going to take something as special as that to beat him.

Few players would have even thought of rolling the ball along the ground like that, but this was Peter Canavan. He could walk on water.

The Tyrone fans erupted. The noise behind me was so loud I felt it was sucking me into the Hill. He raised a finger in the air as he peeled away from the Hill. I just pointed over at him and roared, 'Lethal wee man, lethal!'

He had been slagging me for years that he was always setting me up for scores, and when was I going to return the favour. I was so proud that I was able to set that one up for him.

He had done just about everything in a Tyrone jersey except score a goal in an All-Ireland final. Now, he'd done it all.

We had weathered the storm and scored 1-1 in injury time to lead by four points at the break. Injury problems still dogged Canavan and he had to go off again at half time, but there was no hint of panic. Unlike 2003, I felt great. *I'm going to take this game by the scruff of the neck.*

I felt so fit. I was out in front all the time, showing for the ball and scored another point from play five minutes into the second half.

I was comfortable taking the frees and converted two of them.

We set a relentless pace but Kerry got back into it with a Tomás Ó Sé goal and, for the first time in the game, we were rocking. For the first time, wee doubts started to creep into our heads and Canavan's return came at just the right time.

As ever, his timing was immaculate, scoring a wonder-point from underneath the Cusack from an impossible angle to settle us down. I knew rightly this was probably his last game for Tyrone, and he was going out in some style. But, like the rest of us, he did what needed to be done. When Gooch went through on goal, Canavan just grabbed him and spun him around and took the yellow card. Nowadays, it'd be labelled as 'cynical' but there was no way we were going to let this All-Ireland slip, and we didn't, winning by 1-16 to 2-10.

Some of our boys couldn't stand the Kerry lads and it was obvious Jack O'Connor disliked us as well, you could see it in his face every time we played them. But I was never into holding grudges and, once the final whistle blew, I forgot about everything that went on. The supporters ran onto the pitch and it was just as manic as 2003 had been.

We had seen these scenes before, but you'd take it all day long. I felt total satisfaction. You can only do something for the first time once and, to me, the 2003 win will always be the best one. But, this time, we had proved we were no one-hit wonders, that we were a serious team. We won the hardest All-Ireland Championship ever won, having come through a record ten games. We had won an All-Ireland final of unbelievable quality.

And we had got Cormac his second All-Ireland medal.

◆ ◆ ◆ ◆ ◆

I was up in my room in the City West Hotel having a few quiet drinks with Tina that night when there was a loud knock at the door.

It was Jim Curran.

'Mugsy, are you in there?' he said. 'Hurry up, RTÉ need you downstairs.'

Probably looking for an interview, I thought.

We went back down to the banquet and I was chatting to someone when I heard them calling out the Man of the Match.

'And it's the blond bombshell himself, Owen Mulligan.'

I was over the moon. A lot of people thought Philly or Brian McGuigan deserved it more than me, but I felt I'd played well, setting up the goal for Peter and kicking four points.

Being named Man of the Match in the All-Ireland final is probably my biggest individual achievement. The fact I won Man of the Match in both All-Ireland minor and senior finals is a personal honour that no one can take away from me.

The All Star I won in 2005 means a lot less to me. Tyrone got eight All Stars that year, a true reflection of our dominance, but when Frank

McGuigan threatened to hand back the All Star he won in 1984 because Brian didn't win one that year, I knew where he was coming from. It was a travesty. McGuigan was outstanding that year.

It always seems to me that All Stars are judged from the All-Ireland quarter finals onwards. All Stars should be judged over the whole season and I had not played over the whole season. Tyrone had come through a record ten Championship games and people would say, 'Youse boys must be wrecked'. I used to reply, 'I'm not wrecked, I've hardly played.'

In 2003, I played really well in Ulster but not in the All-Ireland series. In 2005, I was missing in action until the goal. I have a lot to be thankful for in terms of that goal, it turned my whole season around and I played really well in the big games after that. But I didn't want to go to the All Stars banquet. I hadn't enjoyed it last time. I always felt awkward chatting to players I didn't know.

In the end, one day before the event, my da persuaded me to go. He was the site manager of the hotel development at Croke Park and had met a journalist who told him I really should be there, which was a strong hint that I was getting an award.

Da pleaded with me. He had loved it last time. In the end, I went with my girlfriend, Tina, and we squeezed my da in as well.

I even managed to get John McCarthy in, too. Security came and told me there was a man outside looking for me. I couldn't believe it was him and that he had made the effort to come out to the hotel so I got him in somehow.

The place was coming down with Tyrone men. When my name was called out, I was delighted.

In 2003 it was all 'team, team, team' and I was so happy to be on the first Tyrone team to win an All-Ireland, I didn't care less about individual awards. It was only over the next couple of years that people kept saying to me that an All Star would be the icing on the cake.

On top of the All Star, I got a lethal trophy for scoring the goal of the year. I was pleased but I could hardly look at McGuigan. I never spoke to him about it, but he must have been sick. Davy Harte was another man I thought should have got one that year.

The debate raged on for a few days: Did Mulligan deserve the All Star or not?

Personally, I don't think I did.

McGuigan should have got that All Star ahead of me.

I lived like a Premiership footballer for the next six months.

Things were big after our first win in 2003, but 2005 was off the scale for me. The goal seemed to have changed everything. Everybody wanted a piece of me and I was in demand all over the country.

I was switching on Christmas lights, opening shops, presenting medals at club functions. I brought the Sam Maguire everywhere. I took it to wakes, funerals, birthday parties and weddings.

The phone was ringing off the hook. There were bookings flat out. If I had saved all the money I made those few months I'd be a wealthy man now.

Instead I was blowing it, buying drinks for everybody, buying people presents. Partying like there was no tomorrow. I got a taste of what it must be like to live like a professional sportsman, and maybe I enjoyed it too much.

I made three grand one Sunday. My ma kept on at me to go down to a youth presentation for a club down south. I wasn't that bothered, not even for the £700 they were offering. They weren't taking no for an answer. They came and offered me double. . They were desperate for me to go, so eventually I agreed.

They were lovely people and the young lads were looking at me in total awe. I spoke to them about the goal and told them to keep practising their skills. I posed for photographs, signed autographs and when I was leaving I felt an envelope being stuffed in my pocket.

'Thanks for doing it so cheap,' this guy says to me, ' … those Dublin boys are a nightmare to pay'.

I couldn't believe it. What the hell are those Dublin boys getting?

And them that's won nothing!

I headed off, stunned, to my next engagement, switching on the Christmas lights in a wee town two counties away, and headed home that night with three grand in my pocket. It was surreal.

I hadn't a clue about agents and stuff.

I was picked to go on the International Rules squad to Australia that autumn and I was sitting beside Seán Óg Ó hAilpín on the flight out when he asked me what my agent was getting?

I thought, *Agent? What is he talking about? My Ma is my agent.*

My Ma took care of everything for me, she did all the talking and organised where I needed to go and when. If someone was looking for me to do something I'd say, 'Phone the house there … there's a girl there who will deal with that'.

I didn't want to tell people it was actually my Ma.

It was only when I went down to an Adidas shoot in Dublin that I realised how professional things had become in other counties. Most of boys had agents with them, which was a bit of an eye opener.

I couldn't believe it.

I'd worn Adidas boots for years but I had no allegiance to them until they called me after the 2005 All-Ireland final.

They knew I hadn't worn Adidas in the final but they offered me a two-year deal.

I got all the gear I wanted. By the end of it I had the whole Fr Rocks team kitted out too. I tortured the sales people. 'I need new boots.'

'No problem, Owen.' Next day a wee courier would arrive on a motorbike with a pair of boots. Two days later I'd phone a different salesperson. 'I need some gear.'

The wee boy on the motorbike would be back at my house by the end of the day.

I phoned one day looking a pair of boots and got a nice surprise.

'That's no problem Owen, but would you like a pair with stitching on it?'

'What do you mean?'

'Your name or something.'

'Can you do that?'

'Oh yes. It might just take a couple of weeks.'

'Well, can you put 'Mugsy' on the two tongues?'

'No bother. I'll give you a ring when they're ready.'

I'll never forget opening the box the day they arrived. I absolutely loved them. They were class. I got some stick at training, mind you. Typically, McGinley spotted them right away.

'What I can't understand, Mugsy … is why you've never worn white boots like Ricey.'

'Ah no, lad. I don't want to bring attention onto myself.'

He pointed to my peroxide head, laughing. 'Well, what's that about then?'

I didn't feel the white boots looked right on me. I got friendly with Mayo footballer Conor Mortimer through Adidas and he always liked the white boots. He and I are good mates, with the blond hair and all. The only thing we didn't agree on was the white boots! Every single pair of boots I got from Adidas after that always had 'Mugsy' on the tongues, until the gravy train stopped a few years later.

The fan mail kept on coming.

Dominic McCaughey was like a smiling postman. 'Owen, there's a few letters and faxes here for you, they came to the County Board office ... you might be interested in them.'

I got dozens every week for months after the 2005 All-Ireland final.

Most of the time they wanted an autograph or they'd send a picture and ask me to sign it. Sometimes they wanted gear sent to them.

I always hated wearing Tyrone gear over the years and gave most of it away, except for a few jerseys that mean a lot to me. I wore stuff when I was 16 and 17 but that was it.

I didn't want anyone saying, 'Look at him, who does he think he is?' Other players can't wait to get the tracksuits and hooded tops on. When we started getting our initials stitched onto hoodies and tracksuits I absolutely hated that. I'd ring mates up and tell them to come round and take stuff.

If someone sent me a real deadly letter I'd get my Ma to post them something, like togs or socks, or maybe a pair of signed gloves.

I got a brilliant letter from a guy who had cancer who said he got out of bed to watch the All-Ireland final in 2005. He said it had made him forget about his problems for a while. That really touched me. I thought, *That's a real good lad there*. If someone took the time to write something like that, I'd try and send them something extra special.

That went on a lot.

Of course there were some stupid things, silly letters from girls. 'You are the greatest' or 'I love you.'

I kept a lot of them in the glove compartment in my van. One night I was bored and decided, *Right, I'm going to ring one or two of these girls for the craic.*

There was no Facebook or Twitter in those days.

These women were posting photos of themselves with the letters and I liked the look of one of them. She said she was a part-time model.

I was supposed to be going to some function in Aghyaran but that didn't last long. I phoned her up and after a couple of minutes chatting to her, I swerved the car off the road and picked her up in Enniskillen. We ended up in Bundoran. That was a good night.

I was doing some daft things.

A few weeks after the All-Ireland I went to a house party in Dungannon. I had too much to drink and fell asleep.

I woke up in bed, not a stitch on me. I rubbed my eyes and turned around, thinking I must have been in one of the bedrooms at the party.

This girl was lying beside me, wide awake, with her arms behind her head on the pillow.

'Well, how's it going?' I said, as if I had a clue who she was.

'Where are we?'

Monaghan.

'Monaghan? What the fuck am I doing in Monaghan?'

I had no wallet and no phone.

I had to borrow money off her to get the bus home.

In the midst of all the partying, I had one eye on the International Rules series.

Pete McGrath was taking a squad to Australia to try and win the Cormac McAnallen Cup, and I wanted to be part of it.

I had missed most of the training because of our good run with Tyrone but me and some of the lads got to attend a couple of sessions before the Ireland squad was selected. I was played out the field a bit, around centre half-forward, and played well, hitting a couple of killer passes straight into boys' chests.

In the end, seven Tyrone men were picked to go - Sean Cavanagh, Ricey, Philly, Stevie, Dooher, McGuigan and me. Mickey can't have been too happy. He always referred to International Rules as 'that game'. We knew he didn't like it, but this was a trip of a lifetime.

Getting picked to go to Australia was a Godsend. I was desperate to see some of my best friends who had emigrated out there that I hadn't seen in years. I needed a change of scene, away from the partying. *Maybe a few weeks away will settle my head*, I thought.

I ended up having an even crazier time out there – particularly when we went to Melbourne for the second Test.

The first Test was in Perth and it's a city I didn't enjoy, it is far too quiet for me. All the bars were shut by about eleven o'clock.

I was picked to start the first Test, but I didn't play well and was taken off in one of the first inter-change substitutions and never got back on again. The team was stuffed by 36 points.

We had a few drinks afterwards and on the bus back to the team hotel I stood up and said, 'Boys, I'd like to announce my international retirement'. They all started to laugh.

I knew rightly I wasn't going to be togging out in the second Test, but I didn't care less because I was excited about seeing my mates in Melbourne. I hadn't seen my best mate, Barry Devine for five years. He lived in Sydney but travelled to Melbourne to see me, along with a few other boys I knew from home.

It was emotional enough meeting up with the boys again. I met them in an Irish bar and it was all hugs and tears when I saw them.

That was me straight on the beer then. I missed a few training sessions and went AWOL for a few days. I was rooming with Dooher for the entire trip. He said it was the worst three weeks of his life. I completely tortured him.

He covered for me when I skipped training, saying I was sick. Nobody really believed that.

He gave out to me, but I told him to give it a rest - I was on holiday. 'You're not on holiday, Mugsy ... everybody is taking this serious except you.'

I think Dooher would rather have been at home working as a vet than looking after me. I came in at seven o'clock one morning and he had to throw me in the shower to try and sober me up for training.

'I thought looking after animals was bad but it's nothing compared to minding you,' he said.

Worse still, I had run out of clean underwear.

I asked him to lend me a pair of boxer shorts but he threw me over a pair of underpants.

I held them up and looked at them, disgusted. 'Jesus, lad ... who the hell wears these in this day and age?'

'Do you want them or not, Mugsy?' he snapped back.

I said nothing and put them on. They were a bit tight for me, but I managed.

Dooher was taking no chances after that.

He started to do my washing for me, taking two loads of dirty clothes down to the laundry each time.

I wasn't the only one drinking that second week. A few other boys enjoyed themselves too, though maybe not to the same level that I was at. People thought the Tyrone and Kerry lads wouldn't mix, but we mixed too well. I had good craic with Tomas O Se, the Gooch Cooper and Eoin Brosnan. I made friends with Michael Meehan, Ciaran McDonald and Padraic Joyce, who was captain. They were good lads as well.

At a team meeting one day, Sean Marty Lockhart went mental about boys' drinking.

He didn't name names but everyone knew who he was talking about. He said we needed to get our house in order. He was right in a way.

He came over to me afterwards.

'So, what kind of a time are you having, Mugsy?'

'It's an unreal holiday man ... just unreal,' I said.

He just looked at me. 'We're not supposed to be on holiday - we're on tour.' He turned and walked off. He wasn't happy.

I continued to party.

Dooher woke up one morning to find a few of my mates crashed out on the floor in our room.

Him and McGuigan had to literally hold me up and walk me around the pitch that morning, keeping me out of the road of Pete McGrath and Larry Tompkins.

Dooher pleaded with me to take it easy for a few days. I agreed and that night, I went to bed at the same time as him.

I tossed and turned, my eyes wide open. I was in the horrors after so many days drinking. Sleep was not my friend.

Dooher was still awake too, reading a book.

I shouted over, 'Will you read that to me?'

He looked over at me. 'What?'

'Read that book out loud … it might help me sleep.'

So for the next few nights, the All-Ireland winning captain read me stories to put me to sleep.

As expected, I didn't get selected to tog out in the second Test. The team performed slightly better than in the first Test, but was still beaten by 21 points, and it was time for the team to head home.

Poor Dooher gets the worst hangovers so even when it was all over, he didn't take much drink. He was a happy man, though, to be boarding the plane home to get away from me.

When everyone left, I stayed on for a couple of weeks and went to Sydney to stay with my mates to continue the party.

When I got home, I called at Cormac's grave a few times.

I felt bad that I had disrespected the competition and the trophy that bore his name. But I felt sure that he would have been so delighted that we'd won that second All-Ireland title he wanted so much, that he'd have forgiven me anything.

My thoughts were starting to turn to 2006. I wondered how we would carry ourselves as All-Ireland champions. In 2004, we had Cormac's death as an excuse for our failure. There could be no excuse this time.

We had won in 2003 to make history for Tyrone and for the people of Tyrone. In 2005, we won it for ourselves.

Now the challenge was to try and defend our All-Ireland title.

I thought of Mickey's wise words.

'It's not always going to be this good. You have to take every opportunity.

'Boys will get injured … boys will retire … this team is never going to play together again.'

He was right about one thing.

No Canavan and no Cricko.

The Tyrone changing-room was going to be a very different place next year.

13

Dublin came to Omagh the next spring, determined to put us in our place.

It was obvious they were still smarting from our win over them in the All-Ireland quarter final six months earlier and, after two niggly League matches in the previous couple of years, we knew from early on it was going to be feisty.

We gave as good as we got. There was no way we were going to take a step back when Dublin were in this mood and looking for a fight.

It was our opening League match of the season and one of Raymond Mulgrew's first games for us. He was the star of the minor All-Ireland winning side in 2004 and a Cookstown man, like me.

He was being tipped for a bright future and the Dubs knew it. I felt like I needed to keep a close eye on him. It seemed like he was being targeted and he shipped a couple of heavy tackles early on. I was caught up trying to protect him and got too involved with the Dublin lads instead of focusing on the football, but I wasn't alone.

The first scuffle was only four minutes into the game but the thing really kicked off in the second half. The row broke out near the sideline underneath the stand.

As soon as I went in, it seemed to explode.

Dublin players turned their attention to me and it descended into a pure boxing match. Ciaran Whelan was giving bad manners and was chased up the steps by Hub, but there wasn't much verbal slagging going on in the middle of that row. I was right in the middle of it and it was all punches, men hitting as hard as they could, with stewards trying to pull us apart and supporters in the stand getting involved with the Dublin substitutes.

All this aggro meant that Paddy Russell had a tough day at the office. He sent four men off, including Stevie O'Neill and Collie Holmes, and both sides finished with thirteen men. It got really ugly and there was a terrible atmosphere.

Dublin won the match easily, getting some sort of revenge for the All-Ireland quarter final defeat and their League loss to us in Omagh the year before.

I was working in Dublin at the time and got some slagging on the building site from the Dubs the next day, roaring at me from the top of scaffolding, but I laughed it off and enjoyed the banter.

The media kicked up a storm about the match, calling it 'The Battle of Omagh', and we knew we hadn't heard the last of it. Sure enough, the following week, Hub, Ricey and I were among an additional five players singled out by the GAA's Central Disciplinary Committee for our part in the row, and we were charged with bringing the game into disrepute with bans totalling 52 weeks.

We travelled to Dublin for the Central Appeals Committee hearing with Brendan Harkin, a Tyrone official from Killyclogher, who told the panel what great role models we were. He said we were bringing the Sam Maguire around to schools one minute and now we were being portrayed as thugs.

In the end, we got off on a technicality and we moved on.

The game meant it was a fiery start to a difficult year. It was strange not having Canavan and Cricko around, two of my best mates in the squad. Mark Harte also left at the end of the 2005 season, which took balls. After the stick he got from some Tyrone supporters the previous year, no one could blame him for walking away.

I've seen him play seriously good games for Tyrone but it was hard for him being on the team and being Mickey's son. He texted a few of us to say he was taking a break from Tyrone, but I sort of knew it was more permanent than that. I spoke to him on the phone and told him to wise up, that he had a lot to offer, but his mind was made up.

It would have been easier for him to merge into the background and stay in the squad. There've been a few boys over the years who've been happy enough just to be in the squad, who didn't care if they played or not, just so long as they got a few perks and everyone knew they were in the Tyrone squad. Sparky wasn't like that. He made a brave call. He is a great fella and, for a man who didn't drink, he always enjoyed the craic and came out to celebrate with us after matches. We got on well and I was sorry to see him go.

Hub was back after his year in Australia and Calvo was back in, too, having opted out in 2005. Dermy Carlin was another one who returned, all three boys having missed out on our second All-Ireland title success.

We felt we had a good mix again, but the bottom soon fell out of our summer when Brian McGuigan broke his leg in a club game the week before our match with Derry in the Ulster Championship, ruling him out for the season. After the way he'd been playing, it was a huge blow to our hopes of a successful All-Ireland defence.

Derry had all the ammunition they needed coming to Omagh. They were dying to take us down a peg or two while we were struggling up front with no McGuigan or Stevie O'Neill.

I had a really poor game. Kevin McGuckin stuck to me like glue and marked me really well. I got booked after just two minutes and we failed to score in the first half. It only got worse when Hub was sent off and we were out of Ulster before we knew where we were.

The warning signs were there when Louth almost beat us in a qualifier.

Mulgrew played brilliantly and I hit 2-2 from four scoring attempts. The game went to extra time in Navan and we were a point down when we were awarded a free, about thirty-five yards out. Canavan territory, but Canavan wasn't here any more. It was down to me.

It wasn't quite Croke Park in an All-Ireland final, but I knew our season was over if I missed it.

I stepped up and didn't even set the ball down, I just hit it really quickly. Out of the corner of my eye I could see Brendy Donnelly looking over at me as if to say, 'What the hell are you doing? Take your time.'

But I didn't want to think about it. The ball sailed over the bar to draw the game. Relief all round.

Tony Donnelly spoke to me as I walked off the pitch. 'Fair play to you, Mugsy, fair play. What were you thinking there, when you hit that?'

'Do you really want to know?' I asked him. 'I was thinking, "Where's that wee baldy bastard when I need him".'

Tony laughed.

We won the replay in Omagh and then drew Laois away in the next round. The injuries were starting to mount up, with Conor Gormley and Collie Holmes the latest casualties, but I still expected to win. I always expected us to win. Even with McGuigan gone for the year and the other injuries we had, I still thought we would win the All-Ireland.

The weather was terrible, it was a really wet and windy day and our attack only hit one point from play on a dreadful day for us. We lost 0-9 to 0-6 and our summer was over.

The injuries had cost us in the end, but when you're beaten you're always going to look for excuses. We didn't have any. It was an early exit for us and, almost right away, the phone calls started with a few different clubs asking me to go over to America to play football for the summer.

I went to play for St Brendan's in Chicago.

The club asked if I could bring a midfielder out with me, so I asked Calvo to come. The football was of a pretty decent standard and Calvo put on a show. He was absolutely outstanding out there, but unfortunately the same couldn't be said of me. I was terrible and scored just three points in three games.

The club were very good to me in Chicago and I felt bad that I didn't repay them with some good performances. Sometimes I think I would like to go back out there and play better than I did that summer. They thought they were getting the Mugsy who'd played in Croke Park the year before but, instead, they got a pale shadow of my 2005 displays.

Cookstown were out of the Championship when I left and safe in the League, but I still got a lot of stick around home for going away. That pissed me off, other boys had gone while their clubs were still in the Championship.

As soon as the boys slipped into relegation trouble, I jumped on the first plane home. I scored a penalty in our last League game against Clann na nGael to keep us up, but I am still hearing about how I let the club down that summer.

◆ ◆ ◆ ◆ ◆

At the start of 2007, we got an early chance to resume hostilities with Dublin.

The GAA recognised the rivalry we had with them by selecting us to play Dublin in the first-ever floodlit game in Croke Park in our opening League match.

The game was a near sell-out, we were playing my favourite opponents and we owed them one after what took place in Omagh the year before.

Bring it on, I thought.

We had seven regulars missing and were five points down at half time. It didn't look good but we didn't panic. We always felt that mentally we had the upper hand on Dublin and expected them to crack when we put the pressure on. Apart from Alan Brogan, they had no leaders, whereas we had leaders all over the field.

Sure enough, they cracked when we started to come back at them, with Hub coming on and dominating midfield. Mulgrew scored one of those points that I love, a real skyscraper that just falls out of the sky and lands on the top of the net. I hit four points, including the winner two minutes from the end. Another magic win over Dublin, and no less than we expected.

They might have had a few wins over us in League games in previous years, but when we played them on the big days in Croke Park, we just believed we'd win when it mattered.

Mulgrew was starting to dazzle and I was desperate for him to do well. Mulgrew, McGuigan and Cavlan were very similar players and I loved playing with all of them. If they saw the whites of your eyes, if they saw you making a run, they'd give you the ball. They'd try things.

Growing up in the same town, Mulgrew and I were really good mates and I'd watch amazed sometimes at the things he could do. He has all the moves, all the skills, and he's blessed with magic feet.

Our club organised a big gala on the same night as we had a League match against Fermanagh and Mulgrew and I were determined to play well. I thought if I played badly and was taken off, I'd have a shit night at the gala. As it turned out, the two of us went out and raked it, I hit five points and I headed off to the banquet in great form.

My ma was one of the organisers and she asked me to donate something for the auction so I put up the boots I'd worn when scoring the goal in the drawn All-Ireland quarter final with Dublin. Barney Eastwood paid £30,000 for them. I couldn't believe it, what a gesture from a pure gentleman.

We had made a great start to the season, winning the McKenna Cup, and scoring early wins in the league but then it all started to fall apart. Cork hammered us in a match in which I received a straight red card for an attempted strike on Michael Shields.

I got sent off again during that League campaign, at home against Mayo, for a sliding tackle on Ger Brady. I didn't make contact, but I stuck the leg out and the referee was right there. It looked worse than it was.

The problem was, having already received a straight red card earlier in the League, I was hit with an eight-week ban that threatened to rule me out of our Ulster Championship match against Fermanagh.

I sought a hearing for my dismissal against Mayo and Mickey did most of the talking when we appeared before the Central Hearings Committee in Croke Park. He explained that it was a lazy tackle, that I couldn't get back. The red card was rescinded and Mickey was delighted.

'That's you ready to go now, Mugsy, it's going to be good year for us.'

Then disaster struck.

Brian McGuigan didn't come with us on our annual pre-Championship weekend away because he wanted to play a club match for Ardboe. He was still working his way back to full fitness after the leg break the year before and thought an extra game might be more beneficial than joining us on the trip.

Word filtered through that he'd suffered a bad eye injury during the game and that it was serious, that he could be partially blind in one eye.

We were all gutted. I'd been looking forward to linking up with him again and now his season lay in tatters once more.

But Mickey was angry. He was never too keen on us playing for our clubs at that time of year and now this was proving his point. We lost a lot of players to injuries in club games in 2006 and 2007, and we had so many meetings to discuss whether we should be allowed to play for the clubs or not.

I always stood up for the subs and said they should definitely be allowed back to the clubs. I hated when county players had to sit out club matches. When Brian Meenan was in the squad he used to say, 'We're going on these weekends away and we're getting no football. All we seem to be doing is eating big feeds.' He was right. I used to back the subs up in the meetings. Mickey would be looking at me as if to say, Should you not be backing me up here?

I wasn't able to start the Fermanagh game due to a back injury but Mulgrew and I raked it against Donegal in the Ulster semi-final, hitting 1-4 between us. He scored an unbelievable goal that day, and I loved being a part of it. It was the most enjoyable score we ever put together.

It was a tight enough game in Clones and it was hard to get scores, but Mulgrew was moving well. Stevie O'Neill came out, looking for the ball, and switched the play, squaring it to me. I rolled the tackle and fisted the ball over a defender's head to Mulgrew.

I thought he would have carried it in a bit further but he surprised the 'keeper with a wee dummy and the finish was brilliant.

Mickey loved it, it was a classic training ground goal, showing all the drills we'd been doing at training with Fergal – like diagonal runs, running off the shoulder and rolling the tackle.

Mickey always preached to us about the need to give a good ball around the 'D' and getting as much action in and around there as possible. It seemed everything they had been telling us at training all came together in that one move.

I have the photograph of that goal in the bar and in the house, and Raymie also has it up in the Black Horse, the bar that his da owns. Two Cookstown men passing the ball to each other for a goal in an Ulster Championship match in Clones – I'll settle for that.

Despite the injuries, we won the Ulster title again, overcoming Monaghan's mind games to beat them in the final: It had been was agreed that both counties would wear their second kit, us in red and them in blue, but Monaghan came out in their white jerseys.

We didn't realise they were trying to pull a stroke until just before the match started, but we used it at half time as a psyching up session, feeling they were disrespecting us. And it was disrespectful but, looking back on it now, I would probably have done the same as manager Seamus McEnaney did that day. You do what you have to do to try and get an edge.

Our defeat to Meath in the All-Ireland quarter final was my fault, and no one will ever convince me otherwise. I missed everything that day. I scored 1-1 but I should have scored about 1-9. I should have lit up Croke Park and it still annoys me that I didn't.

I was out in front of my marker all day long, he was miles behind me. I would have had fun winding him up only I was missing so much, so I kept quiet.

What the hell is wrong with me? I kept thinking. I was taking free kicks and missing them, too. Dooher really wasn't fit and limped off, and we were two points down at half time. I spoke up in the dressing room.

'Lads, we need to catch ourselves on here,' I said. 'This is not a good Meath team. They're brutal. I've had a shit first half but we have to knuckle down. I'm willing to go out and give it all here.'

Straight away, a free kick from Calvo came off the upright and I stuck it in the net. *Right*, I thought, *let's rock 'n' roll here*. I scored a point straight after that and Mulgrew was pulling the strings. There was only going to be one winner here, or so I thought, but we went on to hit twelve wides in the second half and lost 1-13 to 2-8. It's one of the most annoying defeats I've ever had and I take full responsibility for it.

My ma and da were the first to tell me when I got home.

'What the hell happened you? You were brutal.'

I didn't need anyone to tell me that. It was another All-Ireland title missed as far as I was concerned.

◆ ◆ ◆ ◆ ◆

Calvo had more than a defeat in Croke Park to worry about.

He'd been in court about owning a dog called 'Cannonball' that was supposed to have been involved in dog fighting. When the news came out, I was as shocked as anyone.

Calvo is one of my best mates in football but he is a private person. I would be like that, too. People don't need to know everything about your business and I certainly wasn't going to start asking him questions.

There was stuff in the papers about it during the year but I never once questioned him about it. People may not believe that, but it's the truth.

The only time we spoke about it was when he phoned to let me know the BBC were going to be screening a Spotlight investigation on dog fighting, and that he was going to be pin-pointed. I did think, *What are you doing, Calvo?* I am a dog lover and wouldn't get caught up in that myself. But Calvo is one of the most genuine people you could ever meet, and no one should be judged on one incident.

Sometimes in life you get yourself into handlings where you think, What have I done? and you have big regrets. No one knows that more than me.

I'm sure that is one of Calvo's big regrets. I've been involved in lots of rows in bars defending him, but why would I disown one of my best mates in football, just because he did something wrong? Nobody's perfect. He just got caught up with the wrong crowd. If there was a row on the pitch, Calvo always had my back. He looked out for me on the pitch because I was a 'townie' and so was he. It's the same with me and big Joey McMahon from Omagh, 'townies' have a wee bond and go on the same way, I think. If I needed help, Calvo would be round to my house in ten minutes because he is the kind of guy who would do anything for you.

People gave him a lot of stick over that incident and it pretty much ended his Tyrone career. But, whatever people said about him, he is still one of the most naturally gifted players Tyrone has ever had and no one can take that away from him.

◆ ◆ ◆ ◆ ◆

The year ended with Mulgrew getting an All Star nomination. Considering he was only twenty-one and our year had ended early, it showed what an outstanding season he'd had. It was all the more amazing, considering we were drinking and messing about. At the time he first came into the squad, I had a good bit of money and we were partying more than we should have been. Sometimes I wonder if we had beaten Meath, could we have gone all the way? Mulgrew was on fire that year.

People wondered why he never hit those heights again. Part of it was that his physique was way off. He knew that himself. He didn't do any weights – not that I did but I was naturally strong and I was able to handle myself. Smart managers targeted his lack of physique. They knew he could be pushed around and he was found out a few times.

Personally, I don't think he wanted it enough either. Cookstown is full of lads with loads of ability who didn't want it enough.

Mulgrew is a special talent, though, and I feel guilty that I led him astray and cost him a real crack at making it with Tyrone.

Life was just too easy. Stephen and I were out working for ourselves and making a fortune before the recession hit. I was driving a BMW X5 and had a lot of money. There was plenty of time for drinking and messing about.

Mulgrew and I enjoyed the craic too much, but I was five years older and should have had more sense. He was too good to be messing about as much as we were.

We both were.

Mulgrew and I were still together on the Tyrone team at the start of 2008, and we continued to press the self-destruct button.

Training was becoming an interruption to our social lives. We were on our way home from training one hot Sunday morning, still sweaty in our Tyrone gear, intending to go for a swim in the Glenavon Hotel.

Mulgrew was thirsty.

'I'd love a nice, cold bottle of Corona.'

Not a bad idea, I thought. 'There's a wee carryout in Castlecaulfield, go in there and get us four bottles.'

People were coming out of Mass in Donaghmore chapel when we drove past and there I was, window down, sitting behind the wheel, sinking a bottle of Corona. Mulgrew bust out laughing.

'Ah, Mugsy, you should have seen the look on their faces there, their mouths were wide open.'

I only had the one bottle – I don't drink and drive – but it just added to my reputation as a party boy, a reputation I seemed determined to live up to that year.

I was growing disillusioned with Tyrone. I pulled my hamstring in a League match against Laois and, when I was fighting to get back, I damaged a muscle in my hip. It was just a wear and tear injury but it was holding me back, big time. I was walking with a limp and couldn't even train.

I began to think maybe I didn't need Tyrone any more: *I have my All-Ireland medals, what the hell am I still doing here?*

I also felt there were some players who were playing as individuals rather than for the team. It had always been 'team, team, team' for me. I loved laying off a deadly ball as much as getting a score.

My da always used to say, 'You're not going to be remembered for laying off a ball, you're going to be remembered for Owen Mulligan, 0-3.' I know that is the way a lot of players think and, as the years went on, it crept into the Tyrone psyche far too much.

For me, it's all about a good team score, whether I am at the end of it not. In 2003, I thought we needed to get a result, whatever it took, but I felt that began to slip a bit when Canavan and Cricko left.

I was also putting on weight. My opponents were keen to take every opportunity to remind me of it. A defender said to me one day, 'Mugsy, you're getting wild fat.' I had my answer well prepared, 'Well, if your woman would stop feeding me biscuits every time I call round to see her whenever you're out, I wouldn't be this size.'

I'd love to be able to claim that remark as my own but I'd read that Eddo Brandes, a cricketer from Zimbabwe, had said it to Australian fast bowler, Glen McGrath. I don't know much about cricket but I like the sound of the sledging those boys get up to.

Having been such an integral part of the team for so long, I really struggled in 2008 with my new status as a sub. I was out of the team, out of condition and out of love with the game. The hip injury was giving me serious bother. I could barely walk, never mind train. It was stopping me getting back into shape and it seemed I was in a downward spiral. Nothing was going right.

Mickey brought in another sports psychologist, Caroline Currid. I liked her – she didn't try to tell me what to do, she was a lot subtler than that. She told me to take more time over the frees, that I was hitting them too quickly, and I took that on board.

I was afraid to tell her too much but, when I got on the bus with a hangover one day, she sat down beside me and I started chatting away to her, telling her all the things I was getting up to. She looked shocked.

'It's not sports psychology you need, Owen, it's professional help.'

We both sort of laughed about it.

Her track record says it all, she worked with us in 2008 and we won the All-Ireland, and she was with the Tipperary hurlers when they won in 2010, and Dublin when they won in 2011. I respected her, but I think she knew I didn't put a lot of faith in therapy.

I'd rather talk to a mate, someone who knows me. I've often phoned Cricko or Canavan when I was feeling down about being injured or not playing.

Mickey pulled off another masterstroke moving Sean Cavanagh to full-forward. He was scoring from midfield so, of course, he was going to score from full-forward and wing-forward. He has great feet and is so strong, he was unmarkable in there at times.

It meant that even if I could get back fit again, there was one less place up for grabs in the forward line. But it was a very effective switch, so there was no way I was complaining.

I tried to encourage Martin Penrose and Collie McCullagh, the boys who were starting ahead of me, as much as I could.

When I was dropped from the team during the Ulster Championship in 2005, I didn't handle it too well because it had never happened to me before. This time was different. Injuries and drinking were to blame.

It was a year of pure messing, and a year I ended up in a jail cell sick with myself and sick of the decisions I was making. Or the decisions I was failing to make.

I was on the fringes and felt like an outsider.

Having been a key cog in the wheel for so long, it hurt that I wasn't one of the main men any more.

And instead of working harder than ever to try and get back in, I sank further into a black hole, taking Mulgrew down with me.

◆ ◆ ◆ ◆ ◆

The subs had to do extra training on Mondays and Wednesdays. The rest were doing recovery in the pool on a Monday and we'd be in Augher. The training was brutal. Fergal, Tony and Mickey would all be there. It was voluntary, but it wasn't voluntary: You just knew you were supposed to be there.

We called ourselves the celebrity fat club.

We would do an interval run on the treadmill when the rest of the boys were in the jacuzzi or the pool. We put the nickname on ourselves but it wasn't funny at all, it was degrading. I'd look around at Hub, McGuigan, Mulgrew, Dermy Carlin, PJ Quinn, all sweaty and depressed-looking. I wondered were they feeling the same as me. Do they know that I'm never going to be in this position again?

We used to stop in the Carrickdale Hotel after our back-door matches. Maybe I was paranoid but I always felt the staff were looking at me, laughing, as if to say, *What's that man doing … he was one of the main men on those 2003 and 2005 teams and now he's running after matches with the subs.*

We had men who were happy to do those runs, even though they knew they weren't going to get on the team. They were just happy to be able to say they were in the Tyrone squad.

I put my head down and started to train like a mad man. I was training four nights in a row in a bid to get over the injury that had ruled me out of both Ulster Championship games with Down and a qualifier against Louth.

Mickey was under big pressure after that defeat to Down in the replay in Newry. Amazingly, even some Tyrone supporters were calling for his head. I thought it was poor form by them. After all he had won, who were they to question him? Who would be any better? I do think Canavan will make a great Tyrone manager some day, he and Cricko would be some dream team, as far as I'm concerned. But only when the time is right: Mickey should be manager for as long as he wants it.

My first taste of Championship action in 2008 was as a sub for the last twenty minutes against Westmeath.

Nobody gave us any chance of progressing much further, but we beat Mayo with a late surge of points. I came on late in the game and didn't make much of an impact, but we got over the line and were back in the All-Ireland quarter-finals.

We were paired with Dublin again. We were totally written off in the media, but we knew it was the perfect draw for us.

Our supporters were starting to call us, 'The Beardy Boys' when a few lads stopped shaving. The whole thing was Ricey's idea, of course.

There was a picture in the *Irish News* of some of us sitting in the stand, me with nothing more than stubble on my face. The caption suggested that maybe the Tyrone boys were starting a trend.

I was standing in Asda the next day when Ricey rang me.

'Did you see that picture in the paper, Mugsy? You can't shave that off now.'

'Ah no way, Ricey, I'll have a big ginger beard on me. I'm not doing it.'

He didn't want to hear it. He'd already started to grow one and I was next. Then Joey, then Ciaran Gourley, then Dermy Carlin, one after the other. We were some sight.

It grew legs. The supporters started growing them, too, I was surprised how big it became but I suppose it was another way of uniting everyone as we chased another All-Ireland.

We weren't rated as a team. Stevie O'Neill had surprised everybody by retiring at the start of the year and players like myself and McGuigan were on the bench, struggling with injury, and a shadow of our former selves. People said Tyrone couldn't win an All-Ireland without Peter Canavan. Mickey never said so, but I think that was one of the motivations for him that year. He wanted to see if he could win an All-Ireland without Peter, to see if it could be done. And he did it, nobody can ever take that away from him.

There was a lot of frustration among the subs, however.

Mickey is a lethal manager, but it was only when I was a sub myself that I began to think that he could have communicated better with the lads who weren't getting on.

Sometimes he would ring to tell you that you were dropped, but I thought he could have talked more to lads about what they could do to get themselves onto the team. He always kept a distance, which you have to do. Managers who try to cosy up to players and be their friends never get the proper respect.

We always had one-to-one meetings with him, Fergal and Tony every couple of months, and he'd say to all the subs, 'You are very important to us'. But I thought he could have put the arm around the shoulder more and built us up by saying, 'You're the best about', a bit like José Mourinho or Alex Ferguson would do. I know I would have responded well to that kind of approach. Those two men could be ruthless, as Mickey could be, and you need that to be successful, but I always felt he would have got more out of players if he'd occasionally told them what he was thinking.

That's why I was surprised to see Mickey coming over to me at training the week before the Dublin game.

'What did you think of the draw?'

'I think it's deadly, Mickey, just what we need.'

He smiled.

'I think so too.'

He walked away and my heart started pounding. *Is that man trying to tell me something here? He hasn't come over to me like that for a long time. He knows I always play well against Dublin. Is he gonna play me?*

There weren't enough bodies standing nearby, and he was even helping to pull my harness back during training. Just like always, I was desperate to impress him. We were doing wee sharp drills and tackling. The weight was starting to come off me and I felt good. My mind started to race. *Is this gonna be like 2005 all over again? Will Dublin transform my season?*

I watched from the stand the next Saturday as we annihilated Dublin in the rain.

Everything clicked that day. It was the most complete team performance we put in that whole year, and probably the best since 2005. One of those days when we showcased what a team of natural footballers we had. Sean, big Joey and Davy Harte scored three brilliant goals as we hammered Dublin, 3-14 to 1-8.

The game was long over as a contest when Fergal looked round at me. 'Mugsy, come on down here.'

Oh, no bloody way, I thought. *You cannot be serious here. You can't put me on for a minute!* I seriously thought about staying in my seat but then I considered: *If I say no, what will happen?*

I swallowed my pride and trotted down the steps, running on with sixty-eight minutes gone. I was sure I could hear the Dublin supporters laughing when I came on. I wasn't on the pitch three, four minutes when the whistle blew. I hadn't touched the ball. It was embarrassing.

The boys were hugging and patting each other on the back and I was, too. But inside I felt sick. Tyrone had played lethal and all I wanted was to be out there, to be a part of it.

We returned to the Carrickdale.

I went to the gym with the other subs and hopped onto the running machine. I hit the start button and just ran and ran like Forrest Gump. I ran for thirty-two minutes. Four minute intervals at speed 12, and four minutes at speed 15, jogging and sprinting. Fergal was shouting at us. His voice seemed muffled to me, like he was far away. I thought I was hearing echoes.

There was a big mirror in front of me. I stared at that stupid ginger beard that Ricey had made me grow. I hated myself, thinking, *What are you like, you dick?*

I jumped in the shower, lifted my bag and headed straight for my safe haven, my wee corner at the back of the bus.

Everybody was laughing and joking. No one was drinking but the boys were all going out later. I had to pretend to laugh with them. I was over the moon with the result, but I was heart broken. If I'd made a bigger effort I would have been on that team and it was nobody's fault but my own.

I used to love playing well and then going out with the lads after a good win, it was such a buzz, but I didn't deserve to be out with them that Saturday night because I'd done nothing. That's how I felt. I hadn't earned the right to a good night.

I made up a lame excuse that I had to work and, anyway, I knew I'd be back out with the fat club in the morning. I took a lock of pints on my own in my wee local, feeling sorry for myself, but I was back at fat club in Clogher on the following morning.

I was still in bad form as I drove over with Mulgrew. *Is this what the rest of my Tyrone career is going to be like, sitting on the bench? Because I will never be happy with that*, I bristled, *not at this stage of my career ... when I should be in my prime.*

Mickey used to give the team talk at the fat club. 'This is a great place to be lads, youse are a credit to yourselves and a credit to the team'.

I didn't want to hear it.

Stop trying to make me feel better, Mickey, when I know where I should be. I should be in my bed, hanging, with some gorgeous girl beside me, maybe running her home at this stage. I should have been laughing on the bus on the way home with the boys last night.

And I should have been out on that field last night, helping us stuff Dublin.

I started questioning my own ability, but after one or two good games for the club I began to get the buzz back again. That's why I think club is so important.

Mickey thinks Tyrone is like a full-time thing, but it's not. You should be playing for your club. He would say, 'Are you giving Tyrone everything you possibly can when you're playing with your club?' but, when we were asked about it, I always said the subs should be allowed to play for their clubs.

Now I was in that position myself, I definitely wanted to be allowed to play for the club.

Boys mightn't have got the same stick in other clubs but there were times Cookstown supporters would have been shouting at me to come on. I'd usually come on even if I'd been told not to.

Mickey would go mad if he heard we played friendly games with our clubs at certain times. Other boys agreed with me. 'You need your rest, boys,' Mickey would say, but I always felt I'd rather be playing a friendly with the club than doing weights or something.

I wanted to go to Mickey about my place in the squad.

I wondered whether I should I pack it in and concentrate on club football. I wanted to say, 'Mickey, I'm number 25 at the minute. Any chance of me being number fifteen any time soon?'

Mickey is not the kind of guy you can talk round once he has a set opinion on something. I knew there was a better chance the conversation would go something like, 'Why do you need to be No.15, Mugsy? You're No.25 at the minute, but if I put you at No.29 would you not like that better?' His argument would be so persuasive that I'd have come away totally delighted to be number 29. He would have us believing every word he said and that's what makes him such a great manager.

At the end of the day, I knew why I wasn't in the team and it was nobody's fault but my own. The injury earlier in the year had been a major setback, but I'd been drinking and messing about far too much.

I was training like a maniac before the Dublin game and after it, but it was too late to try to catch up with the other boys now. I knew the best I was going to get was a run from the bench and I was desperate to get on against Wexford in the All-Ireland semi-final. In the end, I saw little of the action again, only coming on in the last minute for Brian McGuigan who'd come on as a sub himself.

Having already seen off one of our great rivals, Dublin, now it was Kerry who stood in our way of another All-Ireland title.

I was going well in training and wanted to ask Mickey if I was in his plans for the final. I went up to see Canavan at the school instead.

I was questioning whether I was good enough any more. When you're dropped, you're your own worst critic. Canavan told me to hang in there. 'If Tyrone are going to win the All-Ireland, then you will be playing a part,' he said.

A few days later, I met Cricko for a few pints in Moortown. Did he think it would be cheeky of me to ask Mickey what his plans were?

'The way you're going at the minute, Stevie O'Neill will get on before you.'

We burst out laughing. Little did we know.

15

The phone rang. It was Mickey. He wanted to meet me.

My heart raced again. *Is he going to tell me I'm starting in the final?* My mind was a blur as I drove to Dungannon to meet him.

Sure, what else could it be? I must be going to start. This man has some faith in me to start me in this final the way I've been carrying on. I suppose he knows I can handle it. Sure, I've never let him down on the big day.

This is unreal.

We met at the side of the road and I jumped into his car, ill prepared for what I was about to hear.

'What way would you feel about Stevie coming back?'

'Oh, right, for next year? I'd be a hundred per cent about that.'

'No, for the final. If he's in good enough shape I'd be thinking of bringing him on in the final.'

I was stunned.

I said nothing for a minute, trying to take in what he was saying. Eventually, I managed to speak.

'Have you spoken to anybody else about this, Mickey?'

'Yes. Hub and McGuigan.'

'And how were they about it?'

'They are happy enough.'

I doubted that. 'Well, if those boys are happy,' I said, 'I'm happy.'

'Mugsy, are you sure you're happy? I need your backing on this.'

'You've got my backing, Mickey. No problem.'

At that time, I agreed with every word the man said but, as I drove away, I was hurting. I'm not the smartest in the world but I worked it out quickly enough. This was going to cost me a run out in an All-Ireland final.

Giving Mickey my support was the right thing to do. I'd played with Stevie all my career and, even though he hadn't been there all year, I knew he'd be in good shape. He doesn't drink and has always looked after himself. I was honest with myself: *Do you really deserve a place ahead of Stevie anyway? Do you even deserve a place on the bench the way you've been behaving?*

I was always big into keeping things in-house but I phoned Mulgrew. He was going to find out soon enough and, anyway, I needed a laugh.

'Lad, what number were you wearing the last day against Wexford?'

'26. Why?'

'Well, you're number 27 now.'

'What are you on about?'

'Stevie's coming back.'

'What? You are joking me.'

'Swear to God, lad, swear to God. We can sit beside each other on the bench and between us we'll have a telephone number on our backs.'

We were in stitches.

A players' meeting was organised to discuss it.

I stayed quiet for a long time, letting everybody have their say. It was the established players who spoke first and one or two were dead against it. 'I have no problem with Stevie, he is a great fella. But under no circumstances should be allowed on in the final,' one of them said. There were a few younger boys in the room who were scared to say anything either way.

I let them ramble on, arguing with each other for about forty minutes. Finally, I'd heard enough. I stood up.

'If we're two points down in an All-Ireland final and Stevie O'Neill is on the bench and is able to come on, I'm going to fully back that.

'I've played with the man all through my career and I know what he's capable of. If he has a chance to come on, if he has a chance to win an All-Ireland title for Tyrone, let's bring him along with us.'

Enda McGinley, who supported Stevie's return, got up and pointed over at me. 'Well that's just unbelievable what that man has just said, boys. Even if he takes your place Mugsy?'

'Even if he takes my place.'

I'm not taking the credit for it, but I think my reaction was one of the reasons Stevie was able to come back.

He trained with us that Thursday night and it was like he had never been away. There was a good bit of banter, no uneasiness at all. In my head, I kept thinking, *If I don't get on, how am I going to go to the banquet and celebrate this the same as the rest of the players?*

There was an in-house game fixed for the Saturday, the weekend before the final. This is where All-Ireland final places would be won and lost. Mulgrew and I had been as good as gold for the three weeks leading up to it. We trained harder than we had done all year to see if we could get on the bench, and then try to push for a spot coming off the bench. Then, the day before that game, we ruined everything.

We set out on the Friday to go to the ice baths in the Carrickdale. The visits to the Carrickdale were becoming quite enjoyable. I'd grown fond of a girl who worked there whom I'd met previously in Australia, and my girlfriend, Tina, and I were drifting apart.

By the time Mulgrew and I were out of the ice baths, the girl had finished her shift so I offered to take her for something to eat. She brought us to Johnny Murphy's pub in nearby Meigh, in the parish of Killeavy. Big mistake.

'Mulgrew, will we chance a pint of Guinness here?' I said.

'Aye, why not, Mugsy? Go for it.'

We were still in good behaviour mode. We ordered wee chicken bites and salad, and fully intended to go home after we'd washed it down with a single pint. That was the plan. Then Mulgrew says, 'Sure, I'll buy you a pint back before we go.'

I didn't need a lot of persuading.

Six pints later and the next thing I see is him walking down from the bar like a waiter, carrying a tray of gin and tonics over his head. I put my head in my hands.

'Lad, don't do this, don't do this.'

'Come on, Mugsy, fuck it!'

Mulgrew and I are just far, far too giddy when we get together. Our parents have often said it. We look at each other and start to laugh because we know what the other is thinking straight away.

I stared at the gin and tonics. They looked so inviting in their lovely tall glasses with big slices of lemon and ice in them. There were four of them, two each. I reached over and took one and that was that. I knew we were there for the night.

The crowd started to come in after work. I was wearing a baseball cap, which is usually a good enough disguise, but I had the stupid ginger beard on me so it wasn't long before we were spotted.

'Aren't you Owen Mulligan? Have you not got an All-Ireland final coming up?'

I denied it flat out, insisting they'd got the wrong person, but I knew people were watching us after that. Thank God there was no Twitter then. Someone would have taken a picture of us and it'd have been viral by midnight.

It was a lethal wee bar. The turf fire was on and as things got a bit rowdy we started doing press-up competitions; Mulgrew and I, and a few other lads and girls.

We were there until three in the morning drinking gins and sinking shots.

We crashed in the girl's sister's house in Killeavy that night. I left my phone in the jeep and had no idea there were search parties out looking for us around Cookstown.

My da and Mulgrew's da had the torches out around the Seven Sisters on the road between Omagh and Cookstown. Because we had been so well behaved for weeks, nobody dreamt we had been drinking this close to an All-Ireland final.

My ma panicked and rang Mickey at five in the morning. He had our physio, Louis O'Connor, and Dooher out looking for us. By the time I got into the jeep the next morning I had something like 70 missed calls on my phone. I listened to one of them. It was from my ma and she was crying. 'Where are you son? Please answer the phone.'

I slumped into the seat, feeling like an idiot. *What the hell have we done? We've worried everybody and now we're sitting in Killeavy with hangovers when we should be getting ready to go to this in-house match.*

I jumped when the phone rang. It was my ma again. I picked it up and she was relieved to hear my voice, but I knew it wouldn't be long before she got mad. I told her we'd be home soon and I'd explain all then. Mulgrew and I had about an hour to come up with a story, and it was going to have to be a good one.

As we headed for home, I spotted a big poster in a field advertising a Mary Black concert in Dundalk for the night before. Perfect. We decided to say we had gone to the Mary Black concert and then to the dogs in Dundalk, where we'd won a few pound, had a few pints and figured it was better to stay over.

We pulled up at my house and my ma came flying out the door in tears. The next person coming behind her was Mulgrew's da. I told him the story. He shook his head. 'Is that the best story youse two could come up with?'

'Aye, that's what happened.'

He rolled his eyes. 'That is the biggest load of shite I've ever heard. You're not gonna fool Mickey Harte with that one.'

My da saw the funny side of it but I could see Annette, Raymie's ma, was gutted, crying in our kitchen. But there was no time to feel guilty, we needed showers and then we had to get to the match.

When we got there, I asked Dooher to do the talking for us without telling him the full story. I wanted to stay out of the way in case there was a smell of drink off me.

'Mickey, it was a misunderstanding, they stayed in someone's house and the battery on Mugsy's phone went dead. I think his ma panicked,' he explained.

I muttered some apology to Mickey on the way past which he accepted no problem. His mind was on other things, like beating Kerry. I would say there was no way he even considered that we'd done anything stupid this close to the final.

Stevie and I started the match together up front, just like the old days.

Stevie came straight over to me with his hand out. Word had filtered through about what took place at the players' meeting.

'I just want to thank you, I believe you stuck up for me at the meeting.'

'Lad, I stuck up for you because it was the right thing to do. It will benefit this team in the long run and for this final.'

'Thanks, Mugsy, I appreciate it.'

I had one of the best in-house games I've ever played, in fact one of the best matches I've ever played, anywhere. I don't know where I got the energy from. I roasted Mickey McGee and scored six points.

Poor Mulgrew hardly touched the ball. He was rank. He couldn't believe how well I had played. 'How the hell do you do that, man?'

He started calling me George Best after that.

The night in Killeavy was probably what sunk Mulgrew. After the way he played in the in-house game, he knew he hadn't a hope of getting on in the final. I definitely led him astray over the years but we both kind of blame each other for that one.

We said we wouldn't touch a drop after that until the banquet, but my mate, Barry Devine, came home from Australia for the final and I went drinking with him on the Thursday night, after our last training session. Just a few pints of Guinness, and gin and tonics.

I knew it was selfish, I knew other players weren't doing it, but I convinced myself that I wasn't going to get on so I may as well have a drink.

Stevie is going to come on and he'll be flying, I reckoned. *He deserves it because he doesn't drink, and he'll do a better job than me in this state.*

I took Stevie's return as a sign that I was about to get what I deserved. Messing about the whole year was going to cost me a spot in an All-Ireland final.

The media were hyping up the whole 'Team of the Decade' talk, but it wasn't mentioned within our camp. We weren't trying to keep score with Kerry or anybody else. It wasn't about stopping them doing a three-in-a-row either. We just wanted to win another All-Ireland.

The 'Twin Towers', however, were very much on our radar. The media were building up Kieran Donaghy and Tommy Walsh as this unstoppable force as a two-man full-forward line. It was music to our ears.

We planned meticulously for them, convinced we had our own 'Twin Towers' in Justy and Joe McMahon. Our two lads were fit and on their game. Every night at training, they marked Sean Cavanagh and Collie Holmes to prepare them for Donaghy and Walsh.

We pumped high ball after high ball in on top of them so they got used to marking two big men and dealing with the kind of deliveries they were going to face in the final. After three weeks of marking Sean and Collie, they were ready for Kerry's 'Twin Towers'.

We headed to Dublin the day before the final, feeling relaxed and confident.

We had only just arrived at the hotel when word came through that John Devine's father had passed away. We'd known all week it was touch and go whether John would be able to play, but it was too cruel. He had to pack his bags again right away and head home.

I didn't even see him before he left. We had a light run out at the hotel and we were told what had happened. I was gutted for JD. I didn't know him that well in the early years but, as we got older, we got really friendly and had deadly craic. I enjoyed his dry wit.

Mickey was upset. He had big respect for JD and their families were close. All the Errigal men were upset and Enda McGinley spoke very well. He told us John would want us to put it out of our heads for now and concentrate on the game.

JD was a real team player, the way it should be. He and Packie had been rivals for the goalkeeper's jersey for years but you'd always see them in the dressing room, heads together, spurring each other on. Now, Packie was thrust into the limelight again, not in the circumstances he would have wanted, but we needed to stand united, more than ever. What happened to

JD brought us even closer together.

We had Mass as usual on the Sunday morning. That year Mickey introduced us to Monsignor Eoin Thynne, who said Mass for us before all our big games. He was Head Chaplain of the Irish Defence Forces and he and I hit it off straight away.

In previous years, I'd usually come into our pre-match Masses late and genuflect with my arms outstretched while the priest was talking, just having a laugh. It got to the stage were they wouldn't begin Mass until I arrived.

This guy was different, though. He had my full attention from the start. I loved the fact that he was from an army background and wore a camouflage stole when he was saying Mass. He had a crucifix that looked like it was made out of bullets and his sermons were real 'blood and thunder' stuff. He got me pumped up every time.

He would just appear out of the blue after games sometimes, he'd wave over and give us the thumbs-up, or occasionally he'd pop into the dressing room.

We needed one of his finest sermons before the All-Ireland final and he didn't let us down.

'When you're going into combat, it is survival of the fittest,' he told us.

'When you have to stick up for your mates, that is when you stick up for your mates.

'In a battle, you have to have their back and they have to have yours. That's the way it has to be if you want to survive.'

You legend, I thought.

All the boys were talking about it, we thought he was deadly.

The dressing room was calm before the game. There were no set speakers in the room. If you wanted to say something, you could say it. For my part, I don't think I was as influential in the dressing room as I should have been. When I think of how good Horse was in 2005, after he'd lost his place, I know I should have done more.

Considering the experience I had and everything I'd won, I should have been more vocal and encouraged the lads who were going through this for the first time. But I was so sick that I wasn't starting in an All-Ireland final that I just crawled into my wee place under my bench and didn't speak.

Dooher, Collie Holmes and Ricey said a few words. Dooher was the kind of captain who led by example and he had the respect of every single player in the squad. The point he scored in the first half, running down the touchline of the Cusack Stand with men hanging off him, set the tone for the day.

Kerry might have thought this was their time to get revenge, but we had other ideas. We were full of running. Joe and Justy were doing the business against Donaghy and Walsh. Everything was going to plan. Ricey was getting their heads with some verbals, all game-related stuff, like patting a man on the ass if he missed a point. 'Keep the head up, lad, you'll get the next one'. Or if they were taking a free, 'This is a hard one, take your time here'.

I knew Stevie would be brought on ahead of me, but I was still taken aback that he was brought on as early as he was. Collie McCullagh went down with an injury after twenty-five minutes and Stevie started warming up.

Brian McGuigan was sitting beside me on the bench and he put his hand up to his mouth, 'Jesus, there's Stevie going on.' I looked up and, sure enough, Stevie was running on, a lot earlier than probably even he expected.

Kerry threw everything at us but they still only led by 0-8 to 0-7 at half time. There was a bit of a scuffle as the teams made their way off the pitch but it didn't faze us. We knew we still had plenty left in the tank and they were already looking a bit tired.

Darragh Ó Sé once said that Hub was the hardest man he ever marked, and how Hub didn't start that game was beyond me, but bringing him on at half time was the winning of our third All-Ireland.

He absolutely bullied Ó Sé and had an immediate impact, setting up a goal for Tommy McGuigan straight from the throw-in. Stevie was out in front and won the ball well, and lobbed a pass over his shoulder straight into Hub's path.

His shot was blocked but the ball rolled loose, giving Tommy a simple tap-in. Kerry were rattled. This was supposed to be their All-Ireland to lose but they knew – and we knew – that if it was close going into the last ten minutes, we had the mental strength to get the job done.

We still had work to do, however. By the time I came on for Ryan Mellon in the fifty-seventh minute, we hadn't scored in seventeen minutes. Tom O'Sullivan came straight over to me.

'Ah Jaysus, Mugsy, look at the state of you! That beard is terrible.' He patted my beard and the two of us burst out laughing. I've always enjoyed Tom, he's a real good lad. I've met him on a few nights out and enjoyed his banter. He'd always give me a bit of verbals about drinking and that, but it was all good humoured.

Some of the Kerry lads' line of patter wasn't very original. They, and some of the Dublin players, were big into calling us 'British c***s' or 'Orange b******s'. It used to annoy some lads, but not me. I mean, so what? I'd get far more annoyed if someone insulted my ma.

There was never the remotest chance of us losing to Kerry in 2003 and 2005 because we were way better than them and had far better footballers. But, in the 2008 final, we could have been beaten. We needed a bit of luck and we got it.

There were only four minutes left and we were a point up when Declan O'Sullivan went for goal in front of the Hill, but Packie got down brilliantly and beat his shot away. It was a crucial moment.

A few minutes later, I did a big 'dying swan' act, looking for a penalty.

I could have fisted the ball over the bar, but I ran around Declan O'Sullivan inside the square. He barely touched me, but I threw myself down, probably the most embarrassing dive I ever did.

But I could see the determination in our boys' eyes. There was no way we were going to let this slip. Enda, Hub and Colm Cavanagh hit a flurry of points and, in the blink of an eye, we were All-Ireland champions again, winning 1-15 to 0-14.

I got on the ball and had a hand in a couple of scores, so I was happy enough. I was also glad that the old guard had got a chance to come on in an All-Ireland final, the likes of Stevie, Hub, Brian McGuigan and myself.

It was nice to be on the pitch when the final whistle blew. It was more than I deserved, but it was a good feeling. I didn't really feel part of it, though, and Stevie must have felt like that, too, because he didn't hang about afterwards.

He was in tears as we stood on the steps of the Hogan Stand waiting for Dooher to lift the Cup. Stevie hadn't played well, although he did set up the goal, but he just kept shaking his head, saying he shouldn't have come back. Michael Harte, our physio, and Conor Gormley tried to console him, but he was in a bad way.

After the presentation, he walked down the tunnel and I shouted after him. 'Come on back Stevie, you're part of this.'

But he kept walking.

He just stayed in the dressing room until we came back in. He went to the banquet but he left early the next morning and wasn't on the bus home.

I felt a bit like Stevie. I had it in my head that if I didn't get on in the final, that I would go straight home because I didn't want to go to the banquet. I knew the subs were needed to push the thing on, but when you've been a part of the starting team for so long, it's tough. I could see where Roy Keane was coming from when United won the Champions League final in 1999. He had done so much to get them there but being suspended for the final meant that he didn't feel part of it. I felt exactly the same. I set myself a high standard and was so used to starting, that I didn't feel a part of this.

The atmosphere was deadly in the room afterwards, everyone was singing and taking pictures. Ricey wasn't long making me forget about feeling sorry for myself. I tapped him on the shoulder while we were celebrating having Sam back with us. We hadn't hit the showers yet.

'Lad, will we head next door and get a few beers?'

'Aye, aye, no bother.'

The players' lounge in Croke Park is fill your boots time. It is total power drinking. You only have a short space of time to sink as many bottles of beer as you can and then stuff a few in your pockets for the bus.

Ricey burst in the door in his socks and did a big slide across the floor. He came to a stop right beside big Kieran Donaghy who had already changed into his tracksuit and was standing at the bar drinking a pint. I burst out laughing.

He turned round, 'All right, lads.'

I don't think he was amused.

That night at the banquet Mulgrew and I celebrated like we'd won the

World Cup, a couple of All Stars and had walked off with a joint Man of the Match award. We were up on tables, we were singing with the band, we were in some form. It wasn't that I thought it might be the last All-Ireland, I never thought that, but I already had it in the back of my head that I was going to give it absolutely everything the next year.

The whole place was going mad, as usual. I met Monsignor Eoin and he was delighted, he squeezed me by the hand and nearly broke it. He has the hardest handshake ever, a good sign of a man I think. I really connected with him and we swapped phone numbers that night.

Even though I was drunk, I wanted to have a word with Mickey.

'I just want to thank you, Mickey, for putting your trust in me and bringing me on today.'

'This is only the start, Mugsy, you'll be back next year.'

'I know I mighn't like it all the time, but you always get it right.' We both laughed and shook hands. I made a promise to myself that night and repeated it going home on the bus the next day: *I'm not going to have this feeling again, the feeling that I'm celebrating but really, deep down, I'm hurting, too. The next time I'm celebrating, I'll be celebrating the way I did before – as part of the team.*

On the Tuesday morning I shaved off the beard, put on my Tyrone suit and went to John Devine's father's funeral.

I was totally hung over but there was no way I was going to miss it. All the boys were there, the Sam Maguire, too. John was choked up to see us all but we weren't there because we were told to be, we wanted to be there to support him.

◆ ◆ ◆ ◆ ◆

The county went into party-mode again but I hardly went anywhere with the Cup. I felt I hadn't done enough to be parading around the place with it. If anybody phoned, I made an excuse that I was away or wasn't able to get the Cup. Maybe it was selfish, but that was the way I felt.

One of the few nights I enjoyed that year was back in Barney Eastwood's house. He'd invited us again for another party. He called me into his games room, back into the room with all the World Title belts and bibs and sporting memorabilia.

'Come here, Owen, I want to show you something.' He pointed, and there were my boots sitting on the shelf inside a glass case, the boots that weaved the magic. I was beaming. I thought they'd just have been lying in a box somewhere, I didn't think they'd have pride of place amongst all of Barney's boxing stuff. It was class.

It gave me a wee lift seeing that, a reminder of me at my best. I was more determined than ever to get back to those days.

16

We had just won another All-Ireland but, as far as I was concerned, 2008 was a nightmare year I couldn't wait to put behind me.

I didn't even bother to keep my jersey from the final. I couldn't tell you where any of my stuff is from 2008.

I don't know if Hub and McGuigan feel the same, but the 2008 medal doesn't mean as much to me as the others. Cricko has challenged me on that and said he was a sub in 2003 and 2005, yet those medals mean the world to him.

But the manner in which I collected a third Celtic Cross was different. I'd been drinking and messing about, and I hated myself for it.

I firmly believe I wouldn't have been a sub if Canavan and Cricko had still been there, they would have kept me right. Still, I should have been able to look after myself. I felt so low that winter but it gave me the kick up the ass I needed. I trained harder than I ever trained in my life trying to make up for what I'd done.

I went into complete lockdown, I gave up drink and I didn't party, with the result that I went into the 2009 season in the best shape I'd ever been in.

My cousin, Brian Mulligan, asked me if I fancied doing the London Marathon to raise money for the Southern Area Hospice in Newry. The training for the race in April was going to coincide with our pre-season training and League campaign, but I was interested immediately. I always loved running the roads, putting the headphones in and just heading out for a few hours. The marathon would be something new, a fresh challenge, and I was in.

I started training, as did my brother, Stephen, our cousin, Brian, and a mate of ours, Barry Ruddy. I lost a pile of weight and was flying fit. Mickey wasn't too happy about it, though.

'Is it true you're training for a marathon?'

I nodded.

He shook his head. 'We're trying to tailor training here to meet everybody's needs and what you're doing is not good.'

He was worried the marathon training would affect my football, that the stamina training wouldn't be good for me, but I was combining it with speed work and I felt great. I felt so fit, I could easily last a whole match.

We played Dublin in front of a capacity crowd in Croke Park in the first round of the League to commemorate the GAA's 125th anniversary. Big matches with Dublin in Croke Park were almost becoming routine.

Six months earlier, I'd sat on the bench as the lads hammered Dublin but this time I was determined to play my part.

Stevie must have felt the same. He hadn't enjoyed his last appearance in Croke Park much either, but he was the star of the show this time, hitting some ridiculous points from acute angles.

Stevie and Sean were flying and we were going that well that I could hardly get the ball, apart from scoring an early point. Everyone felt so confident and wanted the ball. We coasted into a six-point lead but we let it slip, thinking the job was done, and Bernard Brogan's goal drew Dublin level in the second half. Then Stevie hit a superb pass in to me from the end-line in front the Hill.

From where he was, I didn't think he'd be able to whip it in so accurately but, the form he was in, I shouldn't have been surprised. It was a deadly pass. Stephen Cluxton was committed so I stepped inside him, dropped the shoulder and stroked it in at the near post with a wee punt kick.

I fell to the ground after I hit it. I couldn't get up fast enough, I was desperate to see my old mates on the Hill. I stood still, staring up at them. I'd never disrespect them but I wanted them to know I was back in town.

As I came out again, Denis Bastick hit me a wee dunt to remind me I wasn't going to get it all my own way but I felt on top of my game.

I was getting serious space inside but Collie McCullagh ignored me a few times when I was free and Stevie did, too, although the form he was in I didn't blame him. Sean and himself hit three outstanding points in injury time to snatch victory in a fantastic game.

I loved the hype Dublin brought. I was never sick of playing them, though I'm sure they were sick of the sight of us. They huffed and puffed a lot but we felt they hadn't the balls.

Credit to Pat Gilroy, that was only his first League game in charge, and he definitely put a mental toughness into them after that. But, at that stage, they were soft and we felt we had their number every time. We knew once we got on top of them, they'd crumble.

The GAA was criticised for spending so much money on the fireworks that night but I thought it was class. We were lucky to have been a part of such an occasion. It was as close as we get to professional sport across the water.

Highlights of special moments from the GAA's 125-year history were played on the big screen after the game and my goal from 2005 was one of them. It was surreal watching it back on the big screen and nice to hear the roar going up from the Tyrone supporters again.

Over the next few months, the marathon training was getting serious. We were doing eighteen-mile runs for a few weeks before the big day. My Ma was worried about Stephen. 'You need to look after Stephen, I know you'll finish it no bother but stay with Stephen. Make sure he's all right.'

'Yeah, yeah, no bother. Course I will.'

Then, a week before we headed to London, I got a bang on the knee one night in football training.

I had to get a cortizone injection from Noel Napier on the Wednesday and I arrived at the starting gun the following Sunday with absolutely no idea if I could finish the race. After only three miles, I felt the knee starting to go. After six miles I started to limp and I was starting to hold the boys back. They needed to keep at a certain pace, and I wasn't fit for it. So much for me looking after Stephen!

He looked round at me with a worried look on his face and I shouted at him to go on without me. I stumbled on, but the pain got so unbearable I had to pull out after seventeen miles, while the boys coasted home in four hours and ten minutes.

They're still giving me stick about it but I will have the last word. I will definitely do the marathon again and I'll beat their time, too.

The disappointment was huge, but at least I was in great shape heading into the Ulster Championship. All the commentators were saying I looked in good nick, and I felt it, too.

Peter Donnelly quit the panel after the League and I admired him for it. People were shocked when he went, but he was sitting on the bench for three years, what was he supposed to do? It's not nice being in that position. You're training hard, you're going on the weekends away, you're not allowed to play for your club, and for what?

I was never satisfied with being on the bench. Ever. Pete obviously felt the same. Ok, he'd had a few injuries, but if you're sitting on the bench year in and year out, something has to give.

There are players who just want to be on the Tyrone panel. When someone comes up to them and says, 'You're in the Tyrone squad, aren't you?' it makes their day, but Pete set a higher standard for himself than that. At minor level everyone was saying he was going to be the next big thing in midfield for Tyrone, he was even rated ahead of Sean Cavanagh, but it just didn't seem to happen for him. I'm not surprised he is doing so well as a coach in Cavan. Another Coalisland man I thought would have made it was Paddy O'Farrell, a half-back who I always rated when playing with him at underage level for Tyrone.

Pete never missed training and gave everything, he was a really unselfish, class player, and I had big respect for him for walking away.

We regained the Ulster title in 2009, beating Armagh in the first round by three points in Clones followed by a big win over Derry in Casement Park. I was fit, I was leading, I was back playing a key role in the team where I wanted to be.

Antrim reached the Ulster final but we were totally confident we'd lift the Anglo Celt Cup again. After all that had gone on the year before, it was probably one of my most enjoyable Ulster title wins.

I have always rated the Ulster Championship, and valued an Ulster medal highly. Maybe it goes back to the days of the Mulligan clan, all going on the bus to Clones in the '80s and '90s. Any time Tyrone won an Ulster title back then, it was a big deal.

It was just a pity the Tyrone fans didn't feel the same now.

When we went up the steps and took turns in lifting the Cup, there was hardly a cheer from the Tyrone crowd in the ground.

But after the depression of the year before, I really appreciated being back in the team and was enjoying my football. Our post-match visits to the Carrickdale weren't painful either. I was back in the recovery pool, just like I'd promised myself, while the subs were heading in to do their runs. I sympathised with them, 'Boys, I feel your pain, I really do. It's shit.'

We beat Kildare after a really edgy game in the All-Ireland quarter final, Justy McMahon came up the field and scored a brilliant point to get us over the line.

I got an *Irish News* All Star. It was a further sign I was back to my best. We were back in the All-Ireland semi-finals, just two games from retaining our All-Ireland title for the first time. We felt confident of going all the way again and I was going to be a winner on the field this time.

I couldn't wait for the Cork game to come around. Preparations went well and there was no inkling there was a problem with Sean Cavanagh. He had trained the whole week and was flying.

There was no hint of panic on the bus or in the dressing room beforehand, but that was normal, we wouldn't be told things that might make us lose focus. We ran out onto the field first and Sean was with us. He took part in the warm-up and I didn't know there was anything wrong until I saw Tommy McGuigan out there before the throw-in.

I was in complete shock.

Why's Tommy starting, where the hell is Sean? I thought. I looked over to the sideline. Looking at Mickey's face, I don't think he could believe it either.

We were under the cosh for the whole game and nothing clicked up front. Cork were all over us but they were down to fourteen men before half time when Alan O'Connor picked up a second yellow card for fouling me.

Stevie was on fire and drilled over his fourth point of the game at the start of the second half to reduce the gap to four points, but that was as close as we got. I hit a free really poorly, I think I was trying too hard. Even though we had an extra man and there was loads of time left, I just knew it wasn't going to happen.

Sean came on with twenty-three minutes left and lit the place up. He burst through the middle of the defence on one of his trademark runs and went for goal, the ball just hitting the outside of the post.

If he is fit to do that, why was he not starting? I thought.

We were well beaten by 1-13 to 0-11. No complaints.

We left Croke Park dejected. Three All-Ireland title defences had ended in crushing disappointment. This time it was shrouded in confusion. No one could work out what the hell had happened to Sean and we weren't told anything about it. This had been a great chance to put All-Irelands back-to-back but we'd blown it, and I didn't know why.

I doubted it could be anything to do with the pressure of being the reigning Footballer of the Year, Sean had played in bigger games than Cork in an All-Ireland semi-final. He was such a class player but nobody knew the real story, so nobody gave him any hassle. When he walked on to the bus an hour later with a couple of pint bottles of Magners under his arm, however, a few boys were disgusted with that.

When we're beaten we always go out on the Monday, we just pick a bar and go on the rip. It was a tradition that started way back in Art and Eugene's time, and just kept going.

Sean wasn't out with us, though he would rarely be out on the Monday.

It was always the usual crew – Hub, Philly, Ricey, the McGuigans and the McMahons. Sometimes even the non-drinkers, like Gormley or the Errigal boys, would come out for the craic. Fergal and Tony would often come out with us, but Mickey never came.

This time we were in the Black Horse in Cookstown. We were drinking there for several hours when Mickey walked in. I got such a shock I wondered had he come to tell us he was quitting. I doubted it, but that's how surprised I was when he walked in.

I was up at the bar buying a drink and he came over to me.

'Well, what did you think?'

I shook my head. 'Mickey, we can't expect to beat teams like Cork if we don't have our best team on. What was wrong with big Cav anyway, was he injured, sick or something?'

'No. He didn't sleep well.'

I looked at him. 'Mickey, I never sleep well before a big game but I still go out and play.'

'Well, that's what he told me and I have to respect his decision,' he said.

I wondered how the hell a man could be sick and come on and play as well as Sean had done the day before, but it didn't matter now.

Our year was over, all the hard work was for nothing. We'd won Ulster but we were about All-Irelands and this was a big chance lost.

I was nervous about joining up with the Tyrone lads again.

While they had been doing pre-season training and playing in the Dr McKenna Cup and early rounds of the League, I had been on a wonderful adventure with Cookstown.

I was lucky enough to play in Croke Park countless times but winning an All-Ireland club title in Croke Park alongside friends and family was an unexpected treat that we celebrated long and hard.

I still returned to the Tyrone squad pretty quickly and in decent shape.

As myself and Mulgrew drove to training to join up with the squad for the first time, I wondered how the boys would react to me winning an All-Ireland Intermediate club title. I wondered if they'd dismiss it because it was only Intermediate, maybe they would think that it didn't mean anything.

On my first night back, I was delighted when Davy Harte, Enda

McGinley and Conor Gormley came straight over to congratulate me. They shook my hand saying, 'That must have been unreal to do that with your club'. It meant a lot, coming from those boys.

I was pretty happy with how quickly I settled in. We beat Cork and Kerry but still headed into our final League game at home to Dublin needing to win to avoid relegation.

As always, I was buzzing at the prospect of playing Dublin, but I'd hurt my back at work during the week and was worried I might not be able to play. In the warm-up, I felt a shooting pain up my back. Every time I took an impact from the tackle bags, the pain got worse. I had to go to Mickey to tell him the bad news, that there was no way I could play in the game. I think he knew by my face I was devastated.

I have always rated the two Brogans and they destroyed us that day in Omagh, Bernard hitting eight points. The defeat meant we were relegated on scoring difference, along with Derry. Everyone was in shock after the game. We had always been in Division One and this was new territory.

The disappointment of relegation didn't last long.

Mulgrew gave me a lift home from training in Augher one Thursday night. We were driving between Ballygawley and Dungannon when we spotted a familiar car in front of us. It was Mickey.

Mulgrew was at his mischievous best.

'I'll give you £100 if you moon at that man.'

I was up for it. 'I don't need no hundred pound lad, I'll do it for free.'

I don't know what came over me but I didn't just moon, I put my whole ass out the passenger window.

Mulgrew honked the horn as we flew past Mickey in the fast lane.

'Well, did he see me, did he know it was me?'

Mulgrew couldn't speak. The tears were flowing out of him and his nose was running. He was purple until we got to Paudge Quinn's.

'Oh my God I can't believe you did that, I cannot believe you did that! You should have seen his face.'

We had a get-together in Killeeshil on the Saturday morning and Mickey came straight over to me.

'I try to stick up for you most of the time but there's not much I can do about those antics on Thursday night.'

I tried to deny it but he knew rightly.

'Ach, I'm not even getting involved in this. That was you. Good to see you have your shorts pulled up today.'

Harte knew what I was like. He tolerated it. He probably knew he was never going to change me. Maybe in the end he just got fed up with the way I carry on. Even at minor level, I can remember Fr McAleer pulling me to one side and saying, 'Your antics are starting to annoy me, Owen. You are quickly becoming the class clown.'

Ricey and I had worked together on a few pranks but, as I got older, I had my head seriously in the football, most of the time.

We had Antrim at Casement in the first round of the Championship in Ulster, having beaten them in the Ulster final the previous summer.

I was up for the Antrim match. I set Hub up for a goal and then threw a couple of my favourite dummies to score the second.

We beat Down in the Ulster semi-final, and then it was Monaghan again in the Ulster final. People had been writing our obituaries after we'd been relegated, saying it was the end of us, so we took a lot of satisfaction out of claiming back-to-back titles.

It was our third Ulster title in four years but the achievement seemed to pass most Tyrone people by. When we went up for the Cup this time, there was no more than polite applause. The supporters were getting played out with Ulster titles. They wanted the big one. I think they got a bit spoiled, and I've often wondered if maybe that started to rub off on the players. Maybe we started to think that if it wasn't that important, maybe we wouldn't bother trying too hard.

◆ ◆ ◆ ◆ ◆

We had no fears about playing Dublin in the All-Ireland quarter final. Beating them had become a routine thing for us.

They had hammered us in the League earlier in the year, but we thought that was a one-off. Normal service would be resumed when we'd our full team out in Croke Park.

Losing that match was our own fault, it was a missed chance. I was going well and kicked five points, but we kicked seventeen wides and lost 1-15 to 0-13. That was the day the momentum shifted between us.

There were glimpses that Dublin were a coming side under Pat Gilroy. I always rated Ger Brennan and the two Brogans but the new lads like Michael Darragh MacAuley were impressive. Their physique was good, they looked lean and they were hitting harder.

They didn't crumble, the way previous Dublin teams had.

They still needed a flukey goal to beat us, though, when a shot came back off the upright and Eoghan O'Gara stuck it in the net. It was one of the most sickening defeats I'd ever had.

◆ ◆ ◆ ◆ ◆

I was pretty happy with the way I played that year, considering that, off the field, my family and I were facing financial ruin.

Our dream of running a family business had all started well enough. Stephen wanted us to emulate our Granda Eugene and rebuild Mulligan Brothers. My Granda and his brothers, Mick and Barney, were building and painting contractors and, as well as that, my granda used to sell fruit out the back of his house. After he died, that became the pitch where we played for the Mulligan Cup. Stephen and I used to hear stories around the town about what a good builder our granda was and Stephen used to say, 'I'd love to get that good a name.'

Stephen was working for a firm of architects and I was out on site. He always had it in his head that we'd go out on our own, and my da was pushing for it, too. In 2002 Stephen took the plunge and decided to get the family firm back up and running again. He was the brains of the outfit, he always used to say he paid me from the neck down.

We got a van and went out on our own, starting off with a few wee jobs in small residential developments and doing refurbishments. Stephen said we'd have to build up trust and get a good reputation, and it was going well.

Three years after we started, however, everything went pear-shaped. We had looked to make it to the next level in the business, and we used our da's good credit rating to help as our guarantor. The banks gave us money, no problem. But, very quickly, payments stopped coming our way. The whole building business was in trouble.

We were in big trouble.

Stephen kept it to himself for a while, hoping it would turn around but then, one night when we were out, he broke the news to me. We kept working away but things were not adding up. Stephen paid everyone for a while but eventually he had to stop. I had some money saved so I wasn't too worried. But even though we kept working hard, I noticed my money going down and down. Eventually, Stephen told me to try and get work elsewhere. Maurice O'Kane, a plumbing contractor, was good to me and gave me a few jobs to keep me going.

Through advice from accountants, we put ourselves into voluntary liquidation and ceased trading later that year. It was hateful having to scrape the 'Mulligan Brothers' stickers off our vans.

It was embarrassing because it felt like we had failed, even though it wasn't our fault.

We had bought other land that we intended to build houses on but we lost it too. We had meeting after meeting with the bank.

Eventually, even the small jobs were drying up and, by the summer of 2010, I was on the dole for the first time in my life. I signed on every Tuesday morning for about four months and hated every single minute of it. Here I was, playing for Tyrone and going up to the dole office.

What a nightmare. I tried to make myself invisible wearing different hats and scarves and coat collars up, anything to try and not be noticed. I'd have worn a fake beard if I could, I was that embarrassed.

Tina and I had split up, too, and I wasn't living with anybody. I'd no job, no girlfriend, no life. I thought seriously about emigrating to Australia. Tina and I had been on-off for so long, I thought maybe a clean break would be best for both of us.

I tried to convince myself that Tyrone wasn't an issue. I kept telling myself, *I don't need Tyrone any more, I've got my medals*. I'd won an All-Ireland Intermediate club title with Cookstown earlier that year, too. There was nothing left to win.

Then a bar/club in Cookstown came up for lease. I sensed an opportunity right away. We used to go there at Christmas for a drink but I knew it needed a facelift if it was going to work.

I was blacklisted because of what had happened and couldn't get a bank loan. Brian Mulligan, my cousin, was a bank manager. He kept telling me I could raise the money. I needed £20,000 and managed to borrow £10,000 out of the credit union but it still wasn't enough. I had a poor credit rating and racked my brains wondering how I could raise the rest of the money. Who could I ask?

I was still thinking about Australia. *I can take this ten grand with me to Australia and pay it off when I'm out there and working*, I reckoned.

Brian Mulligan didn't want me to give up on Tyrone but I told him I could see my career was starting to decline.

'My Tyrone days are finished,' I told him.

'I can't play football all my life. I want to be remembered for the player I was and all that we won rather than some lad who can't get his place any more sitting on the bench.'

'Well, have you tried everybody you can think of for a loan?'

'I have Brian! Absolutely everybody.'

'Well, you haven't asked me yet.'

'Lad, you're only after having your wedding.'

'I've talked it over with Coleen and we can take this out. You can pay us back over three years.'

I hugged him. I couldn't believe he was willing to take a chance on me. But not only had he given me a way out, it meant I could stay and play for Tyrone, which was what I had really wanted all along.

I was determined not to let Brian down. I paid him back within six months. He winked at me when I gave him the last of it, 'I love it when a plan comes together.' It was our favourite line out of the 'A-Team' TV show and we still say to each other after we win a match with Cookstown.

Mulligan's would never be up and running only for them. Brian and Coleen showed some trust in me and it gave me the push to go for it. Boys from the club like Marty Murray and Jason Quinn and even Cricko, who was managing us at the time, all mucked in and did a lot of the refurbishment work for nothing. Even my old next door neighbour, JB Senior helped out. I could never repay all those people for what they did, but I will never forget their loyalty and their friendship

Tina was still driving our X5 but we decided to sell it because we weren't going out any more. I told her to keep half the money. We had been together a long time and I messed her about that much she definitely deserved it. She came into the bar and handed me six grand, which also helped to do the place up.

But I still had no money to pay for alcohol.

I went to a couple of well-known businesses around Cookstown and Omagh, and they wouldn't give me credit because times were bad. I was disappointed but I understood.

Here I was, with a newly refurbished bar/club, and no drink. Then Raymond Monteith from North West Liquor came and rescued me. He offered me credit for three months. I've stayed loyal to him ever since because he took a chance on me when I needed it.

I'd signed on for the last time.

Instead of sneaking in to the dole office, trying to be a master of disguise, I walked in with my head held high. I'd just got the hair streaked and took off the baseball cap. I walked in, in a new pair of jeans and a t-shirt, looking a million dollars.

I got daggers off a few boys. Everybody knew I was opening a new business. I went out smiling, relieved my ordeal was over.

I got Canavan, Barney Eastwood and Willie Anderson to come to the official opening. The place had been known as a nationalist bar and I wanted to get rid of that.

I'm not a bitter person and have never been involved in any sectarian trouble. I had some mates who were big 'rebels' but I had no interest in it. My granny, Dolores Owens, who I'm named after, came from a Protestant background. I respect anyone for having a different point of view or feeling strongly about those things, but don't do it in my face. I don't want to know.

There was near uproar when I put Aaron Hughes' Northern Ireland jersey up on the wall but, sure, why would you not put it up? He is a Cookstown man who captained Northern Ireland. Our two families are connected through marriage, too. One night some lad ripped it off the wall and I had to chase after him down the street to get it back.

I put up a couple of Ulster rugby pictures and former Ulster and Ireland international, Jeremy Davidson, came in for a drink one night. When the Six Nations is on, I put out the England flag … I put out all the flags. I just try to stay away from the Tricolour and the Union flag. I want everyone to feel comfortable, so if Ireland are playing I put up the IRFU flag rather than the Tricolour.

When I first opened, the place was stuffed every night. Other bars in the town had closed, including the Conway Inn, which to me was the best bar in the town. From Thursdays through to Mondays, our place was packed. I thought of what Mickey always told us after we won the first All-Ireland, 'It's not always going to be like this'.

I knew I had to maximize the interest in Mulligan's for as long as possible and make it a successful venture. The previous few years had been tough, but with a new business up and running and a new season around the corner, I was sure the good times would return.

18

We had a good Christmas in the bar so I booked a trip to Australia for five weeks, to stay with my mate, Barry Devine. He and his girlfriend were working and I was partying, not a good recipe for domestic bliss. I lasted four days with them before I moved into a house full of lads down the road, which is where I should have gone in the first place.

I'd only been in my new place for a few days when I heard about Michaela.

I was on a night out when Tina texted me to ask if I'd heard what had happened, that she had heard that Michaela was supposed to have died in a car accident. I phoned her right away, I was stunned. A few hours later I phoned my ma who said there was talk it might be the same thing that had happened to Cormac. There seemed to be a lot of confusion.

When news came out the next day of what really happened, I felt sick. I couldn't imagine how Mickey and his family must have been feeling. I wanted to be with people from home, so I arranged to meet up with a few Errigal Ciaran boys who I knew were in Australia.

I wanted to be at home. I felt alone. I wanted to be with the boys, I wanted to see Mickey. This was like Cormac all over again, except this time I was on the other side of the world.

I was dreading it but knew I had to ring Mickey. I needed a couple of beers, only a couple though, to pluck up the courage.

What the hell am I going to say to this man? I wondered.

I didn't know what time of the day it was at home or whether he was in bed. All I knew was that if I didn't ring him right there and then, I probably would have backed out and put it off until the next day. And it was a call that couldn't wait.

'Mickey, It's Mugsy here. I'm in Australia.' I was in tears. Mickey was glad to hear from me but I had a lump in my throat so big I could hardly speak.

'I'm really sorry, Mickey, I just wanted to you know that I'm thinking about you. I won't be home for the funeral but there's a Mass arranged here for Michaela and I'll be going to that. There's a lot of prayers being said over here.'

He thanked me and said the prayers meant a lot, and that my phone call meant a lot. Considering I was on the other side of the world, I couldn't do much more.

A few nights later, I carried up the gifts at the Mass for Michaela in Bondi Beach. The place was stuffed. All you could see were Tyrone jerseys everywhere you looked. It was nice for everyone to get together and try to come to terms with what was going on at home.

The next time I saw Mickey was at his brother Paddy's funeral shortly after I got home. I gave him a hug that was long overdue.

◆ ◆ ◆ ◆ ◆

We have had a lot of tragedies to deal with in Tyrone, more than our fair share. While our team enjoyed unparalleled success, we had a lot of heartache, too.

Each time, it was the football that carried us through and gave us something to focus on away from the sadness. It was no different in the spring of 2011 as thoughts gradually turned to what lay ahead.

It was a strange experience starting the season in Division Two of the National League. We had been a top-flight side for so long, and it hurt not to be playing the top teams. Instead of playing early season crackers against Dublin in front of 80,000 people in Croke Park, we were playing Sligo and Antrim.

We all knew the defeat to Dublin the year before meant we needed to work harder.

Mickey was starting to put a big emphasis on weights. In earlier years, he used to go easy on me because he knew I absolutely hated lifting weights. I'd rather do cardio all day long and working on building sites for so long meant that I was naturally strong anyway.

'Weights won't put the ball over the bar,' I used to say, but things got stricter and stricter.

We had always been able to swat Dublin aside and, even though we'd kicked ourselves out of it in the All-Ireland quarter final, it was noticeable how they were starting to bulk up under Pat Gilroy.

We had to keep a record of what we were eating, how many hours we slept, what size of weights we were lifting. I knew it was all part of the more professional era we were living in, but it was too much like schoolwork to me.

Other boys loved it.

'How many reps did you lift this week?' they'd be asking each other.

Smaller boys than me were lifting up to 50kg. Mickey reminded me one day that I was still only lifting 10kg while Cathal McCarron was lifting at least double that. We were training in Eskra shortly after that when McCarron met Ricey in a real 50/50 challenge. Ricey wasn't lifting much heavier weights than me but he sent McCarron flying with a good shoulder.

I went sprinting over to Mickey, delighted with myself, 'There's your weights for you now, Mickey!' He burst out laughing. But there was no getting away from it. The weights were a big deal now, whether I liked it or not.

Teams will do whatever they can to get an edge and Mickey brought someone in to help us with our breathing.

He was a one hundred per cent nice fella, but his methods left me cold. He had us bouncing up and down on trampolines holding our noses, trying to get control of our breathing. We looked like right eejits.

I would drive into training at around seven o'clock in good form, thinking, 'Maybe I'll get a rub before training starts.' Then I'd be greeted with the sight of six men on trampolines, jumping about like kangaroos. Jesus Christ almighty. I would buy into anything if it brought Tyrone success, but this..!

Mickey must have known by my face a few times that I was pissed off. I'd just roll my eyes. I would rather go out before training and practise free kicks on my own for ten minutes than run three laps holding my nose with this man running alongside me.

We were doing really hard training that nearly made you throw up. You'd be wrecked, gasping for air, and there's this boy standing there shouting at you to control your breathing.

He timed us to see if we could hold our breath for thirty seconds, which is supposed to be good for you. When you got off the trampoline you had to run, holding your nose with your mouth shut, to see if you could do it for the thirty seconds.

Of course, I never did it. I would be holding my nose and breathing through my mouth.

I've always got a lot more out of heart-to-hearts with Cricko and Canavan than any sports psychologist or breathing expert. I've always thought my ma should have been a sports psychologist, I think she'd have been great in the Tyrone dressing room! She certainly is brilliant at getting into my head.

I liked the arm around the shoulder approach but I don't mind a kick up the ass either. I have always been lucky, too, that I have parents who are completely honest about my performances. They are my worst critics and that is far better for you than the 'Dotin' Ma, Dotin' Da' syndrome that some boys have.

Whenever I go home after a match, Ma and Da are the first ones to say, 'What the hell happened you today? You were terrible.' Or else it's, 'You should have been taken off earlier,' or, 'You should have taken that shot yourself.'

I loved that honesty from my parents, always. If more people were like that, especially in my own club, we'd be sitting with twenty senior Championships now.

I see it a lot when I'm helping out at underage level. 'Why did you take my son or my daughter off?' and all that. Parents saying to their children, 'You shouldn't have been taken off … you shouldn't go back'. Crazy stuff. The week before we played Monaghan in the Ulster Championship, Mickey was on to me about not filling in my Sporttracker diary, where we were supposed to detail exactly what training we were doing.

I was round in our physio Louis O'Connor's house doing a Vertamax session. I was tied into springs and elastics working up a sweat, going at it hell for leather. I was in the mood for a laugh. I got Louis to video me on the phone clowning about and jumping around for about a minute.

'Mickey, I've decided to take it to a whole new level here, I'm going to send you video clips of me training every day.'

I sent the clip to Mickey's phone. I thought it was funny but maybe it wasn't great timing. It was the day he was picking the team to play Monaghan.

When Mickey read out the team that night, I wasn't on it. I was furious. I was flying in training and playing well in the in-house games. I felt fit and ready to help us win a three-in-a-row in Ulster for the first time.

I was convinced I had heard something wrong, that there must be some mistake. I could feel the boys doing a double-take, staring over at me to see what my reaction was. I was stoney-faced.

When boys are looking at you with their mouths open, you know it's not just you that's shocked. Philly was stunned. He came over to me, 'What did you do on that man?' he said.

Mickey came over to me.

'I tried to ring you to tell you that you weren't starting.'

'Oh right, is there any particular reason?'

'No, I'm just gonna give Marty Pen a chance here but you'll definitely be coming in.'

'I thought I was going well in training.'

'You are, you're looking sharp. I want you to make an impact when you come in.'

There's no doubt there were times in my career when Mickey indulged me and gave me the benefit of the doubt, and showed great faith in me.

In the early years, he gave me the benefit of the doubt and kept me on sometimes when I didn't deserve it. When he dropped me, I always accepted it and said, 'Fair enough'. Even if I was mad, I knew he was right. But I definitely deserved to start that Monaghan game. I was still pissed off about it when I came on in the second half and I was lucky not to be sent off almost straight away.

It was raining heavily in Omagh and I scored a point right away. Colin Walshe was marking me. Cookstown played against his club, Doohamlet, in the club Championship and he is a really good player. He started giving me stick about not being a starter any more.

'Sure, I'm only giving the rest of the boys a chance before the All-Ireland semi-final,' I said to him.

He started grabbing my jersey and nipping me. I lost it. I turned round and hit him straight in the face and sprinted into the full-back line. A bit of a fight started and I was lucky the referee didn't see it.

I was even luckier there was no video evidence. Mickey gave out to me about it and I knew it was stupid. I was annoyed I hadn't started but that was no excuse.

We had Donegal next and, even though Jim McGuinness had just got them promoted in his first year in charge, we were confident we'd beat them.

We set out like we were going to destroy them. We owned the ball in the first half and went five points up, but we shot ourselves in the foot missing chance after chance. We should have been out of sight by half time but we were only a point up.

I scored a point and set up a couple of scores. I felt I was going ok but I lost the ball out on the wing, a low ball in bounced off me, and I was taken off straight after. I was ripping. It was the first ball I lost all day.

There were other men not playing their best either but it seemed I was coming off a lot lately. When I sat down some of the subs asked me if I was injured, which I wasn't.

Donegal were lucky enough to win that match – if Joe McMahon hadn't got injured I don't think they would have. He had Michael Murphy in his pocket all day but Leo McLoone came on and clattered into him. Joe had to go off and, next thing, Murphy is running the show and set up the winning goal. I often wonder would Donegal have gone on to win all they did win if they had lost that day.

I was beginning to feel sorry for myself and the feeling only got worse when I lost my place for the qualifier against Longford.

Mickey always names the team on Thursday nights but he didn't name it before the Longford game, which I thought was strange. Still, I was flying in training and it never crossed my mind I wouldn't be starting.

We had a meeting on the Saturday morning in Kelly's Inn in Garvaghey and that's when Mickey announced the team. I felt sick, pure sick, to the pit of my stomach. *Mickey not naming the team on Thursday night was a cop out. If I can't start against Longford,* I reasoned, *what chance have I of starting anywhere else?*

We had to drive the few short miles from Kelly's to the Ballygawley roundabout to get the bus. I felt so sick I just wanted to go home. I almost did, too. I drove around the roundabout twice in my van wondering what to do. I felt my Tyrone days were over.

This is going to end and I'd rather go before I'm pushed.

Despite my feelings, I knew it would be wrong not to travel with the boys. I knew I had to go, so I drove to the bus and got on, but I felt shit the whole way down the road. I questioned myself. *Am I not good enough for this any more?* When you're not starting against Longford, you should be questioning yourself.

I watched some of the other subs and they were laughing away. If they didn't feel as gutted as me, I didn't think they should have been on the bus. To me there were boys there who were practically cheerleaders. Their attitude seemed to be, 'Great, let's get the Tyrone tracksuit on and go for a spin to Longford. Up Tyrone!'

That's not me.

There are other boys who think they should be on, no matter what. Kyle Coney, Niall McKenna, Mattie Donnelly, Petey Harte, Ronan McNabb and Paddy McNeice all came from the 2008 All-Ireland minor winning team and maybe some of them thought they would walk onto the senior team.

Petey Harte has managed to do it because of his industry and work-rate and Mattie Donnelly proved himself as a senior footballer in 2013. Kyle has been unlucky with injuries. I enjoyed playing with him, I thought we clicked up front, and there is still time for him. He and Aidan O'Shea were the two stars of that 2008 minor final and look at how O'Shea has matured at senior level for Mayo – and to me, Kyle is a better footballer than him.

I believe everybody has to do their time on the bench at the start. I did it in 2001 and 2002. I didn't even expect to start in 2003 but I hit form and got comfortable in my surroundings and I was starting all the time, even ahead of Stevie.

I didn't see the same hunger in these young lads. I used to hear them complaining about not starting and thought they weren't prepared to push themselves to the limit. They had the talent but I didn't think their attitude was right. I let them ramble on. I thought to myself, *They will learn they have to serve their time. They need to trust in Mickey and listen to everything he tells them ... and everything Fergal and Tony tell them.*

Judging by some of their performances in 2013, they are learning and listening now. Looking on from the outside, it looks like they've matured and their attitude has improved. If they do everything Mickey tells them, he will make them champions.

I came on for Penrose in Longford but I had my mind made up that I had just played my last game for Tyrone. It was nothing personal against Mickey, but I couldn't understand why I wasn't starting when I was going well.

I didn't go to training on the Tuesday night or that whole week, and I wouldn't answer the phone. Dooher rang me flat out. The papers got wind of it and reporters were ringing me trying to find out what was going on but

I kept my head down. I didn't want to talk to anyone.

Willie Anderson rang my da, saying I was too young to retire. I'd previously got some herbal stuff from Sean Boylan and he also phoned. Barney Eastwood phoned. The parish priest even came to the door asking me to go back. My sister, Michelle, called round, she was annoyed. My ma was in floods of tears. She pleaded with me to go back.

Then Mickey rang, 'You're making a big mistake,' he said. 'You have to make your own decision but you know the decision I want you to make. We need you here … and you need to be here.'

I knew I didn't want my career to end on that note, quitting mid-way through a season. I felt embarrassed I'd let Mickey down by walking out. After everything he had gone through that year, did he really need me giving him hassle? He had enough on his plate without me doing that. I knew I had to go back.

I felt so awkward when I turned up at training. Everyone knew I'd thrown the head up. *Do they think I'm not good enough any more? Should I really be here?*

Mickey explained he couldn't start me or even bring me on against Armagh in the next qualifier because I'd been away. I understood that, it was completely fair.

We played Roscommon next in Croke Park and I came on for Kyle. There was some mix-up in how the match day squad was registered with the GAA, which meant Penrose wasn't allowed to play. That gave me a chance to get back in.

We drew Dublin in the All-Ireland quarter finals for the second year running and prepared as best we could to get revenge.

I couldn't wait for the game and Mickey rewarded me with a start. Like me, he was probably hoping the sight of those sky blue jerseys would get the best out of me. But they were a different animal now compared to the teams we had hammered in 2005 and 2008.

We had a taste of what was coming in 2010 but another twelve months on, they were fitter and stronger than us. I got the ball and in a second there were three of them there, surrounding me. I fisted the ball off but I thought, *Uh oh, what's going on here?*

They seemed to have their homework done deadly on us and we had no answer. Mickey didn't think they were stronger than us but I was on the field and they definitely were. They steamrollered us.

The match was nearly over when I noticed James McCarthy, John's son, looking over at me. He is a great player and some athlete but I'd never spoken to him. Dublin were winning pulling up so I thought I'd go over and have a chat with him.

'John is your old boy, isn't he?'

'Yeah, he is,' he said. 'He has a good word on you.'

'Aye, I had a couple of good nights out with him. Tell him I was asking for him.' I winked at him and ran on.

There was devastation in our dressing room. Another year over and we seemed to be getting further away from another All-Ireland.

We had wanted it badly, too, for Mickey and for Michaela.

Mickey told us in the dressing room that there was more to life than football, and that we would get over the disappointment. I am sure he wants to win an All-Ireland for Michaela, and I hope to God he does some day. It would be brilliant. I'm just sad we weren't able to do it that year.

19

I never expected, at any stage, to captain Tyrone.

There were a few times over the years when the boys said to me, 'You're bound to be captain for this one, Mugsy, you're the most experienced player here'.

It never happened, and I understood why.

I wasn't exactly captain material with some of the things I'd done over the years, and I wasn't as vocal as I should have been, considering the experience I had. I started to talk more in my last two years in the squad, but I was convinced I'd never pull on the captain's armband for the Tyrone seniors.

So, when Mickey made me captain for the Dr McKenna Cup semi-final against Fermanagh in 2012, I was over the moon. Dooher was gone, after captaining us for eight seasons, and he was on the lookout for a new skipper.

When he said, 'Mugsy, will lead us out tonight,' I was delighted. It wasn't exactly the biggest game of the year but I thought, *This is great, at least I can always say I captained Tyrone in one game.*

I had captained Tyrone a few times at underage level. I captained the minors in 1999 and also for one game for the Under-21s in 2002 when Enda was injured, but never at senior level. I regard it as one of the highlights of my career.

If I was to rank my top five achievements, the 2003 All-Ireland title is number one, because it was the first for the county. Next is the two goals against Dublin in the 2005 All-Ireland quarter-final matches. Winning Man of the Match awards in both the All-Ireland minor and senior finals would be third. Fourth would be the first All-Ireland club title with Cookstown in 2010 and fifth would be captaining Tyrone in the Dr McKenna Cup. It was just for one game, but it meant a lot to me.

I responded pretty well to the responsibility and hadn't a bad game. Marty Penrose set me up for a goal that was just like old times. I was still a good bit out the field when I got the ball and was going to pass it on and then I thought, *You know what? Just go for it.* I threw a fist dummy and ran on to bury the ball into the roof of the net. I was pleased to mark my captaincy with one of my trademark special goals.

Peter Canavan had just taken over as Fermanagh manager and the media were making a big deal out of us playing them twice in that McKenna Cup campaign. It wasn't a big deal to the players. Peter had left a long time ago so it didn't affect us.

I was never a big fan of playing in the McKenna Cup in January but it's funny the way things work out. I didn't know it at the time, but it turned out to be the last trophy I would ever win with Tyrone.

Mickey rotated the captaincy and John Devine led us out for the final against Derry. I scored a goal just before half time to get us back in it after Derry made a good start, and we were delighted to win the trophy again. It was the only trophy Cormac got to lift as senior captain in 2004 and it was always a special one for us after that.

I was a bit surprised at the start of the League when Stevie O'Neill was named as captain for the year, taking over from Dooher. He is not very vocal in the dressing rooms, but he does his talking on the pitch, which is good enough for me. I thought Sean Cavanagh would have got it, and I still think he will captain Tyrone at some stage.

The Tyrone squad was full of new faces that year.

Around a third of our team, so many All-Ireland champions and All Stars, retired after the 2011 season. It was so strange sometimes, I felt like I'd walked into the wrong dressing room. No Dooher. No McGinley. No Philly. No Gourley. No McGuigan. No Mulgrew.

No Hub. Everyone said Hub's legs had gone but I knew it was his back that was killing him. Yet I felt fresh, I felt good. My legs had not gone, I felt like I could go for the whole year no bother.

I missed Hub on the bus, though. For years I'd sat beside him with McGuigan and Philly in front of us. Now, I was sitting beside younger lads like Cathal McCarron and Kyle Coney. Part of me wondered if it was time for me to go but I was a year or two younger than most of the boys who had retired and I still had the enthusiasm.

The demands were getting excessive, though.

After being hammered by Dublin the year before, things had to change, and we started training four nights a week.

Mickey never accepted that Dublin were stronger and fitter than us, but it was obvious how much work they had done. They were a transformed team from the side we'd beaten regularly. They had bulked up, yet they were still flying machines.

We'd always had collective training sessions on Tuesdays and Thursdays, and did our gym work in our own time outside of that. Now, it was being supervised on Mondays and Wednesdays. Mickey and Fergal would stand over me, watching me lifting weights. I hated it.

A decade earlier, Armagh were the first to introduce a new training regime and bring in the tight fitting jerseys, and then Dublin took it to a whole new level when they started training twice a day. In 2012, like a lot of teams, we were out four nights a week.

The game has moved on beyond all recognition now. In terms of fitness levels, I'm all for it, but the game has got so defensive I don't think it's helping the forwards. They're not getting the chance to show what they can do. It's all about athleticism and physique yet the basic skills are being ignored. I'd far rather go out and practise my shooting or kick-passing than lift weights.

Playing in the Interprovincial series was a welcome distraction to the serious work we were doing.

I never seemed to play that well in the Railway Cup. I don't think former Ulster manager Brian McEniff knew what to make of me. One day before we played Leinster he came over to me: 'Ok, Owen, you'll be marking Cathal Daly. Have you played against him before?'

'Eh, what county's he from? Sorry, Brian, I don't know a lot of players.'

He walked away shaking his head.

It was different now. I knew I was coming toward the end of my career and appreciated the opportunity to play in these types of games more than I had when I was younger. I'd played against Joe Kernan's teams in huge games and I was curious. I'd heard he was a deadly manager and when he phoned me up to play for him, I wanted to see for myself.

Being honest about it, I knew I'd a good chance of starting, too. I knew I probably wouldn't have been asked if Jamie Clarke had been available or if Stephen O'Neill had been fit.

Even after all I'd won, I still doubted myself. I looked at flying machines like Mark Poland from Down and wondered if I should even be there, but I was well up for it. *If I start, I'm going to give this one hundred per cent.*

At first I was surprised when Darren Hughes was named captain. *Why the hell is he captain, sure wasn't he put in goals for Monaghan one day?* The whole thing was a real eye-opener for me. I soon realised what a great player and what a good leader Darren is.

Joe told us to enjoy it, that it was a great opportunity to get to know boys from other counties, and I embraced it. I chatted away to Mark Poland, Darren Hughes and a lot of boys I'd never chatted to before.

We hammered Connacht in the semi-final, and then played Munster in the final in the Athletic Grounds. Former Derry All Star, Tony Scullion, gave a really good team talk before the match about playing for Ulster. He'd come to Cookstown to give the odd session and I knew he was good. Joe played me as a corner-forward coming out and I really enjoyed it. It was pure football with not a sweeper to be seen – a forward's delight!

We only led by a point at half time and Scullion lined us up and gave us a right roasting. 'Youse are cowards, youse aren't even going in for balls.' Then he pointed over at me, 'Get the ball in to that man, he is on top of his game.'

I was loving it. Fair play to you, Scullion!

After a dodgy start to the second half, we showed some character to win the game. It was one of the most enjoyable games I ever played in. I thanked Joe afterwards for the chance. I was 30 years old and knew I wouldn't get a chance to play in one again.

Inside twelve months, I went from the high of playing with the best in Ulster to not even being on the Tyrone panel.

Brian McGuigan came out of retirement after some persuasion from Mickey and I was glad to see him back, thinking he would deliver some deadly ball inside.

We had a tough start to the Ulster Championship campaign, drawing Armagh away. I was happy enough with how I played, scoring two points, but it was clear Armagh were not the force of old.

Donegal was where it was at now, and we had them next in the semi-final at Clones. We were confident we would get revenge for the year before, when they'd beaten us and gone on to win the Ulster title. There was no way they should have beaten us in 2011. We felt it was a one-off, that there was no way they'd be able to do it again.

Their style of play made it difficult for me. Every time I got the ball, I was bottled up fast. There wasn't room to breathe.

I hadn't scored and Eamon McGee was giving me stick. I took a swig out of a water bottle. 'Jesus, Mugsy, are you on the drink already? Vodka, I suppose.'

I had to respond, even though things weren't going my way. 'Nah lad, I drink gin. I'll have plenty of it the night after we beat youse.'

I like the McGee brothers and all the Donegal lads. I'd heard all the stories about them being party animals, a bit like Cookstown lads. Apparently, one night when they were out in Dublin, they'd headed to the airport after the clubs closed because there was all-night drinking out there.

They always had the players, but they didn't seem to believe in themselves or give the commitment, until McGuinness came in. I thought Jim McGuinness must have been some man to transform those same players into champions.

It didn't happen for us. Donegal beat us more convincingly than the year before, though Penrose was unlucky with a goal chance near the end. I was taken off just fourteen minutes into the second half.

I didn't fear the men marking me and I'd won every ball coming in to me, but we didn't have enough support runners to lay the ball off to, and I was getting closed down trying to carry the ball. I was throwing a few dummies and getting closed down. Donegal got their tactics spot on but I was disappointed with the early substitution, which seemed to be becoming the pattern.

That night I went out in Omagh with Joe McMahon and a few of the other lads. We hit a few bars and, after throwing-out time, the lads were in the chippy when I jumped into the back of a police car parked out on the street. I'd do that quite often in Cookstown and they would run me home. There were two policemen sitting in the front.

'Any chance of a lift?' I said, waving two £20 notes in my hand. 'Is that enough, or do you need more? I have more money in the house, I can get it after youse run me home.'

They didn't see the funny side of it. 'If you don't get out of the car, you will be arrested,' one of them said.

'Not a problem,' I said, but as I climbed out of the back I lifted the hat off the cop in front. That was it, they arrested me.

They took me to the new barracks in Omagh, which are like a five star hotel. They took my phone, wallet, the lot. They fingerprinted me and even toe-printed me. Somebody who let off a nuclear missile wouldn't have got the same attention.

One of them was getting annoyed at my line of chat. 'You have a lot to say for yourself,' he remarked.

I kept going.

'Are you on the sunbed? You're a great colour.'

He'd had enough. 'Right. You're going to the cell.'

'Why, is there a sunbed in there?'

I was locked up until the next morning but I never closed an eye. I'd hear the footsteps coming down the hall and every time they checked on me through the hatch, I'd be sitting or standing in a different pose.

'I'm still here, boys!'

When they let me go the next morning, a handcuffed Tyrone supporter was coming in the door, still wearing his Tyrone jersey from the match the day before. His eyes nearly popped out when he saw me.

'Ach, Mugsy, is that you? What's the craic with you?'

'Not too bad, lad. What did you do?'

'Ach, sure you know the craic, there was an auld row up the street there. Do me a favour, sign that.'

His hands were tied behind his back but he stuck his chest out, wanting me to sign his jersey. The cop accompanying me to the door hadn't a clue who I was. He was looking at us like we were from another planet. But I noticed the cop had a pen sticking out of his shirt pocket, so I took it out and signed the lad's jersey.

I laughed as I walked out the door a free man, but I wondered how I was going to get home. In the end, I phoned Mickey Moynagh, our kit man, to pick me up and drive me to Cookstown.

◆ ◆ ◆ ◆ ◆

The trial in Mauritius was taking place during our Championship campaign. We felt for Mickey and all the family, but there was nothing we could do except focus on our football and try to give him one less thing to worry about.

Sometimes Mickey couldn't be with us. Tony would say, 'You know why Mickey is not here.' No one needed an explanation, we understood.

I badly wanted to give him a pick-me-up after the 'not guilty' verdict came through from Mauritius, which was just a few days before we played Roscommon in the qualifiers.

Mickey tried to speak in the dressing room but he was struggling, which got me going. I thought, *This man needs us today, we have to deliver.*

During the warm-up I looked over at him and I could see he was finding it difficult. I went over and put my arms on his shoulders.

He said to me, 'Mugsy, we need this.' I knew it.

I played for Mickey Harte that day, nobody else – not for Tyrone and not for myself. Stevie was injured and big Joey was captain, but I felt I wanted to give a real captain's team talk out on the pitch.

'Boys, we have been with this man for a long time,' I said. 'This man needs a result today more than anything. This is pay back for all the things he's done for us. He needs a result, he needs a pick up and this is where he gets it. Let's go out and do it for him.'

I was acting like a captain, running about and pointing and shouting. I was furious coming off the pitch at half time because I saw two men pulling out of tackles right in front of me.

I screamed over at Joey, 'Lad, there's men pulling out of balls here, right in front of my eyes.'

Joey spoke to the boys.

'Mugsy's right, there's men pulling out of balls and Tyrone men don't do that.' I was everywhere that day and scored five points. The way I was feeling, we could have beaten anyone that day.

That's why I still don't understand how we could fall so flat against Kerry. It was the toughest draw we could have got but I still thought, *Bring it on, let's go.* Travelling down to Kerry I thought we could win that game but I knew there were boys in the dressing room who didn't.

I tried to fire them up.

'We win this today, boys, we'll win the All-Ireland. Simple as. This is where you're judged.'

I thought the momentum we would get from beating Kerry would carry us all the way. I didn't think Dublin as defending champions would be able to keep going and I didn't think Donegal were good enough to win the All-Ireland.

But we were terrible.

Darren McCurry was given a start because he'd come off the bench against Roscommon and scored four points, but there's a big difference between playing Roscommon and playing Kerry in Killarney.

Ronan McNamee had a baptism of fire against Paul Galvin. We had mismatches all over the field and Kerry were up for it big time. We had lorded over them for a decade and this was pay back. I was poor but I felt there was no one to create a bit of magic, a wee through ball, a brilliant block or a tackle. I felt sad.

We had lost some outstanding leaders and a few boys threw in the towel. That was something that could never have been levelled at us in the past.

Kerry haven't celebrated as much after some All-Ireland victories as they did when they beat us that day. I looked over at Galvin, crying like a baby. I thought, *Wow, that's how much it means to these boys, that's how much we've hurt them.*

Their supporters were decent and a lot of people shook hands with us. We got a deadly reception but, like, so what? We lost.

I couldn't face going home to the Tyrone supporters and hearing them say 'You were annihilated'. Instead I went on a three-day bender in Killarney.

Sean O'Neill, Cathal McCarron, Brian McGuigan and I had class craic with the Kerry ones on the Saturday night.

A man came up to us in a bar and slipped two hotel key cards to me and McGuigan. 'Stay as long as youse want, boys.' We couldn't get over it. We had a great night, but by day two there was only McCarron (or 'Gorgeous' as he calls himself) still going strong.

I was still in the Tyrone tracksuit on the Sunday, me who hated wearing Tyrone gear at the best of times. A few boys pointed us in the right direction for an early morning cure up some back alley and luckily I fell in with a couple of girls who took me to a shopping centre to get a whole new rig out.

I still couldn't face going home on Monday, so Gorgeous and I stayed on another day. We were a sorry state as the train pulled out of Killarney. We took a few beers with us but it was a long journey home with too much time to think about how the season had turned out.

I was down in the dumps, just like any year we were put out of the Championship. But I'd have felt a whole lot worse if I'd known I had just played my last game for Tyrone.

20

I never dreamt my days as a Tyrone player would end the way they did, with a stuffing match down in Killarney.

We fought tooth and nail our whole careers to compete with Kerry, to be better than them, and for a while we were. Things have gone full circle for me, though, and I've got to accept that it has all ended on that note. I won't get a chance to right that wrong.

My first year outside the Tyrone camp was a difficult one. I struggled with a lack of contact with the group and a lack of identity. Being a Tyrone footballer is who I was for fifteen years of my life.

It's who I am.

After Cookstown won the All-Ireland Intermediate club title for the second time, in February 2013, I thought I would be going back to play for Tyrone.

Mickey came to watch our game against Warrenpoint in the Ulster club final the previous December at the Athletic Grounds, when I was just back after two and a half months out with a hamstring injury and had no sharpness whatsoever. I shouldn't have started the game, but it was such a big game for the club that I patched myself up as best I could to get out onto the field.

The match went into extra time but even by the end of normal time, I was holding my leg. I phoned Mickey a few days later and asked him what the story was with Tyrone for the coming season.

'You can't play because of Cookstown reaching the All-Ireland semi-final,' he said. 'And anyway, you're not fit enough. I saw you were carrying your leg there.'

I agreed with him.

He said that when Cookstown's campaign was over, he would call me in to play in an in-house game to see how I was going. I ended up playing in two in-house games, the first one just three days after the club's All-Ireland final, which we had celebrated hard. Mulgrew and I, along with the Dromore defender Sean O'Neill, were all called in and I played poorly.

In the second game six weeks later, which was the week before the last Division One League game against Kerry, I played well, scoring three points from play off the full-back, Conor Clarke.

In-house games are as good as you make them and our in-house games in 2003 and 2005 were unreal. They always took place before big games and they were hot and heavy, there was no missing each other. Sometimes a scuffle would break out but then we'd be laughing about it afterwards.

We killed each other on the training ground, and that is why we were so good. I remember Ricey getting his head split open one day and he just trotted off, got a bandage around it and came straight back on again, no messing about.

That wouldn't happen now. I can't say for sure when the intensity dropped, but I look back and wonder how the hell I dazzled at the in-house game before the 2008 All-Ireland final, having been drinking for eight or nine hours the night before.

If that had been an in-house game before the 2003 or 2005 All-Ireland finals, I wouldn't have counted. I'd have been a passenger. That's why I was disappointed Mickey seemed to be attaching so much importance to my performance at an in-house game now.

If team selections were being based on in-house games, then Conan Grugan should have been a Tyrone regular because he was unbelievable in that second game I played in. He was class. He looked like an All Star, yet he didn't get a run in the Championship.

I was tortured with people asking me *if* I was going back, or *when* I was going back. It was all anybody wanted to talk to me about. 'Has that man rung you yet?', or, 'Have you rung that man yet?' That's all I heard for months. Other people kept asking me if I had retired.

After the team's League final defeat to Dublin, I got a phone call out of the blue from someone I hadn't spoken to in years.

'Do you know who this is? It's your old mate from 2005, John McCarthy.'

I was delighted to hear from him.

'It's plain to be seen, you should still be on that team,' he said. 'Have you retired or what's happened? All the Dubs were asking where you're at. I can't believe you're not even on the bench. I'm a Dublin fan but I'd love to see you back.' Like everybody else, he urged me to ring Mickey.

I had words with Horse one day when he was drinking in the bar with Kyle Coney.

I played with Horse for years and although he wasn't a great player, he was brilliant in the dressing room, and it was a good move by Mickey to bring him into his backroom team for the 2013 season.

He met my ma on the street in Cookstown a few times during the year and kept telling her that they needed me back. If he thought that, why didn't he say it to Mickey instead of telling my ma?

'Will you stop filling my ma's head full of talk about getting me back?' I said.

'It's up to you, Mugsy,' he replied. 'The only man going to get you back on that team is yourself.' I told him I was training flat out and waiting on a phone call, but he shook his head. He said I needed to ring Mickey.

I didn't feel after fifteen years that I needed to lift the phone. If Mickey didn't want me any more, I would have to accept it, but he needed to be the one to tell me that.

'No, you need to ring him.' Horse was adamant. 'If you don't, you are turning your back on Tyrone. That's all right, sure you're better than the rest of us. You don't have to lift the phone.'

I was furious at that. 'You have a short memory, Horse,' I snapped. 'I have been to two in-house games and Mickey knows me long enough at this stage. If he doesn't want me, he doesn't want me, but after fifteen years I deserve to be told that.'

I still kept hoping for a call from Mickey.

The day I knew it wasn't coming was the day I watched the League final defeat to Dublin on TV. That's when it got me.

I am not saying that if I had been there Tyrone would have won the All-Ireland title, definitely not. But would Mickey have another League title under his belt now if I'd been there to come off the bench? I think so.

I think I could have got a score or bought a free in those closing minutes to win the game, because Tyrone should have won the game. We will never know for sure, because Mickey didn't give us a chance to find out.

I wouldn't have expected to start games if I'd been brought back. Earlier in my career, I would never have accepted being on the bench, but at 31 years of age I would have been happy coming on for the last fifteen minutes and I think I would have made an impact that day. I feel I am still better than some of the players who played that day.

Mickey sent out a real statement in that game.

I could see that he had real trust in the young boys, the way he brought them on at crucial times, when the game was in the balance. I felt sick when the game was over, because I knew I wasn't going to be back.

I know for a fact two senior players approached him after the League final to ask about me coming back, and he said he would see, that the door was not closed on anyone. I have heard that he thought I wasn't up to it any more but I believe if I'd had a month or two months training with the Tyrone team, I'd have got up to the sharpness needed for county football.

Anyway, even if that was his opinion, he should still have come and told me.

All the other lads I played with for so long left on their own terms. They retired when they felt the time was right. I was a year or two younger than all of them and felt like I could give it one more season. I wouldn't even have minded, though, if Mickey had phoned me and said, 'Listen, Mugsy, you're not in my plans any more. It's time to hang them up.'

I would have had my own views on that, but I would have accepted it.

I know he phoned Sean O'Neill after the in-house games to say he was not going to be called up, but I played for him a hell of a lot longer than Sean and I got no phone call.

If you worked for a company for fifteen years and they told you they were replacing you with a younger employee, the least you'd expect would be a thank you and a handshake. That's all I wanted – a bit of respect.

Maybe when the hurt goes away, I will be able to meet him and thank him for everything he's done for me. He gave me the opportunity to play for Tyrone and I owe him a lot.

◆ ◆ ◆ ◆ ◆

I was delighted to be asked by BBC Northern Ireland to be part of their panel for 'The Championship' programme.

It had been a stressful few months and I knew my ma was worried about me. She saw me in bad moods and going through a hard time. It was just what I needed.

It also gave me an opportunity to finally put to bed all the rumours that I had retired.

On my first day on the programme, I said that returning to the squad wasn't my call any more. It was important to me that people knew I hadn't turned my back on Tyrone.

It was tough going to the games and standing on the sideline with a microphone in my hand as the boys were running out past me. Being in Ballybofey for our Ulster Championship match felt weird, but I got pissed off pretty quickly at how our boys were allowing Donegal to bully them.

As a rookie, our goalkeeper Niall Morgan should have been protected, especially when he was taking free kicks, but he was left exposed. Donegal had done their homework on him after he'd done so well in the League final against Dublin, and targeted him. Tyrone teams of old would have done the same, so no complaints there.

But why were so many Donegal men allowed to creep forward and stand nearly on top of him when he was taking the frees?

Conor Gormley was outstanding that day and he was trying to pull Donegal men out of the line, but he couldn't do it on his own.

Our players are still young, and maybe that will come with cuteness. But I know for a fact those Donegal players would have been driven into the ground like six inch nails before the Tyrone teams of 2003 and 2005 would have allowed them to stand there.

The criticism Mickey and the boys got as the season went on was ridiculous. There were far more cynical tackles carried out by other teams in the big matches in Croke Park than the two that Sean Cavanagh got so much stick for, and there wasn't a word said about them.

Mickey Harte never told us to pull men down or take men out of the game. Anything he coaches is within the rules of the game. He always used to think that pulling a man down was lazy tackling. His philosophy was that if you worked hard enough and hunted in packs, then you shouldn't be left isolated.

The two players Sean took down, Graham Reilly and Conor McManus, got into good positions and he was left isolated against them. In previous years, players didn't get into those positions much because we always had plenty of players around backing each other up.

Sean had no choice.

We weren't told how to be cynical but if you're any kind of a smart player, you're going to do what you have to do.

I have always been a big fan of Joe Brolly's over the years but what he said about Sean was totally out of line.

I met Brolly at a club function a few years ago and asked him for his autograph. He thought I was taking the piss out of him but I still have the wee ball I got him to sign.

Tyrone people used to give out about things he said about us on RTÉ when we were winning All-Irelands, but I always thought he wanted us to win. I used to say, 'Wise up and smell the coffee, this man's for us.'

But slagging off Sean and the rest of the boys' character was totally wrong. I'd have a drink with those boys any day of the week.

As for calling Tyrone men cynical, well it wouldn't get me going. Pat Spillane tried it with his 'Puke Football' comments in 2003. I mean, who cares? That never annoyed me. I never used it to fire myself up.

If somebody says you're not good enough, that's a different story.

When Colm O'Rourke said he'd eat his hat if Dooher won an All-Ireland, we used that. It got a lot of boys wound up.

You need to keep the media on your side, because they can turn on you. I've had enough experience of that over the years. Maybe Tyrone haven't been doing that too well lately.

One of Mickey's strengths is that he is able to reinvent himself all the time.

In 2003 our mission was to win for all of Tyrone, for the supporters and for all the players who had gone before us. In 2005, it was about winning for ourselves as a group, and getting Cormac a second All-Ireland.

In 2008 he kept telling us things are not always going to be like this, to make the most of these opportunities.

I know exactly what he'll have told the new boys in the squad.

'No one thinks youse can match up to the old team, no one rates you. People think you'll never be as good as the boys who won three All-Irelands. A lot of you might have won minor All-Ireland titles but you won't get respect until you win a senior All-Ireland with this new team.'

He'll keep drilling that in to them until they win an All-Ireland. Then he'll think of a new reason to convince them why they need another, and then another, more than they need anything else in their lives.

That is why he is a top-class manager.

Reaching the All-Ireland semi-final suggests the young boys are listening to Mickey. If they do everything he tells them and they want it badly enough, then they will be All-Ireland champions some day.

I think Raymond Mulgrew will be there with them, because Mickey doesn't like to be proved wrong and he is on record as saying that Mulgrew will fulfill his potential yet. Mulgrew has serious respect for Mickey and I know Mickey seriously rates him. I've seen his face in training when he's watched some of the things Mulgrew can do. When he shines, he shines.

I've always said his problem was that he didn't want it enough. Maybe he saw how disillusioned I got in 2008 and some of it rubbed off on him.

I have to take a bit of the blame for how his Tyrone career petered out, but if he puts his mind to it he can still make it because he has unbelievable ability. It needs to be soon, though. He is 27 years of age, so it's got to happen in the next year or two for him or it'll be too late.

It will definitely take the edge off my disappointment at how things ended for me, if Mulgrew returns to Tyrone and becomes the player that I know he is.

◆ ◆ ◆ ◆ ◆

I was in the press box in Croke Park working for the BBC when the team lost to Mayo in the All-Ireland semi-final.

When I walked up the steps to leave after the game, a Tyrone supporter shouted over to me, 'That's a disgrace you're in there, Mugsy, you should have been out there.' He was pointing out to the pitch.

The Tyrone supporters around him started to clap.

I felt the tears pricking my eyes. I wanted to say thanks, but I had a lump in my throat so big I couldn't talk, so I just waved at them and walked on.

The Tyrone supporters have always been good to me. When I had the ball in my hands I'd hear them, 'Come on Mugsy lad.' I loved hearing the roar from them when I scored a goal or a point. When I'd warm up or come off the bench they always gave me a deadly reception.

I know it sounds silly but I would have loved just one more chance to run on with the jersey on my back. Just one more point in a Tyrone jersey, one more dummy in a Tyrone jersey, one more clap coming on or off the pitch in a Tyrone jersey. Just to say goodbye to the Tyrone supporters and get a bit of closure for myself.

I always had the craic with the Tyrone supporters, I always enjoyed them and I think they enjoyed me.

You make a lot of sacrifices to play inter-county football. I've missed friends' weddings, family anniversaries, birthdays, you name it, but I wouldn't have changed it for the world.

Tyrone has kept me on the straight and narrow because it's always been, 'Ok, focus, get back to football.'

There were times throughout my career when I was getting a lot of attention that I started to think, *This is deadly … maybe I don't need football anymore*. But that feeling was always temporary. My love of football is permanent and I always came back to it.

In the last few years of my career I knew that I would need something to focus on when the football finished, because it had been my life for so long. Opening the bar and club has given me a new lease of life. It is something I have put my heart and soul into and, even in these difficult times, it has been a worthwhile venture.

All bars need their regulars and you grow attached to fellas who are in all the time. Guys like Kevin McCosker, the bald eagle, Kevin Crilly, Benny McAleer, Emmett McNally are like one big family, everyone looks out for one another. I have loved getting to know them and sitting down and hearing a few stories.

There is a void left when some of them pass away, men like John Joe Donaghy, Seamus Ferron and Francie Devlin Senior, that I enjoyed talking to about their sporting achievements and their lives.

I still use football sometimes to help me in business. Sometimes you get wee breaks in football and in business, and I get wee ideas of ways to help the business from experiences I've had in football.

I'm also lucky to have met a wonderful girl, Niamh Hughes, who I have been going out with for over a year.

The first time I saw her I was lifting beer kegs out the back of the bar and she was walking up the steps of Holy Trinity, where she was working for a short time. The Cookstown manager, John McKeever, introduced us shortly after that and we hit it off straight away.

It is going the right way and I haven't been this happy in years. Niamh is a wee bit younger than me but we get on really well and, along with my ma, she has helped me so much to adjust to life after football.

Looking back on my Tyrone career, I have a few regrets.

I think I could have been a better player if I hadn't messed about, particularly in 2008. Not starting that All-Ireland final is the biggest regret of all.

I didn't maximise my ability. I never did weights and I never really ate properly until later years. I really looked after myself from 2009 onwards, but in the last few years I began to wonder if I should go back out partying again.

When I was out enjoying myself in the first half of my career, I wasn't being taken off.

In the last few years of my career I was being a good boy, trying to start doing some weights and eating right, and I was being taken off all the time.

Having the odd blow out definitely kept me more relaxed, but I suppose, as you get older, your body tells you that you just can't do that any more.

I wasn't partying as much as people thought, but I suppose people will remember the bad times. That is the way the world is.

It's not that important what I'm remembered for, but I hope it will be more for 'The Goal', and for setting up the goal for Canavan, and for being on the first Tyrone team to win the All-Ireland, than for any of the stuff off the field.

'The Goal' is the one thing everyone associates with me. I don't think it defines me, but I suppose you could be remembered for a whole lot worse.

People say us boys who won three All-Irelands owe the Tyrone jersey nothing, but I disagree. I owe it everything.

Tyrone got me everything, so how would I not owe it?

I owe the jersey everything.

Some people commit to something and they commit to it a hundred per cent for life. Other people commit and they go off the rails a bit now and again, I fall into that category. That doesn't mean I love it any less.

◆ ◆ ◆ ◆ ◆

We held a ten-year reunion to celebrate our 2003 All-Ireland success the night before the Dublin v Mayo All-Ireland final.

We went down to Dublin for the night and had a meal and a few drinks. It was brilliant chatting with boys like Deccie McCrossan, Paul Horisk and Peter Loughran whom I hadn't seen in years and it was great to see some of the boys' wives and girlfriends, too.

It was as if nothing had changed. I looked around at all the faces, all a little older and some not any wiser. Everyone was laughing away and enjoying the craic, and I felt so proud of every single one of them. *We created history, everybody in this room contributed to the greatest day Tyrone ever had or ever will have. I am so proud of what we achieved.'*

I have now finally accepted that I'm not going to wear the Tyrone jersey again.

It has taken me a long time to reach a place in my life where I am able to even say those words.

But I am ok with it now, and I look forward to going back to where it all started, travelling the roads the length and breadth of Ireland to support Tyrone.

One thing, though, just as I did sometimes when I was playing, I might skip the McKenna Cup!

Epilogue

My Beloved Club

I was one of the lucky ones.

At the same time as my intercounty career was winding down, I was having the time of my life with my club, Cookstown Father Rocks'.

Getting to play in not one, but two, All-Ireland club finals in Croke Park is the stuff of dreams.

Some people have dismissed our success, saying they were only Intermediate club titles, but for a 'townie' club like Cookstown it was some achievement, given that we have traditionally struggled to get enough players to commit to the cause long enough to hit those heights.

The Cookstown mentality has driven me mad at times.

We've had the talent to win senior championships but the attitude has been all wrong. Some players think football interferes with their social lives. Others are so afraid of their women, that they're letting them dictate when they can train and when they can play football.

The excuses are a complete joke. I've heard lads going up to managers saying, 'Can you take me off at half time? My woman's made plans tonight.'

You might ask a lad if he wants a drink but the girlfriend jumps in and answers, 'No, he's not having another one'. A relationship can't be good if the girlfriend is answering for you. Some of the boys need to man-up. Or it'll be, 'I can't go to training tonight, I have to mind the kids.' Get a bloody babysitter!

I was always disgusted with that. To me, the football always came first and the woman would have to wait. Maybe that's why I'm not married yet!

Partying has distracted me at times, but football is my first love and I always come back to it.

We've had some top-class managers at Cookstown Fr Rocks' over the years. Gary Coleman, Noel McGinn and John Morrison, but even then nothing changed. We had Frank McGuigan, but was he really interested in taking us? Did he really believe we could win anything?

It took Chris Lawn to come in to shake things up in Cookstown.

You can read a manager straight away, whether he's passionate about it and wants the club to do well. Cricko had family connections with Cookstown and when he came in, in 2009, he got the boys' respect straight away.

He was exactly the right man at the right time for us. 'Townie' clubs always struggle to get the same commitment as the rural clubs and, for years, we had boys breaking drink bans and going on holidays whenever it suited them. He brought authority and dropped anybody who stepped out of line.

In our Tyrone Intermediate Championship game against Strabane that year, we were nine points down at half time. Any other manager would have gone mad at half time but Cricko just said, 'I don't really mind if youse are beat, but if you start clawing this back and show the desire you've shown all year, you'll not be beat.'

Sure enough, when we pegged a couple of points back you could see the boys really started to believe it and Ryan Pickering scored our last point to win the game.

I had one of my best ever games for the club against Derrylaughan in the county semi-final. I hit 1-7 and felt so in the zone. Near the end of the game in Dungannon, I took a sideline kick and somebody shouted, 'Try it, Mugsy, sure you've hit everything else.' I went for it, and the wind caught it lovely, the ball sailing through the posts. I turned around to the crowd with my arms outstretched, loving it, with everyone clapping.

I couldn't sleep the night before the county final. We had been waiting a long time to win something. I felt under a lot of pressure to deliver.

I was worried about an infection I'd picked up in my knee after a fall, but we got through the match, beating Gortin to win the Tyrone Intermediate Championship.

It's not like me, but I would have settled for that. We had been so long waiting to win something with the club, I was happy enough, so to go on and win Ulster and All-Ireland club titles was unreal.

It was strange starting off a new year in 2010 not going to Tyrone training, but once we'd won an Ulster title, my head was totally focused on trying to get Cookstown to Croke Park for an All-Ireland final.

We beat a Galway team, Naomh Anna, in the All-Ireland semi-final in Longford and I was buzzing at the thought of seeing the lads' faces when they got to run out in Croke Park.

There was a row within the club about gear for the final, about whether everybody should get tracksuits and bags or just the lads who would be togging out. This wasn't the stuff we should be worrying about before an All-Ireland final. I agreed with Cricko when he said, 'Who gives a damn about tracksuits? It's an All-Ireland medal you should be after.'

We started this craze of dressing up on the Monday after every Championship win. There was a fancy dress shop in town and we'd all go in to get an outfit to wear out drinking for the day. It started after the county final and got more outrageous with each victory.

It really helped us bond as a team, but when Cricko heard boys chatting about it at training before the All-Ireland final, he went mental.

He didn't want any distractions or talk about fancy dress outfits when we had an All-Ireland to win.

I smiled at the reaction of some of the lads when we got into the dressing room in Croke Park before the game. They couldn't believe the size of it. It was familiar territory for Mulgrew and me, but instead of looking around and seeing Hub or Ricey or Brian McGuigan, it was my clubmates in there. I climbed under the bench beside the water tap as usual, putting a towel over my head. Some of the lads were looking at me like I wasn't wise, but this was part of my tried and trusted routine when I played in Croke Park.

We played Spa from Kerry in the 2010 All-Ireland final and it was one of the worst games I'd ever played for Cookstown. Maybe I was trying too hard, but the forwards were poor and nothing clicked up front.

We were behind with less than ten minutes to go when Mulgrew won a penalty. Our captain, Barry Hughes, 'Ginola' as we call him, stepped forward to take it.

I had been surprised when Cricko had named him as captain. A few years earlier, he had pulled out on us when we were in relegation trouble, but it turned out to be a masterstroke by Cricko. Ginola was a leader and he proved it that day.

I whispered in his ear as he went past me to take the penalty, 'Be a legend'. Maybe I shouldn't have said it, it might have put added pressure on him, but he tucked it away in some style.

It was the crucial score. When the final whistle went, it was so emotional. I looked up at the big screen and our club crest was shining down with the words 'Cookstown Father Rocks', All-Ireland Intermediate football champions'. It was some buzz climbing the steps of the Hogan Stand with all the lads I'd grown up with, and a great achievement by Cricko to get us there. It was 'only' at Intermediate level, but I never dreamt we would win an All-Ireland club title. It was huge for us.

Having said that, I never wanted to win another one.

Now that Cookstown were a senior club again, I felt that is where we should always stay. The following year, however, the wheels came off and we were relegated again. I was annoyed a few boys went back to their old ways and didn't give it one hundred per cent.

It always annoys me when players don't give everything to the club. I have played for the senior team since I was fifteen and played with broken hands and broken fingers, I've had injections to patch me up and played in games I should not have played in.

Some lads opt out when they have a blister or the 'flu. I was angry a few boys headed off on holidays when we needed them. Cricko had lost the fear factor. Boys disrespected him and I was ripping with them for it.

Cricko's voice was trembling when he told us in the dressing rooms in Trillick that he was leaving us. He said he would probably never manage the club again, but that we would always be in his heart. I could feel the tears rolling down my cheeks.

Maybe Cricko didn't have the ruthless streak that Mickey Harte and a lot of top managers have. Maybe he fell in love with players and gave them too much love.

But could Mickey have won an All-Ireland with Cookstown? I don't think so. It took a particular kind of person to get the best out of us.

◆ ◆ ◆ ◆ ◆

No matter who was going to be our new manager, I didn't think anyone would be able to fill Cricko's shoes.

Former Antrim player, John McKeever, whom I'd played against and was now teaching at Holy Trinity, was appointed at the start of the 2012 season.

He was amazed to find out that on nights when Tyrone were training at the Mid Ulster Sports Arena in Cookstown, I was leaving before the warm down in order to catch the last ten minutes of club training. I'd been doing that since Cricko was in charge and intended to keep doing it.

I always liked training with the club even when county training was on.

Cricko always said when I trained with the club, it was a better session, most of the time anyway. He hated nights when I was messing about. 'Boys see you taking it serious and they take it serious but when you mess about they mess about, too,' he'd say.

When the Tyrone boys would be starting their warm down I'd say I was away in to get a rub, but then I'd jump into the car and finish the last ten minutes with the club and warm down with them.

I don't think any of the Tyrone boys knew I was doing that but I wanted the Cookstown boys to see me there, doing the last few wee drills and sprints with them.

John said he was asked a lot of times after he took over, 'How do you keep control of Mulligan, is he hard to handle?' He was happy to report that I never missed training and gave it one hundred per cent every night.

I was stunned when he asked me to be captain.

'I do a lot of talking in the club anyway,' I said, 'I don't need to be captain to do that.' He said it was a new start and he'd like me to lead the side. I've never regarded myself as a potential captain of club or county, but I accepted, I thought it was an honour.

Even though Mulgrew was away in Australia, I was confident we would win Tyrone and we did. But when we started beating teams like Doohamlet, Killeavy and Warrenpoint in Ulster, I realised something special was happening again. We hadn't beaten teams of that calibre first time around.

John was good at the psychology and tapping into boys' heads, which was perfect for Cookstown. A team of shrinks is what we needed most of the time. He put a bit of toughness and meanness into us, too, which all 'townies' need. We had been too scared to express ourselves and he finally got us over that.

Our 2013 All-Ireland semi-final win over Mayo champions, Charlestown, in Longford, was the best team performance I have ever seen from a Cookstown team. We were five points down at half time and playing into the wind in the second half.

Marty Murray scored an opportunist goal and we clawed back the deficit, managing to take the game to extra time. We scored the only point in extra time after 23 seconds and then clung on for dear life. Men were throwing themselves into blocks, it reminded me so much of the Tyrone v Kerry swarm tackling in 2003 and our supporters were loving it. You could hear them reacting to it every time we won possession.

Charlestown had a chance to equalise in the last minute to earn a replay when they got a soft free-kick and the referee moved it forwards for verbals.

They brought a sub on to hit it, Colm Maye, who'd been taken off earlier in the game. Our boys gave him nothing but stick and I roared at him, 'Come on, this is a nice wee handy one for you. You don't even need to open your eyes, just tap her over.'

He took the kick and the ball rolled off the top of my fingers and I thought, *Oh no, this is going in the net*. I turned around and saw our midfielder, Conor Mullan, catch the ball underneath the crossbar and kick it into the stand as the referee blew the final whistle.

The scenes were unbelievable. It was so emotional, everyone was in tears. The supporters couldn't believe it. Some of them said it wasn't like watching a Cookstown team, we had shown so much guts out there.

It had never been an ambition of mine to win another Intermediate title but now we were closing in on another All-Ireland medal, of course I wanted it.

The next week, Mulgrew was on a plane home from Sydney.

I knew he'd been itching to get back. He had asked me a few times whether he should come back and I told him it was up to him, even though I knew that with him on board, we would have a better chance of beating Finuge in the final.

Some of the boys didn't think he should be allowed back in. He had been in Australia for two years and some of the senior players stood up at a team meeting and objected to him coming in at such a late stage of the season. It reminded me so much of Stevie O'Neill coming back to Tyrone before the All-Ireland final in 2008. I was listening to the same arguments all over again.

My cousin, Barry 'Groovy' Mulligan, was in the same boat. He had been away travelling for a few months and there were a few boys who thought he shouldn't be allowed back in either.

I could see where the boys were coming from. We had come through this amazing All-Ireland semi-final where we had died for each other and these two boys had missed it. If we didn't need them then, why did we need them now?

I stood up, just like I had done in a Tyrone team meeting four and a half years earlier, and backed the lads coming back in.

'Boys, do you want the best for yourself or for Cookstown?' I asked them.

I used the experience of what had happened with Stevie to show them that it could all work out for the best. Boys started to come round.

Mulgrew came up to an in-house game and straight away I could see he was in really good nick. He had been playing for New South Wales and had put on a bit of bulk. His legs had filled out compared to the wee puny legs he used to have. Some club committee members were angry the two boys were brought back in, but I don't think we would have won the All-Ireland without them.

Both Mulgrew and 'Groovy' were brought on before half time in the final, after we lost Conor Maguire and Conor Mullan to injury. I was playing all right at centre half-forward but those two came straight into midfield and changed the game.

The game had been built up as a grudge match between Paul Galvin and me. During the game, he came over to me and said, 'I'm only after being spat on'.

'Sure, you're well used to that sort of stuff yourself,' I said.

I didn't believe him.

There were some nasty enough verbals going on. I'm all for a bit of verbals but their lads said a few things that were below the belt, though Galvin wasn't one of them. He is not into that.

I didn't mind so much the whole 'British' slagging that goes on, because I am well used to it, but some of our lads were raging. They came in at half time and that's all they could talk about. They hadn't really been exposed to it before but I told them to calm down, that it was par for the course. There was no point losing our focus over that.

We won comfortably in the end, by 1-9 to 0-6, and leading the boys up the steps as captain to pick up the trophy was a fantastic feeling. I had written a speech but I didn't look at it, I just spoke from the heart. It meant a lot, but it wasn't as special to me as when we won it the first time, in 2010. That's because the first time you do anything is always the best, just as the 2003 All-Ireland with Tyrone will always be the most special to me. It meant a lot to my family to see me climb the steps first and pick up the trophy. But I don't rate it among my top five achievements, simply because I didn't think we should have been an intermediate team any longer. We should have been competing for senior honours.

The celebrations were just starting to die down over a month later when a video clip appeared on the internet, allegedly showing one of our players spitting on Galvin. Then Galvin retweeted the link to his 60,000 or so followers on Twitter, sparking huge publicity in the media.

We let it go and said nothing for a few days, but the club's name was getting dragged through the mud so I thought, as club captain, it was up to me to respond.

I released a statement about the abuse our lads had had to put up with during the game. The Derrytresk boys in Tyrone wanted to back us up, because they said they had encountered the same thing in the All-Ireland junior club semi-final against Dromid Pearses the previous year. Suddenly, it was becoming a Tyrone v Kerry row, which I didn't want. I was just trying to defend my player and my club.

A few days later, I got a call from Canavan. Galvin had been in touch. That pissed me off for a start. *Why is he ringing Canavan?* I fumed. *Canavan has nothing to do with Cookstown. He should have phoned me.*

Galvin wanted Canavan to act as a go-between but I wasn't having that. I got his number from Canavan and texted him.

'Paul, it's Mugsy here. Are you ok to talk?'

He texted back that he would take my call, so I phoned him.

'I was very disappointed with your comments,' he told me quickly enough. 'Are you going to take them back?'

'Not one bit, Paul. I'm defending my club and a player on my team.'

'I was spat on,' he said. 'Your club knows it and your county knows it. What would you do?'

'I don't want to fall out with you,' I replied. 'I have respect for you and your club, but this is being built up as a whole Tyrone v Kerry row and it's getting out of hand.'

He agreed that he didn't want the bad publicity either.

The suspensions that were handed down following an investigation by Croke Park were thrown out and the row petered out in the end.

I'm a firm believer in not holding a grudge once a match is over, and I would never have released any statement only that Galvin retweeted that video link of the alleged spitting incident.

I don't know if Paul Galvin is speaking to me or not. I would like to think that if I bumped into him sometime, we could shake hands and have a drink together, and draw a line under the whole thing.

I have a lot of respect for most of the Kerry lads, including him. He is a class player and he's got rough treatment over the years. Of course, he is no angel at times but he is hard done by, too. The time he swiped the notebook out of the referee's hands is a wee bit of craziness that I can identify with.

Paul Galvin and myself, and all the Kerry and Tyrone footballers from a brilliant decade of Gaelic football, are part of GAA history. We wrote a great story together. We are part of each other's lives, whether we like it or not.

It's something, I feel sure, that we will all come to treasure as the years fly by us all in the next decade.

Roll of Honour

1997: Ulster Vocational Schools title, All-Ireland minor football Championship, Tyrone Grade One Under-16 League and Championship titles, Tyrone Grade Two minor title

1998: Ulster Under-18 Vocational Schools title, All-Ireland Under-18 Vocational Schools title, Ulster Vocational Schools title, All-Ireland Vocational Schools title, Ulster minor football Championship, All-Ireland minor football Championship

1999: Ulster Vocational Schools title, Ulster minor football League, Ulster Under-18 Vocational Schools title

2000: Ulster Under-21 football Championship, All-Ireland Under-21 football Championship

2001: Ulster senior football Championship, Ulster Under-21 football Championship, All-Ireland Under-21 football Championship

2002: National Football League Division One title

2003: National Football League Division One title, Ulster senior football Championship title, All-Ireland senior football Championship

2004: Dr McKenna Cup

2005: Dr McKenna Cup, All-Ireland senior football Championship, GAA All Star Award

2006: Dr McKenna Cup

2007: Dr McKenna Cup, Ulster senior football Championship

2008: All-Ireland senior football Championship

2009: Ulster senior football Championship, Tyrone intermediate club Championship, Ulster intermediate club Championship

2010: All-Ireland intermediate club Championship, Ulster senior football Championship

2012: Dr McKenna Cup, Interprovincial series (Railway Cup), Tyrone intermediate club Championship, Ulster intermediate club Championship

2013: All-Ireland intermediate club Championship.

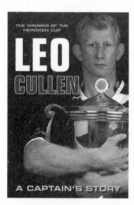

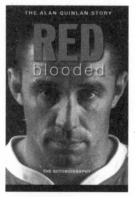

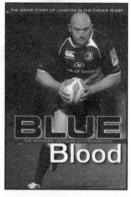

Leo Cullen: A Captain's Story
Leo Cullen
ISBN 978-0-9563598-7-2
€15.99

Red Blooded: Alan Quinlan
Alan Quinlan
ISBN 978-0-9563598-3-4
€19.99

Blue Blood: Bernard Jackman
Bernard Jackman
ISBN 978-0-9563598-2-7
€19.99

In May 2011, Leinster won the most remarkable Heineken Cup title in rugby history, coming from 22 points down at half time in the final at Cardiff's Millennium Stadium to defeat Northampton, and capture Europe's premier rugby trophy for the second time in three years. A year later, Leinster retained the Cup, making Leo Cullen the first captain to raise the Heineken Cup an amazing three times. An Irish International and inspirational leader, the captain of perhaps the greatest team European rugby has ever seen, recorded his incredible journey in 2011 in intimate detail in *A Captain's Story*.

Red Blooded is the story of Munster rugby's most-capped player ever, Alan Quinlan, and his battle to reach the peak of the professional game of rugby. One of the bravest and most honest accounts ever written about the modern game, Red Blooded recounts Quinny and Munster's stories. It details how he has confronted professionalism, tough opponents, devastating injury and personal doubts to become one of modern rugby's toughest, and greatest, characters.

Blue Blood is the story of one man's passionate, thirteen-year fight to reach the highest level of the professional sport of rugby. It's the inside story of Leinster's five-year journey, under their then manager, Michael Cheika, to become the No. 1 team in European rugby. In his revealing autobiography, Bernard Jackman, offers the inside story of that quest and lifts the lid on Leinster in the Cheika years. *Blue Blood* lays bare the ruthlessness required to reach the top of one of the greatest sports in the world.

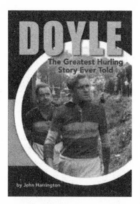